GETTING SCHOOLED

GETTING SCHOOLED

THE REEDUCATION *of*
AN AMERICAN TEACHER

GARRET KEIZER

METROPOLITAN BOOKS

HENRY HOLT AND COMPANY NEW YORK

m

Metropolitan Books
Henry Holt and Company, LLC
Publishers since 1866
175 Fifth Avenue
New York, New York 10010
www.henryholt.com

Metropolitan Books® and m® are registered trademarks of
Henry Holt and Company, LLC.

Library of Congress Cataloging-in-Publication Data

Keizer, Garret.
    Getting schooled : the reeducation of an American teacher / Garret Keizer.
       pages cm
    ISBN 978-0-8050-9643-9 (hardback)—ISBN 978-0-8050-9644-6 (electronic copy)
    1. High school teaching—Vermont—Case studies.   2. High school teachers—
Professional relationships—Vermont—Case studies.   3. Public schools—Vermont—
Case studies.   4. Keizer, Garret.   I. Title.
    LB1607.52.V5K45 2014
    373.110209743—dc23   2013042594

Henry Holt books are available for special promotions and
premiums. For details contact: Director, Special Markets.

First Edition 2014

Designed by Kelly Too

Printed in the United States of America
1   3   5   7   9   10   8   6   4   2

For the Teachers

I know nothing about education except this: that the greatest and the most important difficulty known to human learning seems to lie in that area which treats how to bring up children and how to educate them.

MONTAIGNE

CONTENTS

NOTE TO THE READER

Getting Schooled grew out of an essay of the same title that was published in the September 2011 issue of *Harper's Magazine*. The adults mentioned in these pages have been given their real names or pseudonyms or have been left unnamed as judged best by the author. No student appears with his or her real name. Certain details have been altered to camouflage identities, but none of the incidents recounted have been invented, exaggerated, or otherwise distorted.

GETTING SCHOOLED

BEGINNERS

You go back, Jack, do it again.
—Steely Dan

In the fall of 2010, after a fourteen-year hiatus from the classroom and at the unpropitious age of fifty-seven, I began a one-
year job filling in for a teacher on leave from the same rural
Vermont high school that I'd entered as a rookie thirty years
before. I signed on mainly because my wife and I needed the
health insurance. The reason I trained to be an English teacher in
the first place was my parents' insistence that I graduate from college with a trade, "poet" falling short of the mark in their eyes. It's
fair to say that I have never gone to work in a school with what
might be called purity of heart, though much of what I know
about purity of heart I learned there.

It can still surprise me that I became a teacher at all. I could
have satisfied my parents' requirements by pursuing a different
trade; sometimes I wish I had. With a push in either direction, I
think I could have managed to become a halfway decent attorney
or machinist. I am not one of those high school teachers whose

teenage years evoke such an irresistible nostalgia that they enter the ranks mainly in the hope of chaperoning a prom.

Nor, when I say "surprise," do I mean to suggest that mine is the well-worn path of the marginal student who feels called to the classroom in order to help kids have an easier time than he had. That is often a noble story, among the noblest in the field of education, but it is not my story. I was a good student at school, and when I applied myself, an exceptional student. At the risk of sounding immodest, I should probably add that there are people who would tell you that I am an exceptional teacher. There are former students of mine who would find it difficult to imagine that I could ever have wanted to do anything else.

I never had that difficulty. In fact, there was never a time during the sixteen years I taught when I didn't imagine doing something else. Even in the best moments, when teaching gave me the kind of rush some people find in skydiving or cocaine, I yearned to be at home writing. In the worst, I would imagine putting my name in at the local furniture plant, which I might well have done but for the impossibility of lying about my white-collar credentials to bosses whose kids, nieces, or nephews I'd had in class. I can't recall a single year of teaching that I didn't begin with a burst of enthusiasm accompanied by the fervent hope that come June I'd be done with teaching for good.

There is no simple way to account for that contradiction. From my earliest grades, I was fascinated with teaching and repulsed by school. By second grade I was asking my teacher's permission to "teach the class" about my scientific passions at the time: dinosaurs, rocks, and planets. I still marvel at the number of times she yielded the blackboard—to say nothing of the rarity with which my classmates rewarded my efforts with a black eye. But as early as first grade, I was throwing up my breakfast every morning out of anxiety before the school bus arrived. I had no trouble holding down my food on weekends and holidays. To this day the mere act of entering a school—that first whiff of disinfectant, that crackling interplay of regimentation and anarchy—is enough to turn my stomach.

Becoming a professional teacher intensified, and complicated, the emotions I'd felt as a kid. Teaching could be wonderful, and even when it wasn't, the students I taught could be wonderful. It made me sad to see some of them graduate, though in time I realized that part of my sadness had to do with being left behind. They were going on to do what they "really wanted to do," whereas I wasn't. In a ridiculous but palpable way, I felt less grown up than the gowned graduates who shook my hand and embraced me. After all, an adult is someone who's finished with high school. The distinction tends to blur when you find yourself matching wits with a mouthy fourteen-year-old or asking a principal if you can pretty please leave the building on your lunch break to run home and retrieve the corrected papers—your "homework"—that you left on the kitchen counter. The greatest challenge of teaching is not, as is so often averred, finding a way "to relate to kids." It is rather finding a way to relate to yourself in a process that often leaves you feeling like a kid.

A good part of that challenge has to do with the burden of evaluation. A child's acute awareness of measuring up, and of failing to measure up, exists for few adults with the same remorseless constancy as it does for a teacher. Everything a student fails to learn is something a teacher has failed to teach. (And everything that might be construed as wrong with the society at large can be placed, and inevitably will be placed, at the feet of its teachers.) Work harder, you tell yourself, but hard work is not always enough. Knowledge of material and technique is not always enough. You can still fail. What is more, you *will* fail. Certain social conditions combine with certain working conditions to make failure a foregone conclusion. The realization that I could work every waking hour of every day and still fall short of the most modest expectations was the first great lesson of my teaching career. I ought not to have found it so stunning. A teacher in the ancient world might have had a handful of pupils; he would have eaten and even lodged with them throughout their tutelage. Jesus Christ had twelve. In his first year of teaching, Garret Keizer had around a hundred.

The teaching position to which I applied in 2010 would give me a mere eighty. And I knew more about how to teach English than I did as a beginner. I was also better at the math. I knew, for example, that asking my students to put pen to paper only once a day would give me four hundred pieces of paper by week's end. Giving each piece of paper a scant ten minutes of my attention would require sixty-seven hours of correction. That's a lot of homework, and it doesn't count as preparation, which at its best ought to exceed correction by a factor of no less than two.

Within days after the principal called to say that I had the one-year job if I still wanted it, which is to say, within days after refusing my wife's final plea not to take it, I began having nightmares. I often have nightmares, but these were less obscure in their meanings. Even the fantastic ones weren't hard to figure out.

For instance, I am on a raft on the ocean a short distance from another raft. There is a creature slumped on that other raft that I surmise is either dead or close to it. Still, I hoist and flex the long metal pole in my hand so as to bring one of the leaden balls attached to either tip thudding down on its bowed shaggy head. I don't know how long I've been at this methodical braining, but as soon as I deliver one blow, I hoist the undulating rod above my head, watching intently for when the ball is in the right position for me to deliver the next. I don't dare to relax my concentration for even a second. If I don't make sure to kill this thing, it will kill me. It is easily five times my size.

Suddenly, the creature comes to life, furious, rearing up on its hind legs and sucking the breath from my lungs in the same instant. With one easy leap it bounds over the water from its raft to mine. The weapon in my hand, awkward at best, is now utterly useless, too long to wield in close quarters. With my heart pounding, I wake just as I am about to be eaten alive. Right away I know that the beast is the job I "killed" fourteen years ago and will resurrect in less than six months' time. The symbolism of the weapon takes longer to parse. Perhaps it is the ballpoint pen by which I have managed to earn my precarious living, mockingly elongated and flaccid, my years of hired scribbling revealed in all their humiliating impotence. Or maybe it is simply the ten-foot pole with which I had sworn never to touch teaching again.

Determined to enter my classroom as prepared as I can be, I make an appointment to meet with the principal and department head before the snow is gone. Here in northeastern Vermont that can mean a date as late as May, especially on the higher elevations where I live, but it's March when I make my way off the mountain, along the winding ridge road, and under the narrow railroad overpass that still feels, as it did during my last years of teaching, like the arch of a castle gate: protective coming in, ominous going out. Four miles of the trip are done at that point, followed by another seven that will take me along the train tracks and over the county line, past a lonesome pond and defunct sawmill, the cluttered dooryards and sagging roofs of South Barton, toward the neater lakeside houses laid close to Crystal Lake. Hidden by foliage but known to me are a rusted, battered trailer and backyard scrap-metal business toward the south end of the lake and, with a grand view from a perch above the northern shore, a palatial house of stone and glass in which one of my students once lived. I remember climbing the steep drive to visit her parents one winter night, the tall windows blazing into view just as the radio began to play Mozart's *Requiem*. It was like entering Camelot.

Today, though, I'm entering the village of Barton in Orleans County, its outskirts marked by the turreted Blue Seal feed store and the western-style Crystal Saloon, nicknamed the Snake Pit in former days, when it boasted numerous brawls and at least one homicide on the premises. In the very beginning, before my wife and I had managed to buy our long-desired "house in the country," I had come from the opposite direction, driving south from our apartment in the mill town of Orleans.

Either way requires a turn, left from the present direction, right in the past, onto an uphill road that passes under the interstate. Route 91 reached the heart of northeastern Vermont a few years before our arrival in 1979, changing much though not all of what was then regarded as a wild place. By wild I mean both wooded and lawless. Some of the lawlessness was indigenous, typical of what one might expect of a region at the northernmost tip of Appalachia. Some of it came with the countercultural migrations of the early seventies, the disillusioned hippies and radicals on the lam. No doubt closeness to a desolate border was a factor too. Not far from the high school or all that long ago the maverick inventor Gerald Bull built the long-range "super guns" he sold illegally to South Africa and Saddam Hussein.

The abutments of the underpass were thick with black graffiti when I first saw them, the school's vice principal brazenly proclaimed as an inveterate sucker of "wet donkey dinks" on one cement surface and a more generic "big pud" on another. In later years a depressing run of suicides and drunk-driving accidents lent a morbid, almost macabre tone to the graffiti until the school authorities, apparently as dispirited by the memorials as I was—though I had taken my leave by then—inaugurated the custom of having each graduating class paint a mural on one of the four faces as a legacy to the school. Among those I pass this afternoon is a depiction of rainbow trout jumping the falls, one of the region's more celebrated sights. People still gather every April on the banks of the Willoughby River and watch salmon and trout as long as two feet leap their way upstream to spawn. The iconic trout is also pictured on a granite marker outside the Ethan Allen furniture mill, the area's largest employer, once the destination of most of the able-bodied young males who weren't marked at birth for college or their fathers' barns.

The trout is not the high school's mascot, however, that honor falling to the coonskin-capped "Ranger" of Roger's Rangers, a group of colonial expeditionaries best known for their raid on a tribe of St. Francis Indians beyond the northern shores of Memphremagog and their ill-fated retreat thereafter. I make my turn onto high school property past a granite monument with the Ranger logo carved under the school's name, an addition since I left Lake Region Union High School in the midnineties, when only a few gray hairs salted my head.

The building that emerges as I round the corner is a flat-topped brick structure typical of regional high schools built in the 1960s. But for an occasional tractor parked outside the garage doors of the ag shop, little about the place gives a clue of its geographical location or the diverse sociological profile of its roughly four hundred students. The sprawling grounds suggest an active athletic program and a conscientious maintenance crew. There are tennis courts. Acts of vandalism are not unheard of, but they're painted over or repaired as quickly as possible and, perhaps for that reason, infrequently repeated. There are probably other reasons too. For most of the students, high school represents a heady expansion from the smaller, often less well-funded, small-town elementary schools they attend till eighth grade. For at least a few of them, Lake Region is the warmest, brightest, safest space they know. Kids cry at their graduations all over the world, but they do not cry for all the same reasons.

When Kathy and I first ventured into "Ranger Country" in our late twenties, with newly earned master's degrees from the state university and our New Jersey accents even more noticeable than neighbors claim they still are today, we were searching for two openings in the same school or at least in geographic proximity, one for an inexperienced English teacher and one for a new speech pathologist. Candidates for the first were a dime a dozen, but the latter were and in some ways continue to be a rarity in rural parts of the state. I recall occasions when, after being perfunctorily instructed by a superintendent's secretary to send a résumé and letter of application to such and such an address by such and such a date, I would casually mention that my wife was a master's-level speech pathologist also in search of a job (and therefore able not only to meet new state requirements for special education but to pull in state funding as well), whereupon I was told to hold the line until the superintendent could come to the phone. It seemed we would get some interviews, perhaps even a few choices, though Kathy felt strongly that the state fellowships that had paid our tuitions and duty-free stipends at the state university obliged us to look at school districts where "the need was greatest," or at least beyond the relative affluence of the Champlain Valley.

Not to worry, it was only beyond the Champlain Valley, and quite a ways beyond, that we found a district able and willing to see us as a package deal. We were hired by the Orleans Central Supervisory Union in Orleans County, one of three that make up Vermont's so-called Northeast Kingdom, and one of the state's poorest. That distinction has not changed, notwithstanding the presence of some large prosperous farms (often the aggregated acquisitions of smaller, failed holdings), a solid middle class of small business owners, skilled tradespeople, and white-collar professionals willing to trade an upscale income for a down-home lifestyle, and even a few millionaire squires seeking the same dream on larger acreage. As of the last census, only one of Vermont's fourteen counties (Essex County, also in the Kingdom) showed a slightly higher percentage of its population living below the poverty line than Orleans. Orleans County leads the state in accidental deaths and in the percentage of its children receiving food stamps, is last in the state for longevity among males, next to last for longevity among females. It ranks third for suicides and prominently for drug abuse, domestic abuse, and teenage pregnancy. When Kathy and I announced to our professors where we were going to work, one of them claimed that the region's most popular graduation gift used to be a set of false teeth.

I began doubting the rumor almost as soon as we arrived—if only because I couldn't see how many of the parents could have afforded the teeth. We were not much better off. With a master's degree each, Kathy's and my combined gross salaries were a little over $18,000. We located a high-ceilinged upstairs apartment roughly two blocks from where the rainbows jumped and as many blocks from the furniture mill, whose humming sawdust chutes would become a familiar sound of our summer nights. (We were also within walking distance of a hilltop country club, though we'd live in town for over a year before we knew it existed and would never have guessed from our immediate surroundings that it did.) Our landlords, a first-grade teacher and a school custodian more newlywed than we, though neither was young, sized us up and charged us a rent even less than what our pathetic salaries could have borne.

Theirs was not untypical of the kindness we would meet in that town and in those years. In defense of an eighteenth-century schoolmaster accused of being overly harsh in his discipline, Samuel Johnson notes "with how little kindness, in a town of low trade, a man who lives by learning is regarded." In a region where zoning disputes periodically arise over unregulated junkyards and whose collective memory reserves a hallowed place for game poachers and whiskey runners, the Northeast Kingdom has plenty of what Johnson might have considered "low trade," but the disdain he observed was in our experience mostly confined to harangues against the school budget and mock-wistful references to our long summer vacations. *So you folks are all done work now, are you? Mus' be nice.* What might have been said behind our backs in those first years after our arrival we didn't know, but our faces rarely met with anything but respect. Carolers tramped up our wooden steps and sang outside our door at Christmas. Occasionally students dropped by unannounced, including one endearing, academically challenged lug who, when I choked on a morsel of food one evening, sprang up from our kitchen table and might have broken my ribs had I not recovered my voice in time to spare myself a bruising application of the Heimlich maneuver. When our daughter was born, the minister's wife, a no-nonsense mother of four who handled a baby with the businesslike dispatch of a pizza chef tossing dough and as slim a chance of dropping it on the floor, volunteered to give us a kitchen-table demonstration on bathing an infant (we jumped at the offer) and the owner of the local furniture store came by with his wife and a dozen of her homemade rolls, still warm from the oven. From the other side of the cultural divide, the founders of the famous (or infamous, depending on your poli-

tics) Bread and Puppet Theater in Glover showed up with con-
gratulations and a silk-screened banner bearing a militant red
flower and the word *YES* to hang above her crib. I was a great
eater of pancakes in those days, but I can't recall that we ever
bought a container of maple syrup. It came to us, the way venison
steaks and fresh raspberries would have come to a doctor's back
porch in previous generations.

But we were always mindful of something anarchic in the
shadows, rooted mostly in stories of "what things were like back
then," before the interstate was laid and the down-country bour-
geoisie began arriving in droves to seek "a simpler way of life" or
"an old house with character," but still in living memory and
sometimes on open display. Even in our tamer time, Halloweens
fell just short of what would have justified calling out the National
Guard. Wooden bridges and abandoned barns were set ablaze,
and the house of one unpopular teacher was so mercilessly egged
that he'd gotten into the habit of suspending large canvas tarps
from the eaves to the driveway. In the smaller hamlets on the
farther edges of the district, the older ways lingered on, not only
in midnight devilment but in the comparatively staid conduct of
school business. A veteran teacher's aide we came to know liked
to tell the story of showing up for her first day on the job in the
1960s, only to find the village school locked and empty. When
she went to the superintendent's office to ask if she had misread
the school calendar, his deputy ventured an educated guess that
"Dottie must not have felt like starting school today. Try going
over tomorrow."

The larger point here is that Dottie was still a few years from
retirement when my wife and I arrived at the end of the 1970s.
She no longer used a large handbell to call the students in from
recess, perhaps in consequence of a mishap involving a small
boy who'd ventured too close to the arc of her swing and been

KO'd on the spot. As the story goes, the boy, questioned at dinner by his father as to the plum-sized lump on his scalp, began by saying, "Mrs. J. hit me in the head with a bell." Before he could elaborate further, his indignant father demanded, "What were you doing when she hit you?" The boy said he'd not been doing anything except standing too close to his teacher, but the father was unconvinced. "You must have been doing something pretty bad if your teacher had to bean you with a bell." The child might have gotten some additional knocks had Mrs. J. not rapped on the door just then, dropping by to check on her hapless pupil's head. She assured the parents that he'd done nothing to deserve a hiding.

When we first heard the story, it was used to illustrate how much times had changed—*a parent wouldn't be so quick to side with a teacher these days, that's for sure, call a lawyer more likely*—but it underscored how recently they had changed, recently enough for us to be part of the transition. Of course, we too were destined to be changed by our assignments, as much taught as having taught. By my count I have taken the equivalent of four degrees in my life, one from a college, one from the glue and plastics factories I worked in during college, one from a university, and one from teaching at a public high school in the Northeast Kingdom of Vermont, a region alternately as close to and as far from the Kingdom of God as any place I have ever known.

I walk from my car to the building with my resurrected briefcase (a leather, brass-buckled KPMG "audit bag" given me by my accountant brother and a signature accessory in my former teaching days) and an empty milk crate for lugging home as many course texts as I can carry. On the way I check to see that my old friend Donna Underwood is still included among the various

memorials in the grass circle under the flagpole. It seems the
school's untimely deaths are now consolidated in one upright
monument, and Donna's name is there. Much beloved at the
school, she was my department head until she died of cancer in
between my seventh and eighth years of teaching. She'd been
missing from my application interview—on medical leave to
handle her first, nonfatal bout with breast cancer—and was
reportedly against the hire, her disapproval probably overruled
by my charmed status as the husband of a speech pathologist. In
addition to my lack of teaching experience, she was concerned,
as she later told me when we had become friends and could treat
her confession as a joke, by the number of straight-A semesters
on my transcripts. "You proved me wrong, but frankly, I didn't
think our kids would relate to an egghead."

I sense the current department head also has reservations
about me, and she does, though hers are of a different order,
having to do with my ability to adjust to current trends in education rather than with any distinctions of my transcript or
deficiencies in my toolbox. I will not learn of her caveats until
later, when she no longer has them and I am just beginning to.
For now I'm hoping that by showing up so early to learn the
details of next year's assignment, I will put her at ease.

All trends aside, one thing has stayed the same. As I'm cross-
ing the parking lot, the intercom squawks an announcement
from the outdoor speakers. I have timed my visit to correspond
with the end of the school day, so I can sense the more driven of
the teachers inside the building sighing as the last three minutes
of their lessons are lost—can feel something sigh deep in myself.
"Without the loudspeaker we never would have conquered Ger-
many," Hitler said, and on that point I've always been willing to
give the führer his due. I hated that sound almost as much as
anything else in the school routine, even if I liked the person

whose voice was barking into the microphone. The kids knew I hated it, and the more sympathetic ones would join in groaning with me, a few hinting that in exchange for some extra credit they might be able to arrange a little accident with the wiring. This afternoon's message, "Seniors, remember your picture money for tomorrow," comes with a subtext: *Garret, are you sure you want to do this?*

I am no stranger to the question. I heard it even in the Donna days. After seven years of teaching, I took a sabbatical to write my first book—*No Place But Here: A Teacher's Vocation in a Rural Community*—returning to my classroom refreshed but more convinced than ever that I wanted to write full-time, wanted to work alone, wanted to wake up early with a tranquil feeling in my stomach and to work with no intercom squawking above my desk. I was now the head of my department, Donna having died near the close of my sabbatical. I had fewer classes to teach and thus fewer papers to correct, but more headaches, which is to say, more exposure to problems that were not of my making. What had been my working motto all the years before—stay in your own classroom and out of other people's affairs—no longer sorted with my job description. Nevertheless, I managed to last another eight years, six beyond the two-year commitment required by the sabbatical, largely by alchemizing what was supposed to be "administrative time" into extra tutoring time with kids. But the chairmanship was the beginning of the end for me. I don't think I was an especially awful chairperson, just an awfully unhappy one.

It was my daughter who helped me escape. One evening when she was in fifth grade, slumped as usual over her prodigious homework—it is virtually a natural law that the less educated or educationally involved the parents of school-age children are, the more they will tend to see "lots of homework" as a sign of effective teaching and the more likely their teachers will be to take the hint—I heard her say tearfully to her mother: "I'm not good at anything."

At that point in my career, I was teaching mostly advanced-level courses, a newly devised AP English among them, filled with kids who were "good at everything," or at least had been led to believe they were. Every year I added to my vanity files letters from college admissions offices *written to me* in praise of the detailed letters of recommendation I had written for my students. Every year I received a visit or a letter from a former student or a former student's parent, thanking me for my part in their preparation for college. *You were a good teacher*—but was I an attentive father? If teaching was the best thing I knew how to do, didn't my own child deserve a better share of it?

With my wife's support, in both paychecks and lesson plans, and our daughter's poignantly enthusiastic assent—her only question was whether homeschool would also include "snack time" and if that might be scheduled a little earlier in the day—I took the plunge, requesting a year's unpaid leave and forfeiting a salary that was at the time roughly equivalent to a year's tuition at Harvard. Thus began a labor of love and what I recall as one of the happiest years of my life. I divided the days into halves, with mornings given to conventional, skill-based lessons in basic subjects, and afternoons devoted to hands-on, long-term projects: an archaeological excavation at an old house site in the woods, running our own restaurant for an evening (on the premises of an actual restaurant and after weeks of lessons on foods and finance), and studying "babies" (which included shadowing a pediatrician on his hospital rounds). The local public school agreed to let our daughter come for art and music classes and thus to maintain ties with her classmates. I turned our tanklike '78 Malibu (destined to end its long and illustrious life as the winner of a demolition derby) into a mobile classroom, outfitting it with map assignments and flash cards for long trips and a jerry-rigged bike rack for physical education classes. I resisted the urge to draw up and affix a perverse if altogether accurate bumper sticker—"I'm a homeschoolin' gun-totin' Bible-bangin' . . . SOCIALIST"—though I was not always able to resist giving my stock rejoinder to some acquaintance's sniffing, hackneyed caveat about "the loss of peer interaction": The inmates at Walla Walla state prison get peer interaction too. There are few more trenchant giveaways as to the lack of confidence so many parents have in their local public school, and the anguish they experience in consigning their children to its care, than their readiness to construe another parent's homeschooling as a personal attack.

It had always been our intention that our daughter should return to public school, an institution we strongly believe in. Accordingly, she rejoined her classmates the following year. It had been my plan to return as well, but due to a fortuitous publishing opportunity, I did not—except for teaching an elective first-period course gratis for a single semester, a parting gesture of thanks to a school system that had treated me well. By the end of my semester with an overcrowded and dubiously motivated class, I was readier than ever to be done. And done I was, at least for the foreseeable future. What I could not have foreseen was walking back into the very same school, fourteen years later, and also on another mission I like to think was motivated by love.

Kathy and I had started our teaching careers in the same school district, with the same level of preparation and on the same salary step; for a while we even drove the same type of car, a VW Bug, mine beige and hers white, with a child car seat passed back and forth between them. Notwithstanding the unfair advantage

I had in teaching upper-track teenagers capable of singing my praises or at least remembering my name, both of us managed to achieve a comparable level of excellence according to our formal evaluations and community standing. Beyond that our trajectories were very different. For one thing, hers lasted twice as long as mine.

She had started out as the itinerant speech pathologist for seven schools, with a seventeen-mile spread between the most outlying two. One of our first chores after moving into our apartment was to construct a user-friendly map of their scattered locations and various dirt-road connections, to be kept in her car along with a snow shovel, a thick blanket, and a candle (the heat of a single candle flame reputedly sufficient to prevent hypothermia in a storm-trapped car). After a while her position shifted from working with students K through 12 to working exclusively with preschool children. This had been her aim even before taking her degree. At first she was dividing her time between students enrolled in a preschool classroom and children who received their services at home. When the preschool program began to move away from home visits toward the safer model of site-based delivery, she was also able to reduce her time on the road.

She would soon be spending most of her time in the rented rooms of a church basement, not an ideal site, though preferable to some she had known in the past. In her itinerant years, for example, she had given therapy on the stairwell of a two-story school that would soon be condemned as unfit for human occupancy and had delivered services at another school through whose playground a farmer took his dripping manure spreader every spring.

There was no manure in the church basement but that's not to say it was free of shit. The gatekeepers of the congregation were habitually snapping at the teachers—this trifle or that falling short of their standard of "acceptable" housekeeping—even as the Sunday school felt free to leave the classroom areas in disarray for Monday mornings. Basically there was one classroom and an adjoining room that served the dual purpose of storage space and office for as many as six teachers, aides, and specialists. Whenever I dropped by to deliver some teaching tool forgotten at home or to make a car switch, I'd enter a small metropolis of stacked toys and games, hang a left and then a right past the rainbow-colored skyscrapers, and find my wife (or a chair with just her sweater) sitting in a corner at a broken wooden desk that most people would feel embarrassed to leave on the curb with a FREE sign.

And yet, in spite of the physical circumstances, those years in the basement would be viewed in retrospect as the heyday of an exemplary program. Kathy's closest partner, the program's early-education specialist, was a master teacher (once the district's Teacher of the Year) and also her dearest friend. The other teachers and even the teacher's aides were all seasoned and impressively knowledgeable, as aides often are. (The widespread use of so-called paraprofessionals as underpaid substitutes for teachers is public education's best claim to a racket.) If it's cant to say that women work together more collegially and less "hierarchically" than men, it's a cant these women made it easy for me to believe.

But, just as the beginning of the end came for me when I was promoted to the head of my department, the golden age of my wife's thirty-year job came to a close with what felt at first like the fulfillment of a dream. The program was going to have its own building. The preschool was going to have the amenities of every other school in the district and perhaps even an approximation of the same respect.

The idea and much of the labor that followed came from

Kathy's teaching partner, who at times was working round the clock on the project while still holding her full-time job. Her colleagues took on extra duties in order to free her up for writing grants, consulting with architects and early childhood experts, and pacifying state officials whose greatest single fear seemed to be that a new building funded for direct services to children and families would wind up shanghaied by school administrators for their own purposes. Her colleagues also stirred their ideas into the brew.

Though the plans were repeatedly scaled down from the Reggio Emilia–inspired structure called for in the original blueprint, the building eventually came to be. It included multiple classrooms, individual or small-group therapy rooms, a storage space worthy of a medium-sized hardware store, office space for teachers, additional office space for social agencies (who it was hoped would offset building costs by paying rent and provide the equivalent of one-stop shopping for parents in need of broad-spectrum social services), a combination cafeteria/activities room (for work with gross motor skills), and a cushioned playground with brand-new equipment. Parents of the children, husbands of the teachers, and local business owners all lent a hand in assembling furniture, putting up shelves, moving equipment from former sites, and donating materials not covered by grants. It gave me particular pleasure to sit on the polished floor one evening and screw together my wife's new desk.

With the public declaration of an innovative new model for early childhood education—including the coordination of services between the public school, Head Start, and a nonprofit agency devoted to the area's migrant-worker families—reporters came to snap the pictures and write down the names of the superintendent, the director of special services, the state legislator for our district, and a host of other luminaries (say "cheese," as in "big")—everyone, need I add, but the women who had brought the building to birth. But the building was a reality. A new day had dawned.

It would be a short one. You can build a school from the ground up, but the directing of its destiny will always move from the top down. You can say "the kids come first" till the cows come home, but in practice the kids come fourth behind administrators, parents, and teachers—or fifth, in a dairy economy, behind the cows. Within the space of about three years, a new superintendent relocated his offices to the building. The social service agencies vanished. The storage room was emptied and its contents squeezed into outdoor storage sheds in order to make additional office space. The office for the preschool staff became nearly as cluttered as before with the overflow from the storage sheds. At least one treatment room was rededicated as a transition space for obsolete computer equipment. The spacious "gross motor room," to which children would go for their exercise on days too cold for them to have recess outdoors, was regularly commandeered for district-wide principals' meetings. Worst of all, three out of three extraordinarily gifted preschool teachers had left for other jobs. First to go was the woman whose brainchild the building had been and whose visionary capabilities included that of being able to read the writing on the wall.

Kathy stayed. Now the most senior member of the operation, the go-to person for day-to-day problems, though never for any programmatic decision that might plausibly require some rudimentary knowledge of early childhood development, she was often the first to arrive at the building and the last to leave. She was also one of the few people left under its roof who could recall what the place was originally intended to be. Returning from a sabbatical granted for the purpose of adding to her already considerable knowledge of autism spectrum disorders, she found the building altered and her new proposals ignored. The sabbatical felt like a practical joke. By then the "new initiative" within the district was for "all-day" (as opposed to half-day) preschool, ostensibly predicated on the belief that pre-K education is of vital importance and actually predicated on the belief that pre-K education is nothing more than glorified day care anyway. No one troubled to ask Kathy or any of her frontline colleagues about the appropriateness of a thirty-five-hour school week to a four-year-old. And why should they, given that a teacher of four-year-olds is frequently afforded the status of a four-year-old?

When Kathy dared to tell her imperious new supervisor that she was always open to constructive criticism but not to being snapped at like a stray dog, she was rewarded with the added chore of helping to set out hot lunches, buttering crackers, and wiping plates while postponing the treatment needs of the quasi- and nonverbal children who crowded her roster. Unlike my wife, the quasi- and nonverbal children could be counted on not to complain.

As my daughter had once awakened me from my stupor by saying "I'm not good at anything," my wife roused me to wakefulness by an equally affecting refrain. "Just once before I die, I would like to have a job where I'm treated like an adult."

William Carlos Williams told us that "so much depends upon a red wheelbarrow," and I have wondered if he said so because, as a physician, he wanted to distract us from the fact that so much *more* depends on a Blue Cross insurance policy, glazed with J-Rider, beside the chickenshit job. As my wife continually reminded me when I told her to quit and that I would welcome her home with roses and a loud hurrah if she did, we needed health insurance. My quoting of Thoreau's magnificent line about the folly of working yourself sick in order to have money to pay the doctor wasn't much help. Though Kathy never would have said so, the simple fact was that for years I'd been able to play Thoreau *and* pay the doctor thanks to her.

Indignant and discouraged but not yet beat, I devised two plans of emancipation. Neither one involved my return to Ranger Country, I might add. First, I would try to write my way out of our problem. I seemed close to a solution when the offer of a magazine column promised more income stability than I can usually count on as a freelance writer. The offer seemed almost too good to be true, and it was. The column was given to someone else.

The second plan was to parlay my modest publishing credentials into some kind of prep school or college teaching job. (The expiration of my teaching certificate several years previous made my employment at a public high school seem unlikely.) True, I had no college teaching experience, no PhD either, but creative writing positions sometimes waived those requirements. And hadn't I prepared kids for college for years, including some who were now professors with PhDs?

Knowing this was a long shot but not without confidence, I shelled out for a year's membership (at the peon level) in the Modern Language Association, without which mortals are not permitted even to weep over its want ads, and applied for positions at universities, colleges, and private secondary schools. I'd love to tell you some of the impressive things I said in my interviews, but that would require me to have been invited to an interview.

After every option I could think of had dead-ended, I learned there was to be a one-year opening at the high school where I'd taught, the only place I'd ever taught for pay. Suddenly there was a new and fateful nuance to the title of my book about teaching, now more than twenty years old: *No Place But Here.* For a fee and some hoop jumping, and with the superintendent's approval, the state was willing to grant me a two-year provisional license.

So, you might ask—echoing Dylan's taunting refrain in "Like a Rolling Stone"—*how does it feel* to be walking across the high school parking lot on a balmy spring day in the autumn of my life, just ahead of the school buses now blocking any chance of a hasty retreat, with my old nemesis the intercom blaring at me across the lawn? How does it feel to be back in the building from which I'd ventured fourteen years ago to earn my living with my pen? How did it feel to sit at a table at the one interview I'd managed to garner after all my exhaustive searching, across from a principal, a director of guidance services, and two out of four school board members who are all not only younger than I but also former students of mine and, without telling any lies outright, hedge the desperation that led me to apply? And what did I feel when one of the board members, not a former student, I'm relieved to say, expressed her concern that I might treat the post as a poor relation to my writing career, shortchanging the students while living on the taxpayers' dime, as had been the case with one schoolteaching real estate agent she'd known in the past—a bitterly ironic insinuation given that my refusal to do that very thing in all the years I taught at this school is quite possibly a reason for the arrested development and equivocal success that have brought me hat in hand to the interview?

Ambivalence. That's what I felt at the interview, that's what I feel walking into the school this afternoon, and that as much as any other single word is my best recommendation to whoever gets the chore of coming up with the Library of Congress subject classifications for this book. Teachers—rural high schools—midlife predicaments—freelance hacks, plight of—ambivalence.

On the one hand, I feel a sense of futility and failure, a sense of having been cut down to size, the victim of bad luck, of "systems" both educational and economic, of my own delusions most of all. This has nothing to do with thinking that the profession of teacher is beneath me; I have always said that no book I've ever written or will ever write is as important in the scheme of things, as venerable in the firmament of human accomplishment, and as much sheer fun in its finer moments as teaching the young. I will believe that till the day I die. I would believe it were my name to eclipse that of Joan Didion or Philip Roth. Rather, my discouragement has to do with my apparent failure to live up to the motto I now find blazoned in large letters in the school's main lobby: MOVE FORWARD.

At the same time, I feel an emotion difficult to express without sounding maudlin. As happened more than half my lifetime ago, when no one seemed to want my services or to be willing to give me a chance, this small rural high school is once again opening its doors—and not reluctantly, or on the whole suspiciously, but rather as if little besides its own good fortune has drawn me (what other word can I use?) *home*. I never felt it was a sin to leave the school behind once I was brave and solvent enough to do so, but somehow coming back calls to mind the parable of the prodigal son. Unworthy as I am, Lake Region Union High School has put a ring on my finger and health insurance under my feet. And there may be a more applicable parable. Even as I write this I wonder, honestly for the first time, if I have misinterpreted that nightmare about the beast I was trying to bludgeon to death out on the open sea. Had I dreamed but a moment longer, might I have realized that it leapt to my imperiled raft for no other purpose than to take me in its arms?

AUGUST

High school is closer to the core of the American experience than anything else I can think of.

—Kurt Vonnegut

I lose my black-and-white picture postcard of Malcolm X somewhere in the aisles of Bed, Bath and Beyond, a predicament as ludicrous as I'm starting to feel. I'm in Bed, Bath and Beyond in the hopes of finding some inexpensive picture frames for decorating my classroom. I've brought Malcolm in for a fitting. I'll have his photograph in my classroom for what I tell myself are several compelling reasons; I've gone so far as to memorize them in anticipation of the first time a student asks, "Who's that guy?" and, more to my purposes, "Why do you have his picture here?"

I'll tell them that Malcolm was a pimp and a drug pusher who became the leader of a liberation movement and thus a symbol of every person's potential for redemption. (I'll probably need to define *redemption*; I doubt I'll need to define *pimp*.) I'll tell them Malcolm was an avid reader who found at least some of his redemption in books. "If I weren't out here every day battling the white man, I could spend the rest of my life reading." I'll tell them that although he may at one time have been the most feared man in America, he defied our pop stereotype of the badass rebel by dressing in dark suits and ties and leaving us a body of published work in which you'll search in vain for a single four-letter word.

Not least of all, I'll tell them that until a bullet cut him down, he continued to change and grow, renouncing his own racism no less than that of his opponents. And if I feel the need, I'll tell them that unlike his justly more celebrated counterpart, Martin Luther King, he was no pacifist and nobody's idea of a saint, and neither (all young knaves, take note) am I.

Probably I won't wonder aloud in their presence if hanging his portrait in my classroom amounts to my own bid for badass cachet—the lame attempt of a compliant, middle-aged, middle-class white man to convince himself that he's an edgier customer than he really is. Except that Malcolm seems to have said as much already by vanishing into thin air and leaving me to cope with the embarrassment of losing him in Bed, Bath and Beyond.

Kathy tells me not to be discouraged. For all we know, she says, some bored-to-tears kid who got dragged along on a shopping trip will pick up the picture, ask his mother whose face it is, and turn to Google for whatever his mom doesn't know. I'm braced by her faith, the faith of a teacher, though I feel a bit like a tagalong kid myself to be so much in need of soothing.

If I'm testy this afternoon it has to do with more than a stifling parked car and my general disinclination to shop. The summer is quickly slipping away. Much of it has been taken up with promotional events for my most recent book, published the preceding May like a last hurrah before my writing output dries up to a few doodles. I am using the rest of my time to prepare for my classes, only one of which (Composition) I've ever taught before. Given that I began to do so in March, I'm dismayed not to be further along. I know from experience that while preparation is no guarantee of success, there is no sustained success without it. You can be as prepared to teach *Of Mice and Men* as Milton was to write *Paradise Lost* and still be shot down by a host of exigencies, equipment malfunctions, last-minute changes in the schedule, the wrong thing said to the wrong kid on the wrong day, but you're doomed from the start without an adequate plan.

Any teacher worth his or her salt will tell you that there are gains to be had by laying the plan aside and going with the flow of a class's sudden inspiration, but show me a teacher who sees this as the norm, and I'll show you a teacher living in a pipe dream of delusional serendipity. In a word, I'll show you a slacker. The problem is that time and energy are finite, and the need to be prepared isn't, so that sooner or later even the most conscientious teacher, and most certainly the rookie teacher, walks into a class less prepared than she needs to be, which means anxiously expectant of the moment when the whole thing will begin to unravel at the drop of a hat, or more precisely at the drop of a sheaf of test papers, a roiling test tube, or a photograph that was in your hand just a minute ago and where in God's name did you put it?

I'm gratified to discover that I will have a classroom mostly to myself and that it is one of the few retaining an old-fashioned blackboard. Most of the others have been outfitted with those white glossy panels that take erasable felt markers. I've always found chalk more sensuous, its sound on slate more authoritative than a marker's mousey squeak. I'll be stationed three doors down from the room that was once mine, but with the same view out the windows, the same hilly pastures under the wooded horizon. I might even see cows.

Other details have changed, including the presence of a

television in the room, and a desktop computer that I'm instructed never to turn off. Its wires run up to the ceiling and out to a power strip like an unruly grapevine. The venetian blinds all work; I'll have light through all my windows. For a few bleak years in the mideighties the school directors decided to conserve energy by boarding up one window in every classroom as well as the skylights over the gym. The boards went out on the orders of a new principal. It was during his term that framed pieces of student art began to appear in the lobby and hallways. Now there is scarcely a wall without a painting, though most of the wall space on the floors of the academic wing is taken up by lockers. I don't look forward to the sound of them slamming throughout the day or to the compulsive time wasting they occasion. But the students have always loved them—a small private space in a zone where almost nothing is private—and it is probably still possible to connect with a few freshmen through a bit of extemporaneous safecracking when the combinations fail.

For now my business takes me to the main office, which I find has been reorganized and much brightened since I was there in the mid-1990s. The remnants of someone's birthday cake and a bouquet of flowers are on the counter beside the clipboard on which the staff are expected to sign in and out. Where there had previously been one main office secretary, there are now two, one close to the door and another pulled back slightly from the traffic, but neither invulnerable to constant interruption. By way of a good omen, I'm greeted warmly by two veterans from my first years at Lake Region.

"Back for some more abuse?" asks the music teacher, while the math teacher gives me a bear hug. I always admired these two, especially after I had a chance to see their skills with my own daughter. I'd asked the one to get her through some difficulties with her clarinet and the other to help her prepare for a geometry exam. In both instances, I was struck not only by the deft mid-wifery that characterizes a master teacher but also by the realization that after years of teaching in the same building with these men I had in fact never seen them teach. I fear this is the norm for most schools. You rate your colleagues by your students' praises, by what you're able to deduce from lunchroom conversations or assignments left behind on a photocopier, but you rarely see them in action. Perhaps I'll be more fortunate this time around. For now, it's enough to hear them say "Glad to have you back."

My first appointment is with another past acquaintance, though not a former colleague. I first met Andre Messier as a fourteen-year-old farm boy in my freshman English class, at which age he could have done a competent job of leading the school, though it is only recently that he's become Lake Region's principal. Prior to that he served the school as a math teacher and later as vice principal, the unexpected death of his ranking supervisor putting him at the helm. Well over six feet, with a halogen smile and the broadest shoulders I have ever seen on a human being, he is deferential, resolute, and charismatic to such a degree that he trumps my usual suspicions of charisma. Apparently, the kids like to call him Mr. Mess, and one of my first questions to him is what he would prefer me to call him.

He replies that however I address him, he can't bring himself to call me anything but Mr. Keizer, so he is Mr. Messier to me from then on.

I've never considered myself to have "a problem with author-ity"; most of my tussles have been with men who presume an authority they don't officially have. With authority figures who know their place and honor mine, I have a history of doing well, perhaps too well, to the extent that I wonder if I might in some past life have been a cavalier or a samurai, fierce in my lord's or lady's defense and deferential in their retinue, feudal to the marrow of my professedly democratic bones. Any potential for that dynamic to be strained by the difference in age between Mr. Messier and me is more than compensated by the courtly respect on both sides. That doesn't mean that I won't be held accountable or have my challenges adjusting to what Mr. Messier refers to as "a twenty-first-century school."

As I anticipated, one of these adjustments will be to a computerized grading system, which has been in use at school for a few years now, though this year's version will be new, something called PowerSchool. Mr. Messier is quick to assure me that as long as grades are duly recorded online, teachers are free to keep an old-fashioned paper grade book, as most of the older members of the faculty do.

The demonstration he gives me is less reassuring. I am put off by the feature that allows one to check a student's progress in every course he has. In other words, while I am still not likely to observe my colleagues at work in the classroom, I will be only a few keystrokes away from being able to peer into their grade books. If I so choose, I can cast an appraising eye on how regularly they give tests and assignments and how timely they are in recording their grades. Experience tells me that this will be a favorite pastime with the sort of teacher who looks for any diversion from doing his own job, especially if it affords him the opportunity of learning that another colleague is even lazier than he is. My tongue gets the better of me, and I blurt out, "I'd as soon go through your wife's purse" (the wife in this case being the chair of the math department) "as look into her grade book."

This is received calmly, without visible irritation, and possibly with the trace of a smile—three descriptors I can't claim for my utterance—and I am sorry for my comment. But not entirely so. In time, thanks to some good tutelage from two long-suffering colleagues, I will become a competent PowerSchool user, praised by several of my peers for the number and timeliness of my recorded grades. But I will never be able to return their compliment because I will never be able to bring myself to the point where I would look into Mrs. Messier's purse.

I do better at holding my tongue when the principal sketches out the direction he would like to see the school take in regard to the grades themselves. He sums it up with the motto "Failure is not an option." As I will soon learn, this does *not* mean that no student can receive a failing grade, though the more cynical among the faculty will from time to time contend that it might as well. The principal is rather talking about a shift in emphasis from the grade earned to the material learned. Giving a student a zero for missing work—something Mr. Messier freely admits was his own policy during his years as an esteemed math teacher—he now regards as "the easy way out." It may fulfill some standard of justice or bookkeeping, but if the student is allowed not to hand in an assignment or pass a test, doesn't that mean he or she is being "let off the hook" of learning the material or the skill?

Mr. Messier wants to see a more aggressive approach, one he grants is a difficult sell "for some of the older people on staff." As an example he cites how he searched out a student who'd failed to hand in an assignment for a given class, brought him into the main office during a lunch period, and saw that he did not rise from his desk until the work was done. It seems that leading a horse to water is no longer enough; the horse is going to drink, even if it requires a trip to the principal's office to lower his lips to the trough.

This runs counter to my own philosophy, which has always put a high premium on free will. Based on what Mr. Messier says about the resistance he meets among the older faculty, I gather that free will still has its adherents. But perhaps philosophy is too exalted a word for what boils down to professional pride: I have

always seen compulsion as a poor substitute for a teacher's moti-
vational powers. When the school first introduced a policy on
athletic eligibility years ago, I was adamant in my opposition:
Why ruin something a kid does well on the basis of what he is
failing to do well? And why usurp my prerogative to inspire a
good ballplayer to write good essays about playing ball?

I should be listening to my principal, not ranting in my head,
and what I hear is his heartfelt concern over the drop-out rate at
the school (on the rise in recent years) and the bearing that standardized tests have come to have on its reputation and financial
well-being. (Taxpayers are less apt to support a school they perceive as "failing.") On his side of the argument are some laudable successes in reducing the premature exits and raising the
scores. In the year before my arrival, Lake Region ranked first in
the state in its writing tests. Wasn't I the one who said at my
application interview that I did not have an educational philosophy so much as a work ethic? So why am I wanting to quibble
over philosophy now?

I try to bear in mind that I am little more than an overnight
guest here, with an obligation to cause as little disruption as possible to my hosts. As for educational philosophy, I have taught
long enough to know that it resembles political philosophy in
depending a great deal on the personnel involved. If the king is
Buddha, then long live the king, and if Hitler is elected by popular vote (as in fact he was), don't ask me to give three guttural
cheers for democracy. If Andre Messier says failure is not an
option, I'm ready to bend my beliefs, if only to do my part in seeing that failure is never an option for him.

Sara, my department head, was the second person I saw in
March and we have been in regular touch throughout the spring

and summer. She says she appreciates the time I'm putting in before the job starts. If she has reservations about the hire, as I'm told she has, she doesn't show them to me. I don't expect her to. Very fond of sports, she is also a good sport. She is the only member of the department who is older than I, though not by much. Voluble with peers, maternal with students, and seemingly inexhaustible in everything she undertakes, Sara appears to be the kind of supervisor who for every thing she asks you to do does three herself of the same kind—or four, if you include her assistance with the one thing she's asked you to do.

What I've asked Sara to do is to bring me up to speed on my teaching assignments and the current English curriculum. She has everything in readiness on my first visit. In addition to copies of the required texts for all my courses, I receive three-ring binders outlining the 2009 Vermont Common Core of "standards-based instruction," the department's own "scope and sequence" for its 9–12 offerings, and the NECAP (New England Common Assessment Program) test, an annual examination given since 2005 in order to comply with the federal No Child Left Behind Act.

One thing is clear from the outset: the biggest change in education since my departure from the classroom, bigger even than the place of technology in the curriculum, is the move toward uniform instruction. Students and teachers are obliged to be on the same page, or the same screen if you will, in terms of the "desired outcomes." In many ways the changes are mutually supportive: the technology allows for greater standardization and oversight; it also provides the rationale for greater standardization and oversight. *Our kids need to be prepared for the digital age and we need to be sure our teachers are preparing them.*

Despite some strong misgivings—the "digital age" is not my god any more than the "global marketplace"—I want to work in concert with my colleagues. I want to do a good job. I recognize the dangers of the self-styled contrarian whose "different drummer" lesson plans amount to little more than a list of pet peeves and arbitrary waivers. I've met more than one English teacher, for example, who claimed that "writing can't be taught" or that "grammar isn't important." At the same time, I'm not sure students are best served by a faculty of conformists, by teachers who are less shepherds than sheep. Sara probably imagined me raising just such a caveat when she objected to my hire.

Nevertheless, it's obvious she wants me to succeed. She has seen that my teaching assignment includes three sections of the same class, midlevel tenth-grade English, and has assured me that I will have a sufficient number of the required texts to teach the same book to all three classes at the same time. Effectively this means that for a five-class teaching assignment, I will have only three preparations, perhaps as close as any public high school teacher ever gets to the teaching load of a tenured university professor, which admittedly is about as close as Neptune ever gets to the sun.

My semester-long elective courses, offered exclusively to juniors and seniors, are Literature of Vermont and Popular Fiction in the fall, and Composition and another section of Popular Fiction in the spring. These, too, are geared to students of average ability, who account for roughly half of the school's total enrollment. While that doesn't discourage me, it does make me slightly uneasy. In general my preferences run to the advanced (top third) and the remedial (bottom fifth) tracks of the school's ability groupings, where the stakes tend to be higher, though they're not often the same stakes. The brighter kids are driven to succeed; the more challenged kids are driven not to fail. The middle are more complacent; it can take a heap of kindling to set them afire.

As if reading my mind, Sara tells me that I can choose a new book to add to my Popular Fiction class. It seems she wants the course to be an elective for me as well as for my students, though it's just as likely that she wants to add a little fresh blood to the reading syllabus. I'm happy to oblige, and I know, as Sara undoubtedly does, how much the students stand to gain if I can teach a book I love. But I have other criteria besides my own enthusiasm. I want the book to be recent enough in copyright date to qualify as contemporary. I would also like a book written by a woman or at least a book in which a fully drawn female character figures prominently. Few of the books at my disposal meet this requirement. Not least of all, I'd like a book that might do for my students what *The Autobiography of Malcolm X* did for me.

It so happens I have recently read what seems like the perfect selection: Elizabeth Strout's *Amy and Isabelle*, a poignantly class-conscious predecessor to her Pulitzer Prize–winning *Olive Kitteridge*. The book has two major female characters, a mother and a daughter, a working-class setting not unlike the grittier parts of our school district, and an author whose unsentimental compassion for her characters is on a par with Thomas Hardy's. As a bonus, the novel contains what is possibly the sleaziest teacher in all literature, a sexual predator who seduces the daughter. The problem is that some of the students I teach may already have met his type. Sara suggests as much, with little commentary but with a strong recommendation that I select another book. She's afraid of reopening old wounds. This is classic Sara in its sensitivity, but it also strikes me as indicative of a major change between schools now and schools then. The self-censorship that once was predicated on the wish to spare students exposure to aspects of life they were "not ready for" now is based on the dismal job we've done in providing that very sort of protection. In other words, much of what we now deem "inappropriate for children" is deemed as such because it depicts what has already happened to children. The unmentionable is no longer the same thing as the unthinkable.

Anyway, *Amy and Isabelle* is out. When Kathy and I go up to school one night at the end of August to make final adjustments to my classroom, I lay another novel on my department head's desk for vetting, with the juicy passages flagged to save her time. I'm surprised by the number of flags; I'd never thought of the book as racy. *You're in a different setting now*—it occurs to me that I will need to flag some of my own daily expressions. I'll need to relearn the skill of listening with the ears of a child and the ears of a parent too.

Kathy and I set down the plants we've carried up through the stuffy, darkened halls and throw open the windows to the air and the moths. When the students show up in another week, I intend to have a bouquet of fresh flowers on the sill. I hang up framed photos of the Vermont poet James Hayford and his wife, Helen, both deceased, who befriended Kathy and me in our first teaching years, as well as a new Malcolm X (with a more suitably priced frame from the Dollar General) and a flyer from an ACLU Banned Books Week event in which I'd participated the previous year. I tape up larger posters of Billie Holiday and Eleanor Roosevelt, the latter quoted as saying that no one can demean you but yourself, the former seeming to say "I'm not so sure of that." I roll up two large sheets of paper into horns and tape one to each side of the TV. If I have to give the devil his due in my classroom, I'm also going to give him his proper insignia.

My predecessor has left the room in immaculate shape, including the desk and filing cabinets. There's a rumor that his year's leave is in fact a prelude to his farewell—that he's not coming back after this year is done. Judging by the shape the room is in, that seems plausible, though an equally plausible explanation is his regard for his former department head. He liked to call me

Boss in those days, which he explained was not a gesture of subordination but a tip of his hat to my Jersey roots and our shared love of Springsteen. In front of his room stands an arti-fact from my old boss, Donna Underwood, who died before he joined the faculty, a massive wooden podium built for her by a former student in his shop class. I'm cheered by the sight of it, a bit worse for wear but still solid and, to my eyes at least, still Donna's.

Tomorrow will be the first official day of duty for district teachers and staff, all of whom will meet in the high school cafeteria en masse before going to their separate buildings. The program will be the usual mix of orientation, goal setting, and possibly a speaker, workshop, or activity designed to hone our skills and boost our morale but almost certain to depress me. For the past fourteen years Kathy has come home from these staff development days and said, when I asked how they went, either "It wasn't so bad" or "It was pretty awful" but always "I am so glad you're not there anymore." Now it's my turn to be thankful, though hardly Kathy's turn to gloat. Her eyes are wet, the next morning, when she kisses me good-bye.

By custom, staff development days begin with the introduction of new staff and the noting of departures. The superintendent makes a statement to the effect that the district has lost one Keizer and gained another, and it takes just about all the self-control I possess not to blurt out that the district has hardly broken even. Several others speak of Kathy's "retirement," and I want to correct them with the word *resignation* but I'm committed to holding my tongue as much as I can.

Not much of the morning will pass before I become aware of my need to exercise another kind of self-discipline: that of holding my bladder and bowels. I won't need to ask permission to use the restroom during staff development days, but once school starts, I'll not be able to step away from my room without asking another teacher to keep watch on my class. There are four minutes between class periods, roughly five hundred students and staff spread out on three floors, and a single toilet for each gender on mine. This is going to pose a challenge, especially since my only proven strategy for avoiding what were once almost daily headaches is constant hydration.

For her part, the "retired" Kathy Keizer is doing well in a new job. After my acceptance of the teaching position and shortly before resigning from her own, she located a part-time position as the speech-language pathologist in the pediatric neurology department at Dartmouth-Hitchcock Medical Center, an hour and a half's drive from home and several light years away from what her public school job had become. The headiness of the change is hard to describe. Courted and now regularly consulted by a former Georgetown specialist and a PhD-level nurse practitioner with multiple tours of humanitarian work in Colombia and Afghanistan, shadowed by earnest interns in their first white coats, Kathy has found herself in what is commonly called "another orbit" though "different universe" might be more apt. Where once her insights counted for naught among supervisors with little or no knowledge in early childhood development, now among specialists with breathtaking credentials she is asked to weigh in. Of more surprise to her than me, her decades of frontline work with underprivileged children and families amount to gold-standard currency among people smart enough to know their own limitations, which is to say, among people whose advanced degrees are not in education.

My low opinion doesn't lessen with the superintendent's address. It strikes me as typical of the profession's schizoid synthesis of lamentation over prevailing trends—"the newspaper is dead," "the World Wide Web is dead" (presumably a casualty of social media), on-site classroom instruction by teachers will soon be dead—and zealous promotion of the same. But "typical" is the whole point: the schizophrenia is not the superintendent's so much as the profession's. We teachers will make the world a better place, our masters tell us, and we will do so by finding more effective ways to keep our students in lockstep with the world as it is.

Consider, for example, the "30-million-word gap." Citing statistics from a famous study, the superintendent notes that students from the lower strata of society reach the age of three having heard 30 million fewer words than their middle-class counterparts. They've also heard 400,000 fewer parental expressions of praise. Possibly because I'm scrambling to get these figures into my notebook, I'm not sure what point they're intended to illustrate. That this is what we're up against, or that this is what will ultimately defeat us, or that this is the wrong that a handful of people armed with Ho-Hum State diplomas and Payless shoes are responsible for making right? Or perhaps, given that we are one of the poorest schools in the state according to the criterion of students who qualify for "free or reduced lunch," the implication is that the wrong has already been righted. After all, our top-notch students perform satisfactorily on their AP tests; nearly two-thirds of our graduating seniors go on to some kind of college or technical school.

In vain I wait for someone to remark that if our students are subject to such appalling inequalities, even before they enter school, then educational reform is a pathetic substitute for social revolution. At the least, I want someone to assert that the best reason for educating children is not to put them and their descendants on the winning side of the 30-million-word gap but to equip them to destroy the gap altogether. As the lecture continues, and throughout the school year, I will repeatedly be struck by the sense that the professed goal of creating "a level playing field" through education is little more than the goal of sorting winners from losers with a steady hand and a clear conscience. The single greatest expression of the American project, American public education is also its most cynical lie.

I'm still straining to keep my mouth shut (for all I know, dozens of my colleagues are engaged in the same struggle) and figure that if I've made it silently through the 30-million-word gap, I'll probably manage the same feat with the segments given over to technology, though that is likely to be a longer slog. Here, too, I wait in vain for what strikes me as the ultimate, unavoidable question. As we're told that 10 percent of all high school education will be computer-based by 2014 and rise to 50 percent by 2019, and as the PowerPoint throws up aphoristic bromides by the corporate heroes of the digitally driven "global economy"— the implication being that "great companies" know what they're doing, while most schools don't—and as we're goaded mercilessly to the conclusion that everything we are, know, and do is bound for the dustbin of history, I want to ask what kind of schooling Bill Gates and Steve Jobs had. Wasn't it at bottom the very sort of book-based, content-driven education that we declare obsolete in the name of their achievements?

Like an act of clemency, we're informed that after a short break we will have a presentation on blood-borne pathogens by the same school nurse who used to do the program when I taught here before and has done it ever since. Fair, freckled, and willowy, looking only a little older than I remember her, and with the same fetching display of good-humored embarrassment she's always shown in front of a group, Joannie steps on stage to sing her old standards about what to do when a kid starts bleeding all over your shoes. It's not easy to describe the effect this has on me, after so many years away and after several hours of biting my tongue, though it's clear that my companions are also moved, especially the old timers. Our cheering only serves to make Joannie more blushingly adorable, which brings on a whistle or two besides. Joannie and the Blood-Borne Pathogens. Bennie and the Jets. It's like coming back to your hometown and finding so much altered, the storefronts new, the gas pumps automated, and the dogs all dead, but then, just around a corner is your old bar, still open, with the same girl at the taps. Just as she did in years past, Joannie's handing out the rubber gloves, offering extra pairs to anyone who wants them. It was Joannie who told me to drink more water and I'd need fewer Excedrin, Joannie who will tell me to go easy on myself as I get back in harness. I'd as soon start the day over as miss a minute of what she has to say about her old buddies the blood-borne pathogens. So glad I am to see her that it takes me a few moments to realize that I'm less than a week away from walking elbow-to-elbow in a tense throng of jostling adolescents, where the eruption of a fistfight is always possible, to say nothing of contracting a case of hepatitis from a combatant's bloody nose.

On the second day of staff development, the district's teachers report to their respective schools, with each building principal in charge of the day's agenda for his crew. I greet the prospect with relief, though the agenda item labeled "Let the games begin" gives me pause. I tell myself it is probably a metaphor, something like "play ball" or "to your marks, get set, go" and completely in keeping with the athletic sensibilities of our administration. Even when the vice principal appears before us dressed in a catcher's outfit, I wonder if this is merely a theatrical touch, no more, something to raise the hungover spirits of those still sobering up from their summer breaks. I ought to know better.

The vice principal tells us that no one has to participate in the game he is about to describe but urges us to consider the number of times each of us, in our role as teacher, has asked students to do things they found uncomfortable and even embarrassing. In short, he asks us to consider whether feeling like a fool might not, in the long run, be preferable to looking like a hypocrite.

It is acting like a prima donna that I fear most and so I resolve that I am going to play along, though I will never in the course of the year feel more tempted to walk out of the building than I do right then. Without going into tedious detail, the game is basically a treasure hunt that each team of tablemates is to conduct while holding on to a length of clothesline. Since this is a timed race, it behooves each team to move quickly, which is to say, as quickly as its slowest member allows. Since the clues are scattered throughout the school and over the sprawling school grounds, and since I have spent the last weeks of the summer taking medication for an injury to my feet, it does not take long for me to be in some pain. It takes even less time for me to feel humiliated.

Finally, I drop out and return to my table. I tell my teammates that I can only slow them down. I rather feel as though I've let them down. This has been my first real challenge on the job, and I have failed—something I'd not have done had I either flatly refused at the beginning or followed through to the end.

I also see it as an occasion for repentance. Over the past fourteen years of my self-employed life, I've gotten rather smug about my appetite for work. Well, Garret, this is what "work" means for most people. Although the vice principal's words about putting on the shoe we often ask our students to wear conjures up few associations for me, I find I'm thinking of a whole array of wage earners: the HarperCollins sales people I saw at a book conference who'd been forced by the publisher to wear Lemony Snicket armbands, the junior executives ordered to examine one another's auras in sleepover seminars on Gurdjieff, the counter clerks who risk reprimand and even the loss of their jobs for failure to get you your burger and fries within one minute flat or to ask if you want a hot apple turnover to wash down with what remains of your supersized soda, my teacher colleagues today not least of all, who fall into the drill without complaint and perhaps with a more informed sense than my own that this could be, and in some years has been, a whole lot worse.

These are my musings at the time, though not at present, when my thoughts are mostly of the vice principal. I made a note to keep my eye on "that guy" then, little knowing that his eye was already on me and that he was showing me with as good a metaphor as any I can imagine how our relationship would work. In the ensuing nine months he would stand with me in every difficulty I brought to his attention, as though a rope were holding us together, and he would never once let me go.

After almost a week of meetings, the arrival of the students is like a breath of fresh air. Their voices course through the hallways like molecules of oxygen through tired blood. Literally, though, the air is hot beyond belief. The temperature in my classroom, which is directly above the flat tarred roof of the downstairs lobby, hovers around 90, which is to say, a few degrees above what the temperature is outside. I have a fan for my room, but turning it on makes hearing more difficult, and opening the door to the classroom exposes us to noise in the halls. I lower the blinds to block as much sunlight as possible and turn off the overhead fluorescent lights, leaving students with barely enough light to see. The last time I recall working in heat of this intensity was during the summer after high school, when I worked in a glue factory. Even there we had an open garage door and a handy water hose for dousing ourselves.

One of the rooms adjacent to mine is fully air-conditioned. It contains several banks of classroom computers, which will run erratically if they get too hot. I remark to my students that if they were made of wires and silicon instead of nerves and blood, they would be sitting in a cooler room. They do not seem to grasp the irony. Born at the close of the twentieth century, they know their lowly place in the Great Chain of Being. They show remarkable patience as the day drags on, complaining as well they might, but not whining or using the heat as an excuse to slack off or misbehave.

Much remains to be seen, but the kids seem fairly similar to those I taught in the past. The voc-ed boys still carry baseball caps, putting them on between passing bells, and stalk through the hallways in high-topped boots. The girls still take hot weather as an invitation to bare as much skin as the dress code allows, though décolletage was never the rage it is now: one has the impression of being in the court of Louis XVI on a casual Friday. Everyone seems to have a cell phone; school rules dictate they be turned off throughout the academic wing. There's also more obesity than I recall in past years, though that was probably always more prevalent in this region than in other parts of the state. (Only someone utterly unacquainted with the cruel ironies of underclass life would see a contradiction between high rates of obesity and the fact that an estimated one child in four in the Northeast Kingdom is "food insecure"—that is, unable to take the likelihood of three meals a day for granted.) If anything, the students seem more cooperative, even more friendly on first contact than I remember kids being in my first years, but I am of the same generation as their grandparents now, and I was a mere nine years older than my oldest student when I first started out. Toward the last half of my first tenure I enjoyed the benefits of a cumulative reputation, of dos and don'ts handed down from older siblings—I'll enjoy less of that benefit now. It turns out I might have something better. "Do you remember having a student named Mary LaClare?" "Yes, and fondly"—and a sudden perceived resemblance tells me what's coming next. "She's my mom."

Unlike most of the men on the faculty, especially on those first sweltering days, I wear a tie, and a jacket too, hanging up the latter as soon as I enter my room. In an offhand expression of solidarity with the blue-collar parents of our community, but mainly as a concession to my falling arches, I add a pair of well-oiled work boots. For the first time in many years, I have what might be called a look—like me and like the white-collar trade of teaching itself, a strange amalgam. A girl passing in the hall tells me I look "spiffy." "I'd have thought I looked *old*," I say, and she counters by asking, "How old are you, thirty?" I take this as a compliment and beam accordingly, though she may in fact be doing nothing more than agreeing that I am old.

I have decided to begin each class period with a selection of music chosen for that day, writing the selection and artist on the board above my class agendas and keying the selection into a small CD player. For the students' first day, I choose John Coltrane's "Welcome," at the closing bars of which a hush comes over my chattering students, proof of what I've always believed about the divinity of Coltrane's inspiration and the wellsprings within even the dopiest-seeming kid. "This is nice music," one boy remarks, and no one sneers.

As I imagine is true for most teachers, I believe in stating my expectations from the start and in getting out of the gate as fast as possible with a first assignment. I stress the importance of courtesy and mutual respect. I stress that I will expect reading assignments to be read, a requirement I've been given to understand is alien to the experience of some of my older students, whose past English teacher is no longer employed at the school.

I also lay down what has always been one of my firmest rules: students who've been absent are to see me *on the morning* of their return to school, before classes begin. Few things can deflate a class period like devoting its first ten minutes to catching up students who were absent the day before—at the cost of neglecting students who were there. Often with the best of intentions, schools consistently telegraph the message that missing school is more advantageous than attending it. The suckers who show up live by the deadlines; the rest do their work and take their tests according to their own convenience. The trick is to convince students that you value their presence, you value the class period, you value the taxpayer's dime as the equivalent of a sacred trust. I personify that trust by asking my students not to forget "the man who works in the woods." As I explain, I mean any local logger who cuts pulp in a cedar swamp at thirty degrees below zero in order for us to have light and heat and books and in order for yours truly to have the health insurance and pension fund that the logger doesn't have. (Please, somebody, ask "Why not?") We insult his sacrifice if we waste our time.

Strict as I sound, and decent as most of these kids seem, it doesn't take them but a day to learn that as a matter of principle I will not refuse anyone's request to go to the restroom. I find the request itself demeaning, to me no less than to the student, and my answer has always been yes. It takes an explanation from another member of the faculty for me to realize that the requests are about answering the call of a cell phone as much as the call of nature. Texting in the boys' room is the new version of smoking in the boys' room, though to their lasting credit the addicts of yesteryear were usually able to go an hour without taking a puff. My strategy, at least initially, is the same as the one I used in years past when dealing with the Marlboro Man: keep the classes focused enough and intense enough that there's really something to be missed by staying away. Make the students *want* to be there. But already I can see that this approach may prove inadequate. Given that my classes this year are on the whole "less academic" than those I used to teach (now designated, to my considerable distaste, as "honors"), test scores and report card grades may not be the sticks and carrots they were for me in the past.

What is more, I'm competing for students' attention on no firmer foundation than I'm competing for air-conditioning. In other words, I'm up against the orthodoxy of a virtual religion, much more powerful than any narcotic, of which teachers themselves are the chief apostles. My comparison of texting today with smoking in years past amounts to a weak analogy unless it can be shown that schools in times past were evaluated by how thoroughly they integrated tobacco products into every aspect of the curriculum. With some teachers conducting class discussions via keypads and others following their students on Facebook, decrying the students' obsession with their cell phones seems disingenuous at best—like Al Capone decrying the amount of time Chicagoans are spending in speakeasies and brothels.

At the end of that first sweltering week, with the Labor Day weekend bobbing like a life raft at the end of it, a large boy, tall and wide, stops by my door and asks if it's true what he's heard, that I'm a writer. I tell him it is, at least insofar as I've managed to make a modest living doing that work. He says he's a writer too. I say I'm glad to hear it. I could be meeting myself as I was forty years ago, though I was much skinnier and not so tall. I probably can't expect to have the same effect on his literary aspirations as young and lovely Miss Pombo had on mine, but maybe I can have a small one. The boy is not in any of my classes. I shake his hand.

When I ask his name, he says that everyone calls him Ox. I search his face to see if I can detect whether he is happy about that, but it's possible he doesn't know himself. I tell him I'm not sure I'm going to be able to call him Ox, but that in the absence of a given name—he doesn't seem to want to tell me his—I might decide to call him Writer. Would that be okay?

It would. He says that maybe he will show me the book he is writing. I tell him I would love to see it. I will restate my willingness at least once more in the coming weeks. As time goes on, I will realize I am not going to see Writer's book—no more than I am going to see any of the other books my students claim to be writing, including one incredible tome that reportedly vanishes into cyberspace during the composition of its final, 700-and-somethingth page.

But now is only the first week of school, when I stand ready to assist and possibly rechristen every one of the budding authors who I am almost certain will approach me as a matter of course, ready for that moment when a framed photograph of El-Hajj Malik El-Shabazz, formerly Malcolm Little and best known as Malcolm X, will incite a life-changing discussion that in fact never occurs.

— 3 —

SEPTEMBER

Americans must resist the coming of fall, . . . because Americans want to remain individual. The classroom will teach us a language in common. The classroom will teach a history that implicates us with others.

—Richard Rodriguez, *Days of Obligation*

Within a few days after classes begin, I've formed my routine, which for all its appearance of self-discipline is grounded mainly in my desire to avoid panic. I rise most mornings by 4:00, hoping to carve a few more productive hours out of the day and also to convert the psychic energy that might otherwise go into making nightmares to creative energy for making assignments and tests. It occurs to me that had I risen as early to write during the past ten years, I might be writing still.

By 4:30 I'm showered, dressed, and at my upstairs desk, where I can usually accomplish a couple of hours of solid work. I know from experience they'll be worth twice that many spent at the tail end of a tiring day. By 6:30 I'm out the door, toting a full briefcase and a lunch cooler my wife has carefully packed for me, including at least three containers of fluid, usually two of water and one of iced tea. I could easily have another hour at my desk and still be to school by 8:00 as required, but I have my

reasons for leaving when I do. I can get situated with fewer interruptions if I'm there by 7:00 and possibly have first dibs on the
photocopier. I can blow some of the stale air from my classroom
and suck the last of the cool morning air in. I probably won't be
the first to arrive—there seem to be more early birds on staff
these days than in the past—but I'd prefer not to be. I'd prefer
not to risk setting off the school's security alarm when I punch
in the code that deactivates it.

Once I've unlocked my classroom, opened the windows, and
observed a moment of silence, I set up my fan and head down
the hall to the photocopier in the teachers' workroom. I'm a regular there, having no leftovers from past terms to fall back on. In
addition to being fast, the magnificent machine collates, staples,
and punches holes for a three-ring binder. The first automatic
washing machine could not have looked more magical to a laun-
dress than that copier looks to me. I came up through the ranks
in the days of mimeograph machines, typing my masters on a
typewriter without a ribbon in order to maximize the clarity of
the keys' impressions, correcting mistakes with a razor blade
and a fresh scrap of inked backing, and creasing the sheets carefully onto the drum lest the slightest wrinkle lay a blue jagged
scar across each page. Then it was staple, staple, staple, or find a
kid willing to staple for a few bucks. Even when the first copiers
arrived, they were reserved for use by the administration. Now
there are four copiers in the building; if there's a queue at this
one, I can try my luck downstairs.

With the copies warm in my hand, I walk quickly back to my
room to set up for my first class. This includes writing an agenda
on the blackboard, posting the title and artist for that day's
music, and arranging my desk and worktable as neatly as I can.
A teacher's battle with chaos follows the lines of Norse mythology: we know that the frost giants will eventually win but that

doesn't mean we can't smack a few down in the meantime. I uncap one of the water bottles my wife has prepared, the bottom third of its contents frozen solid against the heat. I chew an Altoid left over from the gift bag I took home from a television interview last summer. There was a bottle of vodka in that bag too, but I'm not to that point yet. I wait for my first arrivals.

I ask absent students to see me at the start of the day for the reasons I gave above, reasons I will have to repeat before the rule sinks in, along with warm praise whenever the rule is followed, but the fact is that I might keep the rule even without the reasons. Seeing a student first thing in the morning, telling him that he was missed the day before, asking her how she is feeling today, basking for a couple of minutes in the backstage banter that the audience of a classroom seldom allows—this is the only shot of spirits I need. There are school days that would seem close to wasted but for that first half hour with a few sparkling, sometimes still damp-haired kids.

At some point before the first passing bell I will need to turn on my laptop and log onto PowerSchool in order to take attendance as quickly as possible. The process is always slower than I hope. My habit in past years was to take a few minutes at the start of each period to set a positive tone, tell a joke, praise a student's achievements in another school activity, recount a current event, or read a passage I'd come across that seemed worth reading aloud, all the while taking attendance out of the corner of my eye and noting it in my grade book. The present system is more jealous of my attention. Often my first words to the class are related to the minutiae of the record keeping. We are expected, for example, to record missing homework, so that teachers in subsequent study halls can follow up and see that it gets done. To start a class by asking for a show of hands from those who haven't done their homework (something I've always preferred to do confidentially and at least a few minutes into the period by walking discreetly among the students) is hardly the best way to set a positive tone. If I hit the wrong key, I need to cancel out my notations and do all of them again. If a tardy student walks into the room a minute after I've hit "submit," then I need to call up the screen and do the entire roster over. As noted by the outside consultants who manage the system, it "currently lacks the capability" of maintaining a daily record of absences beyond "total to date"—a must for any teacher who hopes to keep track of when a student was and wasn't in class and therefore was or wasn't responsible for a missing assignment or on hand for an essential presentation of material. This means I must take attendance twice, once on the computer and once in a notebook I consult whenever I wish to know for sure what a student may have missed on a given day.

The bottom line here—and I use the phrase with an eye to the mind-set that promotes these "systems"—is that I am increasingly devoting more time to the generation and recording of data and less time to the educational substance of what the data is supposed to measure. Think of it as a man who develops ever more elaborate schemes for counting his money, even as he forfeits more and more of his time for earning the money he counts.

At least I do not lose more of my first period to morning announcements, which come at second period, when I have off. Instead of being read over the intercom by the principal as in years past, they're presented as a televised newscast by students in a media class. Included are a weather report and a notice of student birthdays. Thus the reason for a television in every room. I dehorn mine on the day of the first broadcast, sorry for my snarky gesture, not that it arouses much notice. Neither do the bulletin boards I've put up, including one that displays a medley of pop culture profiles, arresting photographs, incredible statistics, and hilarious cartoons and another that provides a space for students to write their "blues" (right next to Billie), complaints, and suggestions. The space will remain as blank as a broken TV for the next nine months; apparently no one has the blues but me.

My first-period class, Literature of Vermont, is small (ten students), docile, mostly unmotivated, and overwhelmingly (though not boorishly) male. Our one young woman sits in the middle, geographically, academically, and as a sisterly moral center. Among the texts I inherit, all of them chosen with the strictest regard to the permanent Vermont residency of their authors, I choose to begin with the longest, an all but forgotten novel by Mari Tomasi called *Like Lesser Gods*. It represents one of the state's first ambitious works of fiction (1949), was written by a woman, is based on almost-local history (that of the Barre granite quarries), and treats two themes not commonly associated with Vermont: Italian ethnicity and organized labor. The latter seems especially pertinent. The local furniture plant has no union, nor do the region's numerous underpaid child care workers (though an effort is afoot to organize them), nor do many of those employed in the building trades. Tomasi also develops a theme remarkably missing in much of the literature we assign to young people: the choice of a life's vocation. Study of the novel in years past has included a field trip to Barre, where Tomasi lived and where granite is still quarried and carved—an incentive for students to read the book but also for the teacher to assign it early, before any snowstorm can cancel a bus.

On the other hand, the book is long, the exposition dense, the vocabulary ponderous, the allusions plentiful—obstacles that seem all the more daunting after I've spent more time with the class. One student tells me flat out that he has never read a book in his life. Even over the summer, ignorant of my students and about a quarter of the way into my exhaustive annotation of the book, I began having doubts as to the wisdom of teaching it, but I told myself that if "midlevel students" in the past had managed to read it, students in the present should be able to do the same thing. I bet an awfully big wad of confidence on what proves to be a monumentally big *if*.

I consider bailing at one point, but conclude that would be a mistake. Abandon a book because it's stupid, not because it's hard, which always risks sticking the "stupid" label in the wrong place. I press forward, using almost every trick I know—study guides, character lists, in-class oral readings, real-life tie-ins, pop quizzes, alternatives to quizzes, student-designed quizzes, student-designed crib notes to be used on quizzes, close analysis, revised syllabi, donuts, imaginative identification with the novel's sentimentally drawn characters—but for most of the students, most of the time, the book is a loss. I'm an experienced teacher, but it seems I have a few lessons to learn.

Some of them come to me in offhand, stunning ways. I've been instructed that the policy for study halls requires teachers to assist students with their work before attending to their own (which was always my practice anyway) and prohibits allowing students to catch a few winks at their desks (something I never minded, especially once I discovered how taxing a school day could be to my own child). I have a small, highly cooperative lunch-period study hall, and a most delightful girl on the list, someone whose studiousness and affability seem to rub off on her neighbors. One day she has nothing to do, claiming she's managed to complete all of her homework. I have no reason to doubt her. Either because I've noticed her drawing or because I know she has a class in the art room, I ask her if she likes art. Yes, she likes art very much. Music to my ears—among several of the books I've brought to school for browsing is an expensive coffee table compendium of painting and sculpture by three

Italian masters, Leonardo da Vinci, Michelangelo, and Raphael, costing more than even I would shell out for a book (it was a gift) and including (though I don't mention this in my pitch) some very buff guys depicted as only a gay Italian genius could depict them. The girl glances at the book without opening it. "Thanks," she says, "but I guess I'll just draw," by which she means penciling in the scribbled loops on a torn-out page of lined notebook paper. So much for the Renaissance.

More troubling is the small fiasco I cause in the Vermont Lit class by pulling out my old chestnut on the fallacy of saying you're "no good with grammar." Every class I teach does some writing, and I try to offer a few pointers in composition and usage whenever I return a batch of papers. One thing I've always enjoyed impressing upon students is the idea of language as a cultural inheritance—it doesn't belong to English teachers, it belongs to them—buttressed by a demonstration of the fact that they know more "grammar" than they realize, however alien grammatical terminology may be.

"For instance," I will ask, "which of you can tell me the difference between an objective case pronoun and a nominative case pronoun?" (Few people then, no people now.) "All right, no surprise there, most people can't. Yet every single one of you knows the difference, and, not only that, you've known it most of your lives, since you were about two or three years old, which is to say long before you began to be intimidated by the word *grammar* or the likes of me. Look at these two sentences, please."

I will go to the store this afternoon.
Me will go to the store this afternoon.

"If I speak the first sentence, what does *I* refer to? And if I speak the second sentence, what does *Me* refer to? Exactly. The pronouns mean the same thing because they refer to the same person. But one of them is used correctly in its sentence and the other one isn't, and all of you know that, even if you don't know why. A show of hands, please. How many of you say the first example is right?" Hands up, all around, as always, ready to catch the big eureka. "How many of you say the second example is right?" Of course, no one will.

Except that a hand shoots up.

Wise guy? No, sir. Just a boy, often in trouble, or so I've heard, though never with me, frequently absent, always dressed as though he's just got out from under the chassis of a car, with his hand raised boldly, proudly, not afraid to be different or, in spite of my prefatory remarks, wrong.

I backpedal as fast as I can, as far as possible from the insinuation that he doesn't know what most people know by the age of three—and what he certainly seems to know based on his spoken language. Fearing I've done him harm, I go after class to the specialist he sees for academic support, prepared to make full confession of my sin and do whatever penance she prescribes.

"He has some challenges," she says, which are compounded by poverty and a very tough past. But I shouldn't be worried. "In fact, he really likes you. I've rarely seen him this motivated." Moving as this is, it leaves me unable to picture him reading *Like Lesser Gods*.

In the weeks to come he will give evidence of doing just that—with some tutorial help, I'm sure—but even now I'm impressed by his answers to questions and his contributions to discussions, and I tell him so. Outside of class, we talk about cars, the truck he'd like to buy if he can pull together the dough. But his attendance grows more sporadic, probably because he is out working when he ought to be in class, and I can see already that he's going to fail. He gets into some kind of trouble I don't fully understand, and suddenly he is gone from school, leaving the objective *me* and the nominative *I* to parse their anger at the world's injustice from the shame (admit it!) of their own relief.

Martin Luther King said that a person who doesn't know what he would die for doesn't know what he's living for, and I decide I'm going to live or die on the value of books. That's a pretty tame stand for a high school English teacher, though perhaps no more so than that of a twenty-first-century Democrat who stands by organized labor or a twenty-first-century husband who stands by his wife. The girl who refused to open the art book is a partial inspiration; so is the sight of a school library that resembles a NASA control center in which the technicians occasionally break for a little light reading after lunch. More provocative than either is a curious window display outside the library prepared by our energetic first-year librarian and grossly misunderstood by the older man in necktie and work boots whom she treats with the kindest regard. The display consists of a dozen or so new acquisitions, graphic novels and topical books of particular interest to teens, standing on a pyramid of steps made from the glossy black volumes of the Library of America, laid flat like bricks. The library began collecting these volumes, each devoted to the works of an American literary master, some years back and has managed to amass an encyclopedia-sized collection. What can the display be if not a celebration of the old and the new, and perhaps an acknowledgment that the new stands on the old, "on the shoulders of giants," to use an ancient metaphor. Faulkner, Whitman, Dickinson, and Wharton are the building blocks of our American literary project, our stepping stones to the future . . .

Actually, what they are is discards. The symbolism of their position under *Pride and Prejudice and Zombies* is comparable to that of the dragon under the foot of St. George. As the librarian has explained to my department head, her space is limited, the books are hardly ever used, and so she's decided to give the library a freshening up by moving the Library of America out of the Lake Region collection.

I decide at once that one of my goals for the year will be to find a tactful way of persuading her to restore the volumes. I say tactful because I understand her predicament: she has a budget she must either spend or lose, she oversees a space that no electorate has agreed (and at least one has adamantly refused) to expand, and she has even fewer shelves for books than there were twenty years ago because of the space required by the computers. I'm also mindful of her prerogatives; this is her classroom, this is her first year, and if I would not take kindly to her telling me how to teach, I imagine she might not take kindly to my telling her how to run her library, a presumption that would be compounded by our respective genders and ages. I'll need to bide my time on this.

What I want to say to her is that school libraries exist to serve all the students, yes, but they also exist to serve that student who comes along once every twenty-five years, who is likely to go almost totally unnoticed during his four years of haunting the stacks and is about as likely to be the graduate who puts his small-town alma mater on the map. I'm thinking in particular of a former student of mine from years back, now a professor, writer, and dear friend, who probably would have set herself the task of reading as many of those Library of America volumes as she could carry in two arms had they been around in her day. By her sophomore year she was dropping by my classroom to discuss what she'd newly gleaned from Plato and Montaigne, a good deal more in both cases than I'd received in my formal education. When she asked me whether I'd recommend Saul

Bellow's *Herzog* as a suitable read for her and when I confessed that it was but one of many gaps in my background, we made a pact to read it at the same time and discuss it as we could, an arrangement in which I was often scrambling to catch up. She prompted me by leaving whimsical reminders hidden in places where I was likely to find them; more than twenty years later, I will still pull a book off my shelf only to have a scrap of colored calligraphy fall to the floor: *Herzog!* I won't try the same stunt with the librarian, though if I did, I might use my former student's name.

Faculty meetings, always a trial for me, are softened only slightly these days by my affection for the person leading them. What most vexes me, ironically enough, is that we have been asked to read a book. Mr. Messier has assigned us monthly chapters in a text called *Raising the Bar and Closing the Gap: Whatever It Takes*, the first time in my experience (another irony, to be sure) that an administrator has given teachers a book for homework. I love the gesture, but I hate the text. Its four authors, two of whom are married and share the surname DuFour and all of whom self-identify as "active consultants" (i.e., those who've managed to figure out that there are easier and more lucrative ways to make money in the education racket than by teaching kids), have devised a program for organizing faculties into "professional learning communities" (PLCs) and schools into a network of "intervention strategies" dedicated to the premise that every student can—nay, must—learn. The goal is laudable; its underlying assumptions trouble me.

I am troubled, first of all, by the pseudoscience of the authors' "evidence," according to which a successful (usually middle-class) school is invariably one that has adopted their nomenclature and bought into their program. I see no hint of a suggestion that a rose by any other name, which is to say a PLC in everything but their franchised acronym, can smell as sweet. Equally unscientific is the utter absence of any evidence that doesn't support their hypotheses or any measure of success besides such dubious indicators as performance on standardized tests or the number of students signed up for Advanced Placement courses. Surely any "educator" worthy of the name would be scholar enough to raise an eyebrow at this.

I'm also troubled by the repeated, snide, and almost sinister references to those recalcitrant teachers who insist on acting as "lone wolves" and on treating their classrooms as "personal kingdoms." Admittedly, these are fair descriptors of one of the worst kinds of teacher: the self-described maverick whose primary aims are to amuse himself and do as little work as possible. Not for him a plan book or a comprehensive exam; such trivialities are at odd with his "style," his "philosophy," his plans for the weekend. At the same time, the authors seem to indict the very teachers who played the biggest role in my own formation. Those teachers were never lazy but they were indeed lone wolves, sleek-furred beauties who preferred howling at the moon of their own lunatic inspirations to sniffing hindquarters among the faculty pack. One of their type, a foreign language teacher still going strong after my last stint at the school, still whisking kids away to France on a wing and a bake sale, even as she brings France to them by the vivaciousness of her instruction, will say to me, "I'm afraid the day of the teacher as artist is dead."

More than anything else I'm offended by what seems to be the main subtext of the authors' argument—and no doubt the principal reason that they're getting plugged by such luminaries as Lawrence W. Lezotte, "CEO of Effective Schools Products, Ltd." and embraced by school reformers who count past presidents as personal friends—which is that poverty need not deter achievement (*Stand and Deliver* redux) or overly concern us so long as we can get the children of dysfunctional families and blighted neighborhoods to achieve grade-level proficiencies and have a few AP courses under their belts when they get shipped off to their fourth tour of duty in Afghanistan. We must shift "from an external focus on issues outside the school," the authors assert, to what business consultant Jim Collins calls "the brutal facts" of our "organization."

Taken at its best and shucked of its corporate jargon, the authors' argument sounds like a modest and perfectly reasonable appeal for schools to focus on what they're actually able to do (impart basic skills and information) as opposed to what they might wish to do (guarantee a decent life for all of their graduates). But taken as an overarching solution to the "problem of American education"—our preferred euphemism for the problem of creating a democratic society within a decidedly undemocratic economic system—the DuFour agenda strikes me as an argument for ignoring every "brutal fact" save those that can be blamed on poor teaching. Out with the pedagogical lone wolf! In with the political ostrich!

I've often said that it's a good thing Jim Jones wasn't an educational consultant, else the halls of America's schools would be littered with the corpses of self-poisoned teachers. As if reading my mind, some of the teachers who've returned from the DuFour workshop held in Boston the previous summer jokingly refer to having drunk the Kool-Aid. They mean having replaced their initial skepticism with unconditional conversion. They're only half joking. I don't hear a single caveat or criticism when we break into small groups to discuss the reading assignment, and I don't expect to. Excepting the misfits and the burnouts, public school teachers are the original true believers: show them the latest thing in education and they'll soon be bowing down to it as to a god.

The reasons are not hard to discern. For one thing, educators are naturally predisposed to hope that someone better educated than they are will have a better method for addressing the vexing challenges of universal public education. The key word here is *method*—usually an implication that people up a creek without a paddle can be taught a strategy for maneuvering their boats that eliminates any need of buying them paddles. Teachers see method as an alternative to going mad; politicians see method as an alternative to spending money.

For another thing, anyone who can go to work each day believing that every student can learn, which every good teacher needs to believe as an article of faith (and which, to their credit, the authors of *Raising the Bar* seem to believe without reservation), has to have cultivated a prodigious capacity for belief. Students marvel at their teachers' gullibility in the face of lame excuses, and skeptics like me sometimes marvel at their colleagues' willingness to imbibe the most noxious concoctions of snake oil, both of us failing to appreciate that the best teacher has already fallen for something much more outlandish: the potential for magnificence in every human being.

So it happens that even as I'm inwardly fuming at passages I've underlined and asterisked as "tripe," "crap," and "what every Republican wants to hear" (for I make it a point of honor to read every assignment, a resolution I have good reason to suspect is not universally shared by those of my colleagues who take their seats whispering, "What chapter were we supposed to read?"), I'm moved by the heartbreaking earnestness of men and women who, after years of being bored and bamboozled by every sort of con artist, from those with pimples to those with PhDs, still worry over their students enough to hope for a messiah, or at least a miracle or two. No less than I'm convinced that Jim Jones had what it takes to be a successful educational consultant, I'm convinced that the fishermen Jesus chose for disciples in his day would have been schoolteachers in ours. True to type, they'd have misunderstood much and wrangled among themselves not a little, yet they would have held on to their implausible faith with a fervor sufficient to subvert an empire, which is what I in my own credulous way am always waiting for teachers to do.

Meanwhile, back in the classroom, I have smaller subversions to deal with. Going to school is like going to prison (as generations of schoolyard songs attest): you have about two weeks to establish your credibility, failing which you're either a punk or as good as dead. Depending on the school, some students can manage to avoid those stark alternatives, but even at the best school, no teacher does.

I seem to be doing all right so far. I have nothing that could fairly be described as a discipline problem. Experience helps. Age helps. Good class size helps. (None of mine exceed twenty.) Mr. Messier sticking his head in the doorway now and again to tell my students how lucky they are to be in my class certainly doesn't hurt. And to give the devil his due, having a school dedicated to the idea of being a "professional learning community" doesn't hurt either. I've never before seen so much collaboration among the faculty. Lone wolf I might be, but I never feel alone.

Not least of all, I'm helped by the relative good nature of a student body served by a well-functioning school, and, as I'll show, by particular students who are pulling for me every bit as much as I'm trying to pull for them. It's a tentative negotiation day by day, like the courtship of an unlikely pair. At our first meeting I told all of my classes that they were going to have to remind themselves at least once a day that I was not seventeen years old, and I was going to have to remind myself at least once a day that they were not fifty-seven.

The reminders are more or less built in, of course. Some of our differences are "generational" in terms of the normal stages of human development, and some of them generational in the sense of cultural changes between historical generations. It's not always easy to parse which is which, and it doesn't make much of a difference in practice. For instance, I'm repeatedly struck by what seems a compulsive, almost uncontrollable communicativeness on the part of my students. It's curious to watch a class taking a test. No sooner does a student turn over his completed test than his head goes up like a prairie dog sniffing the wind. Who else is done? Whom else can I talk to? According to a rule I enforce with inflexible strictness, the answer is no one—not until everyone is finished. It's tempting to ascribe the failure to respect a neighbor's concentration as nothing more than adolescent solipsism—and in my more sarcastic caricatures, I sometimes do: "The most important person in the whole wide world has just finished *his* test, so, like, what's the problem?"—but that is to pay short shrift to all the ways in which students show touching concern for one another's welfare. A true solipsist wouldn't be so charitable as to slip his needy neighbor the correct answers during a test. What drives my students is rather this ahormonal lust for communicativeness, this need to fill up silence with any kind of sound, something that's always been true for adolescents, to say nothing of adults (just watch a group of teachers trying to settle down for a meeting), but that I suspect is also the technologically conditioned enhancement of a habit (what human beings are likely to do) into *a habit* (what junkies have no choice but to do).

There sits my student Jack, sideways in his seat, his sizable forearm resting on the desk behind his, and his attention directed to the girl beside him, not in admiration as nearly as I can tell but in constant solicitation. *Talk to me.* I tell him to turn himself forward; he does so, and the next time I look back from the blackboard he's turned sideways again. This goes on to the point that I invite him into the hall for "a word." I can't figure out if he is playing dumb or is dumb, but there's a denseness in his responses that I find unsettling—is this a tactic or a disability? (I've already checked with the school nurse to see if he has problems hearing.) I tell him that along with violating his neighbor's right not to be eyeballed for forty-five minutes a day, he's starting to get on my nerves. I'm quick to add that I like him personally. "I like you too," he says. "You're a good teacher." *Then why can't you just shut the fuck up and turn around in your seat!* Not what I say, but the substance of it. "I'm not comfortable sitting the other way," he says. Well, he's a big kid, though I've taught bigger specimens who had no trouble fitting into a desk. Eventually, I offer a compromise; I'll sit him in the back, next to an empty desk, and he can sit however he wants. He likes that idea, perhaps because it affords him greater license for scribbling on his desktop on those days when he manages to bring a pencil. Now the girl who sits in front of him starts turning sideways in *her* desk.

But something else besides communicativeness or restless youth may be contributing to the occasional disruptions surrounding tests and in-class assignments. Increasingly I design the latter as cooperative exercises in the hopes of exploiting communicativeness in a positive way. But just as the tests are not proofread by the early finishers, the group exercises are often completed in a slapdash way—leading to the same disruptions I observe on tests. Probably the slapdash aspect is also cultural, but in a more localized sense. My wife's friend, the one who worked with her in the district preschool program, once said that she moved out of the region because she had gotten sick of hearing the expression "Good enough." Another she might have cited is the quasi-obscene "Get-R-Done," prominent not only on the bumpers of innumerable pickup trucks in the Northeast but also and shockingly on one of the superintendent's PowerPoint slides. I do want my students to "Get-R-Done," but not at the expense of producing quality work or working in concert with their less speedy peers.

Cashing in on both their sociability and their love of the screen, I take my Popular Fiction students to the library for an online treasure hunt relating to the scores of allusions in Sue Monk Kidd's *The Secret Life of Bees*. What happened at the bombing of the Birmingham church? What was Apollo 11? Who were the Supremes? Immediately, I see I've taken the right tack: they go to the computer banks like little children set loose on a beach, diving into Google images as into a surf, splashing one another with hints and links, chattering happily but mostly on point. I make a mental note to incorporate a visit like this into our weekly routine, add a competitive element, say two "hives" with two "queens," prizes, presentations the next day. But even in this case, communicativeness joined with a Get-R-Done ethos works against us, augmented by the Internet-fostered illusion of a world at your fingertips, instant gratification, no sense in lingering, no need to dig. "We're done!"

Also observable, especially among some of the more sullen students and especially though not exclusively among the boys, is a kind of built-in defeatism. "I ain't smart enough to take this course," says one of the boys in Popular Fiction, to which I reply that if I were the one saying so, he'd be within his rights to knock me down. I wonder, though, how much of what he says is an attempt to describe not his intelligence but his having grown up without books. Even more I wonder how much his having grown up without books is the result of his belief that as a natural-born "redneck" he has no business reading one. We shake hands after I sign his drop slip, and I tell him he'd be welcome back to try again, with all the help I can give, if he changes his mind. When he turns to join his friends out on the sidewalk, I notice the NASCAR insignia on the back of his shirt. Does he see it as the obvious emblem of a young man "not smart enough" to take my course? If he does, I want to tell him that I don't.

No doubt some of his attitude can be explained as the passive fatalism that has dogged working-class life since the dawn of the proletariat. But there is another, more recent factor at work. So much of what passes for authentic "redneck" culture—the Confederate flags, the macho strut, the trailer-park mores—like so much of what passes for authentic inner-city culture, is in fact a fabrication of the market. This first dawned on me several years ago when I realized that certain former students of mine seemed more "local" in their dress, speech, and mannerisms than their parents. How could that be, given that the students were generally less insulated in their rural environment than their parents had been? The answer is that what I took for local wasn't really local at all. Instead it was a countrified getup created by the savvy (and, needless to say, nonlocal) marketers of beer, mass entertainment, and motorized recreation. This is the flip side of the truism that capitalism destroys local cultures in its relentless drive to dominate the globe; it also *creates* cultures, mostly caricatures of the tribes it has displaced. The self-described rednecks, more likely to be young folks than old, see themselves as the "real Vermonters," the last of the Northeast Kingdom holdouts, when in reality they are no more indigenous than a Quebecois truck driver line dancing in cowboy boots. The sad irony in all this is that on some deep level the self-identified redneck wants to rebel against the economic forces that have run roughshod over small-scale agriculture and agriculturally based community, even as he buys his prepackaged rebellion from those very forces.

Suffice it to say, the brokers of those forces would much prefer rebels who shop to rebels who read. More than once it occurs to me how many of my conflicts revolve around a book. I come to understand why some of my predecessors, if I'm to believe what I've been told, gave up and simply read the texts to the students or had them watch based-on-the-book movies instead.

I try to remain flexible, with reading as my constant and the approaches up for grabs. Discovering that a mere handful of the sophomores in my last period have read an assigned short story, I opt for a different-strokes-for-different-folks agenda: those who've yet to read it can have today's class for a grace period, provided they will stay on task; those who have read it are invited to hold a literary powwow with me on the floor outside the room. I know this is going to be dicey, but it works rather well. The kids reading need only a reminder or two to settle down, and the kids on the floor become positively dazzling in their insights. So far, so good.

The next story on the syllabus is more difficult, and so I forgo the quiz and suggest we read the story aloud together, strengthening whatever comprehension each of us achieved the night before and discussing passages as we go. Immediately, one of the girls from yesterday's hallway symposium balks at having to sit through the oral reading of a story she's already read. It seems that without meaning to I've created an elite. Within the next thirty seconds several other girls, all friends of the first one who spoke, claim the same conscientiousness with respect to reading assignments and the same distaste for reading a story twice. They want to leave the room and discuss the story out in the hall.

My best course here would be to say that today we are doing something different, that good literature stands up to repeated readings, and end it there. But I make the mistake of giving way to baser motivations, namely, guilt over having created a false expectation, fear of offending a kid who seems to have gotten the message about reading assignments, and vanity in wanting to show that if you try to play poker with me you best be ready to have me call your bluff. I might be amenable to some people going out into the hall, I say, but just so there's an appearance of good faith all around, I'll ask those who've applied for the privilege to answer a few questions about the story or simply to formulate a few relevant questions of their own that the rest of us might use in our close reading of the text.

That's enough to set off a sniping contest with several students, one of whom volunteered to kick off our oral reading but now refuses to do so. I'm not at my best; it hasn't been an especially good day, I'm running on four hours of sleep and unfortunately find less humor than humiliation in the thought that at almost sixty years of age I am reduced to debating my professional prerogatives with fifteen-year-olds. One of them has been yanking my chain for weeks now. In time, she is going to become one of my best, most reliable students, but at the moment I'm wondering how much more of her I can stand.

Until—another girl stuns the class, and me, with a remark that I must say, at the risk of sounding older than I feel, no girl would have said back when I was going to school:

"Ladies, it's starting to get a bit estrogeny in here."

This isn't the only time a kid saves my bacon; in fact, it isn't even the first time today. I got off to a bad start by losing my cool with a boy in my first-period class whom I had to remind for the third or fourth time that school rules prohibit food and drink in the classroom. There he was with his can of Monster drink in

his mitt, and there I was in the doorway, standing next to my
department head and feeling especially ineffectual in her presence. We all have our triggers, and one of mine is feeling that my
courteous requests are being ignored, all the more galling because
I've gone out of my way to be so courteous. After barking that I
wasn't going to tell him about the rule again (a rule he probably
and accurately sensed was of complete indifference to me beyond
the school regulation), I added in sheer frustration, "It's like talking to a tree stump!"

One is often startled by the sensitivity of the seemingly insen-
sible, which is to say, by all the life that remains latent in the roots
of a tree stump. I clearly hurt his feelings. After class began, I
apologized to him for my harshness. I meant it too. I walked to
his desk and offered him my hand. He took it warmly, to the
relief of us both I think, and everything between us would be
good thereafter. Still, there was an awkwardness in the room as I
tried to get on with the class as though nothing had happened.

Then, out of the blue, with no pretext in anything I have ever
said or intend to say in this or any other class, one of the students
blurted out, "Mr. Keizer, somebody told me you were on Comedy
Central."

I was, I said. When I'm not making an ass out of myself here,
I like to do it for a television audience—I didn't say that but wish
I had. Instead I revealed that last summer I'd briefly appeared as
a guest author on a program called *The Colbert Report*. In contrast to yours truly when his publicist had first told him of the
show, everyone in the room was familiar with it. They wanted to
hear the details. There was more light in their eyes than I'd seen
since the start of school. Even the guy with the Monster drink
seemed to feel an extra buzz. In a New York minute, and as the
result of what I have to believe was a very calculated maneuver
on the part of a very sympathetic student, I went from a testy old

fart to a television star, someone who just might be worth listening to after all. I was so relieved at the change in the atmosphere that it took me a while to realize that my larger problems were still waving in my face, that it was not my authorship of a book that gave me credibility in an English class but the six minutes I spent as a straight man on TV.

I often stay late. It's not uncommon for mine to be the last car in the faculty parking lot. Sometimes I stay to meet with students who want extra help, though the good work of the tutors in the academic support areas throughout the day and the transportation needs of a regional high school tend to keep their numbers down, as do the constraints of after-school jobs. Just as often I stay to record my grades and tidy up my school e-mail account. The dial-up Internet service at my house doesn't permit me to do much with the Lake Region site or the PowerSchool account it links to. There's a certain unfairness to this: I'm kept from going home because broadband Internet service hasn't gotten there yet. It can feel especially sharp when the 4:30 display on my classroom clock marks my twelfth hour on the job. But it's a trifle compared with the predicament of students who lack personal computers or Internet of any kind. Social inequality has gone digital along with everything else—disguised somewhat by the fact that even the poorest of the poor seem to have cell phones.

One of the kids who lives in an "unwired" household is my former nemesis Jack. I say former because by the end of September he's gone from one of my daily irritants to one of my daily delights. His detention today is for a brief relapse; I heard him say "Fuck you" to another student just before class was dismissed. As I explain to him, and as he readily agrees, I have to respond in the same way I'd want my daughter's teacher to respond if another kid said the same thing to her. The at-home digital handicap doesn't surprise me because I know he lives as far out in the boonies as I do and because he admits to interests of an off-screen nature. For example, he tells me he's interested in World War II. I haul out another coffee table book on the subject, fully prepared for him not to open it. He doesn't at first—because, he says, he was working down in Ag Shop, and he ought to wash his hands before handling such a nice book. I ask if he'd like to take it home. It will not come back for a while, the reason being a little brother who's interested in the same stuff. "Then maybe you better keep it," I will tell him.

Ag Shop gives us another thing to talk about. He tells me he loves everything to do with farming and works part-time for a farmer after school. He doesn't live on a farm, however. In this he is typical of most of the handful of students I have who belong to the FFA (Future Farmers of America). At first the sight of their regulation dark blue corduroy jackets seems like a thread of continuity between the present and the past, when kids came to school after a round of morning chores with the barn smell still in their clothes and sometimes the muck still in the tread of their boots, but it's not long before I realize that most of the members I have in class are children of the Past Farmers of America. Like other businesses in the nation, small-scale agriculture has increasingly been displaced by larger operations and consolidated holdings. In my first year at Lake Region, there were well over three thousand dairy farms in Vermont (compared with three times that many in the year I was born); now there are slightly over a thousand, about a quarter of them in the Northeast Kingdom. But the dream of "a family farm" remains. Jack makes a statement that will stay with me as much as anything that anybody will say to me in the course of the entire year—this rough-and-tumble young man who tosses off a "Fuck you" for a fare-thee-well and says he's going to join the military straight after high school. "I wish I was a farm child."

Unlike "Fuck you," this is the sort of endearing, unaffected utterance one seldom gets to hear during class. It sounds more natural after school. No less than a city after dark, a school after hours is a different place, at once spent in its disheveled appearance and flexed for more passionate engagements. The student body's complacent middle class is mostly gone, leaving the felons and the stars, the former in detention and the latter running drills down in the gym or practicing their scales in the band room. Usually, you can get more than a scheduled minute with the colleagues you need to see, you can carry a cup of hot tea through the hall without risking catastrophe, you can finish a thought before someone interrupts it with "Can I quick go . . . ?" Custodians who drop by to empty the trash cans and dry-mop between the desks pause to talk politics and sports. Better still, the children of younger teachers occasionally stick their heads in the doorway, either because they've got the wrong room—*Whoa, you're not my mom*—or because the right room has gotten pretty boring over the last ten minutes and they're wondering if your plant might need watering or your blackboard want some chalk-drawn daisies by way of decoration.

One of the things I find I need to relearn, want to relearn, is the art of casual visiting. This is seldom a challenge where a student of mine is concerned—in that case even "irrelevant" exchanges count as productive—but occasionally an annoyance when I'm scrambling to finish work that another person seems not to have. For years I have worked entirely at home, by myself, where my few conversations have been confined to my family, a writer friend who phones, and editors or agents who are usually even more eager to get off the phone than I am. My situation has changed. For very different reasons but with very similar results, not a few of a school's denizens, both students and staff, are starved for adult conversation. I try to cultivate the practice of feeding that hunger without opening an all-you-can-eat buffet. As for my hunger, hungers, I should say—all of them bend toward home.

I enjoy coming home from work, which I've not done for years, setting down my valise like Willy Loman and collecting my breadwinner's kiss, though it turns out my wife is still kneading her half of the loaf. Against my advice, Kathy has cut short what I had hoped would be a time for vocational self-exploration and has added another job to her Dartmouth gig, delivering speech services several days a week to children at an elementary school. They're older than the preschoolers she's used to and perhaps, she worries, too far from her core of expertise. At least it won't be just one of us talking school over our predinner glass of wine. And we certainly won't lack for money, though each of us earns what would be a beginner's salary in another profession or in the school system of a warmer state.

Never so sweet as the destination, the drive home is still sweet. When we first moved from Orleans to another county in the Kingdom, I appreciated the longer drive to work, the opportunity to warm up going and cool down coming, and I appreciate it even more this year. September is my favorite month—if youth is wasted on the young, September is wasted on the academic year. Make us sweat out July in a classroom if we must, but leave us September in which to roam free. The leaves at this latitude begin turning midway through the month; I see red and orange tinges in the mountain, a small litter of yellow maple leaves on our lane. In my happy-hour mood I might stop for a drink—not at the saloon and not in a bottle, maybe a fortifying cup of coffee at the convenience store, where I can also buy gas—for the sensation of my real-world tie blowing like a signal flag as I operate the pump. If I see someone I know, a former student or the parent of one, they're likely to have heard I'm "back teaching" and almost as likely to ask me how that feels. "Good," I'll say, as expected, though I refuse to give the stock response when someone starts to hold forth, possibly in sympathy, on how incorrigible "kids these days" can be. Not really, I tell them. Only if you expect them to read a book, I say to myself.

If someone should add, "Thank God it's Friday"—an expression that's always tasted to me like a watered-down death wish—all I have to offer is a devout amen. Friday nights have never seemed so luminous. I've never felt such a Sabbath ease as I sit down to my meal. I ask my wife to light the candles before we eat. My peace has to do less with not having to get up early the next morning (something I'm likely to do anyway) than with not having to be prepared to go on stage. I need offer nothing to the next two days but myself. I try my best to do nothing school-related once the sun goes down.

By Saturday morning, though, I'm no longer taking my cues from the Mishnah. I'm correcting papers, planning lessons, developing assignments, my goal a fully unloadable briefcase come Monday morning and enough materials to get me partway through the week. One of my first batches is the four-page student-interest questionnaire I've given to all eighty-plus of my students, not only to get to know them better but also to assess their proficiency at following directions, writing complete sentences, forming good paragraphs. I'm up to speed enough to know I should refer to the last of these as "constructed responses," the current state jargon for a unified block of prose. It won't occur to me until much later how my questionnaires must strike at least some of the kids as a horse-and-buggy version of a Facebook page. I don't ask them who their friends are, true, but I do ask them to weigh in on some of their likes and dislikes. I also invite them to post a comment, as it were, advising me on how to be an effective teacher.

I write my responses sitting in my easy chair, with the books I used to read on weekends close at hand but effectively out of bounds. By Monday, I know much of what can be gained by asking students their favorite foods ("macaroni and cheese"), their future plans ("to go into the militerry"), their mailing addresses ("don't know"), their greatest weaknesses ("math and reading"), their greatest strengths ("being a good friend"), their heroes ("my dad"), their hopes ("that my parents would get along better"), their writing (better than I'd have dared to expect in the past), and I've finished my quota. I've also learned what comes of keeping a middle-aged hand and elbow in the same position for the waking hours of two whole days. When I go to write Monday's agendas on the blackboard, I can scarcely raise my arm.

4

OCTOBER

No man who worships education has got the best of education. . . . Without a gentle contempt for education no man's education is complete.

—G. K. Chesterton

October is the month when schools administer the NECAP (New England Common Assessment Program, pronounced "kneecap") test, which as a temporal benchmark, an event to prepare for, and a reason to live probably ranks on a level with the senior prom. All disclaimers to the contrary, the results will be the chief measure of our effectiveness as a school, the pretext for hanging our heads low or holding them high, the news the local papers will print on page 4 if it's great and on page 1 if it's not. The metal storage cabinet in my room contains stacked photocopies of complete and partial NECAP tests from previous years, selectively "released" by the testing authority for our practice and general edification. The reproducible originals are gathered in a three-ring binder on the cover of which my satirical predecessor has scrawled the words TEACHING TO THE TEST.

That is essentially what we are to do in our English classes for a week or two prior to the examination. So, I assume, will our counterparts in math and science, the other content areas to be tested along with reading and writing. Although I don't think highly of teaching to the test, I do admire how the school as a whole acknowledges the game it's been forced to play without yielding any more ground than necessary to out-and-out crassness. There are no General George S. Patton–style pep talks from the principal about the enemy we have to kill, no directives to the students other than to do their best and not to fret. Nor is there any pretest automated robocall such as comes to our house from the school where my wife is now working part-time, reminding parents to see that their children "eat a nutritious breakfast and have a good night's sleep" because . . . *tomorrow is the day when the elementary schools take their NECAP tests.* Let no child be left behind for a good breakfast on the day of a standardized test. The message stops short of suggesting that children might also have shoes on their feet and kisses on their foreheads, but then there is less data to support that such amenities raise scores.

If I'm impressed by the sobriety of my colleagues, I'm even more impressed by the dedication of the students. I expect many of them to blow off the pregame drills, but there's almost none of that. Granted, those who perform exceptionally well on the reading and writing parts of their NECAPs will get the option of not taking their final exams in English, a privilege formerly extended by some teachers for high academic performance in a given course but now denied by school policy in all cases except the one mentioned. Still, it's doubtful that many students expect to win that plum. The motivation seems to derive more from pride in their school, affection for their principal, and not least of all from having performed above par in the recent past. Success with taking tests is not unlike success in making money: the more you have, the more you want and the more you're likely to get. Regardless of the reasons, any evidence of motivation for a test that "doesn't count" among students conditioned from the age of nine to regard grades as the only reason on earth for lifting a pencil strikes me as pretty remarkable.

The strategies we employ are remarkable, too, if not so inspiring. The five-paragraph model of an essay (each paragraph consisting ideally of five sentences) is by this stage totally ingrained—not only as a way of taking standardized tests but as the definitive taxonomy of English prose. I meet no student who believes the universe was created in six days, but Darwin himself never saw so many open mouths as greet my meek suggestion than an essay might once in a while achieve six paragraphs or, more shockingly still, complete its work in four. Among the recommendations that come from the teacher who seems to be the department's NECAP guru are "address the prompt" (i.e., feed the question back to the examiners in your first paragraph, a virtual death sentence for any impulse toward writing a captivating lead) and "fill the space provided," which means precisely what it says. He's made a study of test results and has determined that the higher scores invariably go to those students who fill the space. Perhaps because our department head senses that some of us, including the guru himself, might be a little embarrassed by this observation, she attempts to dull its edge by noting that there are occasions in life that require a person "to bs" and that our kids might as well learn that now. This is realism, to be sure, though hardly an inspiration to teach rhetoric.

For all my grousing, the NECAP process hands me one reward and one small vindication, both in an offhand way. My elective courses contain junior and senior students, but only juniors take the tests, and so I must have an alternative activity for the seniors. Sara suggests that we coach them in writing college application essays while juniors are at work on their practice tests. This means I get to do some of the intensive one-to-one work with students that was once a mainstay of my routine (especially when I was department head and shamelessly devoted most of my "administrative" periods to giving extra help to students) but is now a less frequent occurrence, at least outside of class, because of a full teaching load and because the school's academic support areas have absorbed much of the tutorial work that used to fall to classroom teachers. Refreshingly, the act of coaching a college essay is in some particulars the exact opposite of coaching a NECAP essay. In a standardized test, you're urging kids to conform to a template; on a college application, the trick is rather to inspire the drowsy admissions officer who's slogged through scores of generic essays to open his eyes and ask, "Who's this and where did she come from?" In other words, part of the coaching boils down to convincing students that their own lives are interesting.

I need no convincing to believe that some of their lives are hard. Reading over these essays amounts to a refresher course on social dysfunction. Two of my seniors have a parent in prison; not a few of them have at least one parent who might as well live on the moon, and the phrases "lost his job" and "drinking too much" occur often enough to make an out-of-town teacher suspect plagiarism. At the same time, there is a movingly recurrent theme— *especially* from the kids who have only one functioning parent—of admiration for a mother's or father's struggle to provide enough emotional and financial support for a child to thrive.

None of the essays are defeatist. On the contrary, some seem to strain for a sense of triumph unsupported by the details of the narrative. I'm given a better understanding of my Popular Fiction class's standoffish response to Russell Banks's *Rule of the Bone*, the novel I thought they'd connect with most easily. A few kids do, though just as many seem to hold it at arm's length, refusing to infer its grittier implications. In the prevailing view of my students, the novel's young delinquent protagonist owes all of his troubles to his abuse of drugs—not to his parents' virtual abandonment of him, much less to his society's virtual abandonment of his parents. As they see it, he needs to give up doping and try harder in school. *He needs to make up with his mom*, some write, even though his mother has essentially told him that she'd rather hang on to her pedophiliac boyfriend than to her emotionally needy son. The tendency of at least some of my students to blame themselves for predicaments they did not create seems all too clear. Not that I'd want them to become fatalistic—I'm encouraged that they believe in the merits of "making the right choice." But to believe that every calamity results from a poor choice is fatalism of another kind, existence reduced to a standardized test with a karmic scoring key.

The vindication I mentioned comes in the form of one of the essay questions on this year's NECAP. Essay questions are framed according to specifically designated modes of discourse—"procedural" (what we used to call process analysis), "persuasive," etc.—and one of this year's turns out to be a "reflective essay," a type my colleagues have seldom seen on past NECAPs, to be written in response to a quotation, a subtype my colleagues can't remember seeing at all. As reports of the test's contents begin trickling back from students to teachers, one hears a grumbling in our department, and among some of the kids too, as might be heard among baseball fans who've just seen an umpire call a third strike on a player who any idiot could see was pitched a ball. I can't resist mentioning to my department head—having at least enough decency not to mention this to my peers—that though the past tests and practice exercises gave us no forewarning of such a prompt, I've been having my Popular Fiction students write reflective essays on quotations taken from the novels we've studied. Ironically, I may have made my best contribution to the NECAP effort when it was furthest from my mind.

Of course, the joke is on me in that the vindication seems less mine than the test's. *See, this emphasis on standardized testing isn't just a matter of teaching to the test, as cynics like to claim. The testing has a much broader focus, and your own assignment proves that!* Sara doesn't say this, but someone else might. Parse it either way, the two most pertinent questions remain. First, how much better might my students be at writing reflective essays if they and I were permitted to get on with our work? And second, how confidently can we assume that the sort of people who sign on to score NECAP tests would know a decent reflective essay if it hit them in the head?

Whatever the answers, one is left with the "brutal fact" that the headquarters from which educational policies emanate are always at a comfortable distance from the frontline troops. At a department meeting I watch as two of my colleagues have a heated disagreement over the creation of our own mandatory "summative assessments" for year-end mastery of the English curriculum, not over the mandate itself but over the best way to implement it and interpret the data. This is not the sort of turf war that erupts between the teacher who wants to do things in a new way and the teacher who wants to stick to the old, nor is it the more dismal sort of turf war that erupts between the teacher who wants to do things in a new way and the teacher who doesn't want to do anything at all. These are two accomplished and highly dedicated practitioners, neither of whom appears to have a cynical or lazy bone in his or her body. They also happen to be young parents. Often I see them working late into the day as their children, dropped off by the bus, sit dangling their feet in the big kids' desks while munching on carrot sticks and crackers and wondering aloud when it will be time to go home. I never see either one of them with a child in tow that I don't recall with an ache what my own daughter once said when she was small: "I wish I could make two daddies, one who would grade the kids' papers and one who would play pirates with me." And it's impossible for me to witness their dispute this afternoon without wondering which of the tipsy potentates reconvening at the Red Lobster after a day of designing NECAP exams or writing "new state standards" or conducting a workshop for school administrators has ever in his or her life or wildest dreams worked as hard as either of my colleagues or cared half as much as they do about the well-being of their students. In short, it's impossible for me to stand among the frontline troops without dreaming of a mutiny. And wishing I'd been a better pirate.

In total the NECAP tests and preparations cost me nearly two weeks of teaching time and a considerable loss of momentum in our study of literature. At first I tried to combine goals, sticking to the reading syllabus while devising multiple-choice exercises based on our texts and modeled on questions in the reading section of the NECAP test:

> *The closest meaning of the word* homely *as it appears in the first paragraph of* Like Lesser Gods *is*
>
> A. ordinary and domestic
> B. plain and unattractive
> C. familiar and comforting
> D. foreign and strange

In the end, I lacked both time and confidence; I couldn't be sure that my NECAP impersonations were on the mark. I laid the books aside and went with the canned materials from previous tests.

Even without the NECAPs, October has a way of impeding September's best-laid plans. It takes but a few weeks for enthusiasm to make the acquaintance of entropy. I begin the year with two ideas for enriching my connections with students and for superimposing some of my own rhythm on that of the regular school day. First, I invite students (and their friends and parents if they wish to come) to have breakfast with me every Thursday before school. For a meeting place I choose a luncheonette in the village of Barton, roughly midway between my house and the school. It opens at 6:00 a.m. and sits catty-corner to a stop on the school bus route. (I am advised by both the principal and my own judgment that giving rides to students, as I used to do without scruple, is probably not a good idea.) I plan to be drinking my coffee by 6:30 a.m. and leaving for school an hour after that. Students are free to drop by at any time and leave whenever they want. I'm careful to emphasize that there is absolutely no credit to be gained or lost, academic or otherwise, by coming or by staying away. In the unlikely event that we pack the place, I might ask my guests to kick in a small amount as they are able, but otherwise the cost of the breakfast is on me.

I know enough to keep my expectations low. I'm not surprised when no one shows on Thursday. I sit by myself at the long table in the back room kindly provided by the owner. He is probably more disappointed than I am by the lack of takers. I eat my bacon and grade my tests with easy resignation, reminding myself that no one ought to go fishing who isn't prepared to get skunked. After a few weeks of this, a new kid appears in my homeroom, a tall and affable young man who divides his coursework between the high school, community college, and homeschool instruction from his mother and who seems to have no designated homeroom on his schedule. He's come to mine, he says, because he thought he ought to report *somewhere* on homeroom day and he knows that mine is one of the homerooms assigned to seniors. I tell him that I'm happy to have him aboard if he can get the guidance office to do the paperwork. Later he asks: "Are you still doing that breakfast thing?"

He and I will have breakfast on and off for the remainder of the year and once or twice after he graduates. For a while I'll repeat the invitation to my classes, with the added reassurance that students will almost certainly not wind up eating alone with their English teacher, but in time I feel the invitation is going to seem like a nag and I drop it. Anyway, I'm content with my companion, one of those homeschooled kids whose presumed lack of socialization skills does not include the inability to socialize with adults and even to pose pointed questions about my two professions. For his own he intends some kind of law enforcement. He's quick to laugh and doesn't take himself too seriously. He's a good head taller than I and probably has a good twenty pounds on me for weight, but I'm his equal for a morning appetite.

The project serves to remind me of what has to be one of the most central paradoxes of teaching: that you must reach out to every student with the belief that no student is beyond your reach and that you must, at the same time, hold to the conviction that having served one student is worth the effort of having tried to serve them all. Losing sight of the first is a quick slide to elitism; losing sight of the second is a recipe for despair. As for the recipe for pancakes at Parson's Corner, it's a good one and, this being Vermont, the maple syrup is real.

My other intention at the start of the year is to take a few moments before I leave on Fridays (when I also water all my plants) to send at least one brief handwritten note to the parents of some student who has distinguished him- or herself during the course of the week by an insightful remark, an extraordinary effort, or a remarkable courtesy. I buy a small box of note cards embossed with the image of a golden tree bearing red fruit and keep it in the left top drawer of my desk. I use the student questionnaires, which I've kept on file, to determine the names and addresses to which the notes should go. I stamp them at my own expense because I want the gesture to be mine alone. I assume the notes reach the parents, and I hope they're gratifying to the students, though I hear nothing to indicate that the notes ever make it home. I don't expect to. It takes a bold adult to compose a note to a red-pen-wielding English teacher, and it takes an even bolder kid to acknowledge a teacher's appreciation where another kid might overhear. The proof is in the repetition of the action praised, and I see plenty of proof. Still, I wonder if my gesture is so eccentric as to arouse suspicion. Is it but a step down from offering to drive a student home—or, for that matter, to buy him a plate of scrambled eggs and toast? I wonder now and then what the regulars at the Parson's Corner counter make of the "spiffy" middle-aged man who waits for the blue-eyed boy with curly hair to join him for breakfast, though I suspect their dirtiest thought is that we're eating our sausage patties on the school's tab, as if my long summer vacation weren't extortion enough.

My notes home become a moot point after a while because my Friday afternoons—chosen for my latest stays because of the hour and a half it takes my wife to get home from her Friday job at Dartmouth—are soon taken up with other tasks, many of them occasioned by the modern school's almost insatiable thirst for "data" and the timely (i.e., as close to instantaneous as possible) recording of the same. In addition to grades and homework assignments, we are required to do a "productivity rubric," which must be tallied for each student for each marking period and for the "progress report" periods in between; in other words, eight times a year. The productivity rubric is a feature of the PowerSchool grading system that allows teachers to assign numbers of 1 to 4, with 4 being the highest, to criteria presumably not subsumed by academic grades, such as "initiative," "cooperation," "attendance," "behavior," and "responsibility." A faculty committee has designed a two-page spreadsheet that defines the meaning for each criterion of "productivity"—what distinguishes a 3 for behavior from a 2, for instance—and also attempts to reduce the vexing overlap between categories like "initiative" and "responsibility." It goes without saying that the guide creates as many questions as it answers. What score should I give to a student who is missing far too many days of school but who does a better job of meeting her deadlines than a number of students with close to perfect attendance? Do I give her a number that amounts to a wink at truancy or a number that turns a blind eye to the efforts of a kid who's anything but a deadbeat? What conclusions will she, or her parents, draw from the word *unsatisfactory* or the word *acceptable*? I can only give a number that designates a word; I cannot put the word into a sentence.

Though I approach the process with as much care and diligence as I can, vowing to myself that I will never allow skepticism to be a cover for shoddiness, I resent the chore deeply. I see it as part and parcel of the way in which "the school of the twenty-first century" is continually trying to mask the ambiguities of evaluating student performance by a pretense of rigorous objectivity. In English classes, for example, we avoid assigning an "arbitrary" grade for a piece of writing by constructing a "scoring rubric" of roughly ten criteria and assigning ten no less arbitrary scores to each, adding them up to achieve a grand total of subjectivity that is undoubtedly as solid as a Freddie Mac mortgage or a Miss America scoring card.

Even more I resent the way in which our jobs are increas-ingly dictated by the tools we employ. Form doesn't follow func-tion; form dictates function. I don't want to sound dogmatic or, worse, ungrateful. Without a doubt, the PowerSchool pro-gram, once mastered, offers a more efficient way of recording grades than I've ever encountered. Every time you add a grade to the roster, the student's average for the marking period is auto-matically computed and displayed. The end-of-marking-period all-nighter with a roped-in spouse doing backup duty on a cal-culator has mercifully gone the way of the mimeograph blues. But digital technology abhors a vacuum even more than nature does; it insists on reinvesting whatever time it saves, and it insists on doing so according to its own agenda. The purchaser's need to justify the cost of the technology also plays a part. If a school system invests money in a sophisticated computer program that includes a feature for calculating the daily growth rate of a user's moustache, then don't we owe it to the taxpayers to see that every man, woman, and child capable of growing a moustache begins doing so at once?

The first time I try to do my productivity rubric it takes me several hours. I have roughly eighty students and five criteria, which means four hundred separate considerations and data entries. Times eight, that comes to thirty-two hundred by the close of the year; I try not to think too much about that. There are few people still left at school on a Friday afternoon, but I have received a good tutorial in advance. I should note that I never find myself floundering with a computer task because someone has handed it off with an attitude of sink or swim. But somewhere in the inner sanctums of the school's IT system, or in the empyrean of cloud computing, or perhaps in the domain of PowerSchool itself, there resides a spore of latent indignation. Suddenly my screen is taken over by red headlines accusing me of things I'm not sure I even understand. The launching of a North Korean nuclear warhead could hardly produce a more alarmist screen. I'm unable to give a precise account of the wording because my screen goes black before I can read it a second time. Fearing that one inadvertent keystroke may have caused a digital meltdown, I run for the English teacher in the room next door, who is also working late, and ask for her help. She is a compassionate, careful woman who teaches both Advanced Placement and remedial-level English with the gentle hand that each requires, and I can tell that my stress is causing stress for her. I can also tell that she is doing her best to avoid any insinuation of stupidity on my part when she asks, "As you were going along, did you happen to hit save?"

Not once. I feared that saving before I could double-check my entries would lock in mistakes that I might not be able to change, a foolish notion perhaps, though not inconsistent with what I've seen so far of the system's potential for capricious finality. As for the Armageddon screen display, it strikes my colleague as nothing more than *what these machines will sometimes do*. Every so often a gargantuan gorilla will seize a woman in his paw and climb to the top of the Empire State Building—just the nature of the beast, I guess, no different from the way that an exhausted human being overcome by a sense of futility will sometimes break down and sob. I will do that only once in the entire school year, and I keep myself under control until my colleague leaves the room. Anyone who stops in thereafter might wonder which member of my family has died. But there are no casualties to speak of beyond the loss of an hour or two with my wife and the jettisoning of a few quaint intentions. I entered the scores first in my paper grade book, so it seems I've "saved" them after all. I'll find some other use for the fancy note cards.

———

Like a scene changer in a situation comedy, the sky opens up and rains to the point of flooding on the day scheduled for my Vermont Literature class's field trip to Barre. We've been preparing for the trip for weeks, holding sessions in the library to research the sites we hope to visit, and voting to decide the weighty matter of where we'll eat. Our plan is to tour the Rock of Ages quarry, the plant where the quarried granite is carved, the renowned town cemetery where generations of stone carvers have left monuments to their skill and to one another, and, if there is time, a museum that promises to pay more attention to labor history than the novel does. By the time I get to school it's raining so hard that some of my wryer colleagues can't resist a bit of ribbing—brought on, in part, by the hubris of the enterprise. Field trips are not for the superstitious. I know of more than one teacher whose career was suddenly on the line because of some shenanigans involving an AWOL kid or a bottle of booze smuggled onto a bus. But drowning, not drunkenness, is my concern today.

In spite of the miserable weather, I'm reluctant to cancel, and any teacher can tell you why. Canceling a field trip is like calling off an invasion. We have had to reserve a bus, a guided tour, and a restaurant. I've had to notify the main office several weeks in advance and have the trip approved on three tiers of administration. My department head has had to submit a purchase order, the school has had to hire a sub, and I have had to devise lesson plans comprehensive enough to prevent her from being eaten alive. The students have had to obtain their parents' signatures on permission slips from home in addition to a sheet signed by all their teachers indicating that they've taken the trouble of finding out what they're missing on the day of the trip. These documents are only a little less difficult to get signed than a stay of execution; repeatedly they're lost, misplaced, forgotten, and often, I have no doubt, forged. The thought of starting the process all over again, perhaps only to be drenched on some other date or in some other way, is too much to bear. I'd rather get wet today.

At the last minute, it seems that a couple of students have decided not to take the trip. Loath to leave anyone behind, I check to be sure. I'm especially sorry to learn that one of those who've opted out is probably the novel's most devoted reader, a notable distinction given that he spends a good part of his time jockeying between the households of separated parents, one of whom lives beyond the borders of the school district. At one of his way stations he reportedly received a quantity of fleabites sufficient to keep him out of school for a week. There's no time or pretext to discover his reason for not going on the trip today. It isn't money; all costs are covered by the school. His classmates have already boarded the bus, a large one for our handful. I've asked the school's female guidance counselor to come with us as an extra chaperone, believing we ought to have at least one woman along for the sake of our lone girl. The windows are fogged and streaming when I take my seat, the aisle mats muddy from the morning's pickups on dirt roads. I make it a point to tell our driver that we're leaving in plenty of time so there's no need to rush. The roads are bound to be slick with wet leaves.

The students are in good spirits in spite of the rain; if anything, the weather outside makes ours a cozier ark. Plus we're leaving school grounds, and I share their sense of release. The worst thing I have to contend with is a couple of boys with a fondness for coarse language. I dutifully reprimand them, but not harshly since it's not directed at another kid. By now they've probably been with me long enough to deduce the distinction I make between saying that life's a bitch and calling someone else a bitch, my greater tolerance for *shit* than for *shithead*. It is virtually a ritual for kids to swear and for teachers to tell them not to, where-upon the kids say "sorry" and keep a lid on things only to begin swearing again—and I have wondered sometimes if adolescents swear for the same reason that baby animals bawl, as a way of making sure they're alive and that their mothers haven't forgotten them. So it's "fucking this," and "fucking that" followed by a "Gentlemen, watch your language." After a while, they do.

Our first stop is the Rock of Ages hangar-sized workroom. From a catwalk visitors can watch the craftspeople carve and polish monuments, mostly for graves, though a master sculptor in the distance is at work on a statue of the Virgin destined for the Vatican. None of them seem in a hurry. They walk their massive blocks along tracks of rollers with all the studied non-chalance of Frank Sinatra strolling onto a stage. Music from different work stations drifts up to us along with the drone of the dust collectors. The silica dust that once disabled quarrymen and stone carvers as early as their late twenties and is virtually a character in Tomasi's novel, an airborne angel of death, is now controlled by air-filtration systems, their effectiveness certified by routine visits to a doctor. I expect the students to grow antsy after a short time but I underestimate them along with the sustained fascination that comes of watching a skilled person at work. They, too, are in no hurry.

I wonder if they feel the same twinge of envy that I do. I wonder if they have the sense of watching an elite. Like the characters in Tomasi's novel, and their Italian contemporaries in the textile mills of Paterson, New Jersey, where I was born, the people on the floor below us are proud masters of a craft and members of a union. Schools devote too little time to labor history, but a decent labor-based curriculum would also need to address the awkward subject of labor's debasement, not least of all in the popular conception of what it means to be a "manual laborer."

The workers of Paterson and Barre who wove the cloth and cut the stone also played musical instruments in their spare time and attended public lectures, they dressed in their Sunday clothes to have their pictures taken in front of the grape arbors they'd planted, they made their own wine and drank it, they went on strike believing in nothing so much as their own worth. They sent their children to school with the same belief. They would have had a hard time seeing their reflection in the stereotype of the Joe Sixpack proletarian. The symbolism of what is being chiseled on the floor below is not lost on me—I keep waiting to see a grave marker inscribed with the words "Meaningful Work," "Collective Bargaining," "Made in America"—"Rest in Peace."

If the cemetery above town isn't one of Vermont's best-known tourist attractions, it deserves to be. There you can see a life-sized married couple holding hands in their granite bed, a rare gendered angel with her legs crossed demurely as she sits atop a stone, an entire grove of stylized granite tree trunks (symbolically cut off like the lives of those interred beneath, but putting out shoots for the future), and the likeness of socialist Elia Corti, victim of an anarchist bullet in the days when the Left was robust enough to have family feuds, sitting in contemplative dignity with his elbow resting on a pillar and a palm branch spread over his carving tools. Unlike most of my students, I have been to the cemetery several times before, but this is the first time I see the monument erected to Louis Brusa, wasted by silica dust and dying in his wife's arms, the curve of her hip, the cuffs on his pants, a worker's pietà. Brusa agitated for the recognition of silicosis as an occupational hazard and was instrumental in getting the quarry owners to acknowledge the disease and take steps to prevent it. His image finds its way onto several smartphones, along with the cross-legged angel he created. I wish I could give their photos a caption.

"What does labor want?" asked Samuel Gompers in 1893, in a passage I encountered, also for the first time, several weeks before our trip. "We want more schoolhouses and less jails; more books and less arsenals; more learning and less vice; more leisure and less greed; more justice and less revenge; in fact, more of the opportunities to cultivate our better natures, to make manhood more noble, womanhood more beautiful, and childhood more happy and bright." And what did labor get? Fleabites. Obesity. NAFTA. My kids live in a country that holds more of its citizens under correctional supervision than the gulag did under Stalin, that at one point spent two billion dollars a week on a war in Afghanistan, that has experienced the most devastating financial meltdown since the Great Depression, that counts childhood lucky, if not happy and bright, if it manages to avoid being raped in its bedroom or shot dead in its school. The roads are washing out. Wires are down. Sports and drama practice have been canceled due to weather. I don't want my students driving home after sunset, and so after making a call to the school, we skip our visit to the labor museum and head straight home from the cemetery. The sky looks even darker than it did when we started out.

Sometimes I wonder what my students will do for work and what I ought to be doing to help prepare them. The simplest answer is that I ought to be teaching them the basic skills they'll require to get into college or hold down a job: how to communicate, collaborate, and reason. How to comprehend an assigned task and see it through. I would like to go further. I would like to think I can play a role in helping my students to discern and develop their talents. At the very least, I want to help my students to resist any notion of their lives as a done

deal. I hope that in the course of my teaching career I've managed to do both.

But if teaching has taught me anything, it is to be wary of
any easy assessment of my influence, for better or for worse.
"For us, there is only the trying," T. S. Eliot said. "The rest is not
our business."

A student hands me a rambling short story loaded with every
imaginable error and only marginally suited to the assignment I
gave, but that's what creative kids often do, and this kid is clearly
trying to announce her creativity. I already know that one of
her dreams is to become a writer. So I attach what amounts to
an editorial letter to her story, showing that I've read the work
and care for the work, trying with all my might not to patronize
the work or belittle its shortcomings. I also include several
recommendations—all with this intended subtext: "I take you and
your aspirations seriously." In short, I write the letter I wish an
English teacher had written to me. The student receives it with a
single comment: "I find it hard to read your handwriting." She has
never mentioned this difficulty before.

Another student in the same class hands in a quiz fifteen
minutes after all the papers have been collected, claiming that in
her absent-mindedness she stuck it into her notebook instead.
This sounds a bit suspicious, but I tell her I believe her, though
I also believe in holding to certain matters of form for the sake of
a classroom's collective good faith. Therefore, I'd like to give her
a different quiz during her next free period. Would she be willing to do that? Yes, she says, and she takes it, performing about
the same as she did on the first one. But in the process I have
made an impression I hardly expected to make.

"No teacher has ever given me another chance like this," she
says. I doubt this is so—especially in a school that prides itself
on accommodating the needs of individual students. It would

have made more sense coming from the student with the short story. But this is the student it comes from; my job is to be ready for what comes next.

Eventually she will volunteer to write news articles for the local paper on her after-school club's activities and enlist my editorial help. We go over her efforts line by line. Watch her be the one who wins the Pulitzer Prize, which is not to say my help was all that important, merely that the ultimate result of our help is unknown.

I decide that it might be a good idea for me to devote the twenty minutes I usually have between lunch and study hall to taking a walk around the building as opposed to doing a bit more work at my desk. I need the exercise, for one thing, and it wouldn't hurt me to keep the school's big picture in view.

My usual route takes me past the academic support area at the foot of the stairwell, two flights down from my second-floor classroom and several steps up from the level of the lobby and the main office. It's the one where I'm likeliest to find my students though not the only place they can go for help. After the ubiquity of technological devices, the school's tutorial component is the most notable of the changes I've seen. What was previously one highly stigmatized "special ed" room is now a bustling network of four study areas, all staffed by unflappable, die-hard tutors, most of them proficient in several subjects. Some of those areas are devoted to students with identifiable special needs, but there's a laudable blurring of the boundaries, at least on the surface, that seems to make it easy for kids to feel comfortable in any given room. The word *retard* sadly persists in the hallways but is used mostly as an all-purpose, gender-neutral alternative to *peckerhead*.

It's rare for me to walk by these areas without at least sticking my head in. Sometimes I can help clarify one of my assignments for a kid or his tutor, but mostly I stop by simply to enjoy the heady sight of so much application, to breathe the easy camaraderie in the air. Everybody's welcome, and so am I. I also go for the no less heady sight of three of my former students running the show. One of them tells me that my class played an important part in her youth. "I always felt safe in your English class, and at that time in my life I couldn't say that about every place." She's glad her niece has me for a teacher this year, she says, though she can hardly be more delighted than I am to teach that bright and intrepid child, who sports a "Girls Rule!" T-shirt about once a week.

Today her aunt is working on math with a small group of students, one of whom, a big kid in short pants, is complaining bitterly about how much "things suck" in his life. She is sympathetic but doesn't gush. Summoning an authority for which she's paid her dues in full, she says to him, "Then what you need to do, Charlie, is get a good education. It was the way out for me."

The ag shop is at the farthest reach from my classroom, at ground level on the opposite side of the building, so I make it the turnabout for my walks. I've already reestablished my credentials as an honorary member of the FFA by prominently displaying my old blue cap above one of the blackboards in my room. (The honor was bestowed on me in response to a chapter I'd written in my first book, and so it counts as one of my first literary awards.) I'm happy to see that the garage bays still hold tractors in various stages of repair, though no students are working on them today; they're in their classroom with their backs to the door, lined up at a bank of computers. It's fall so there are no new chicks in the incubators, though I'm greatly relieved to learn that they still hatch chicks in the spring.

As for seeing the country's future farmers glued to computers, it's no different from what I witness everywhere else. Teachers I would have seen one-on-one with a kid fifteen years ago are now as likely to be seen one-on-one with a laptop, though the picture is somewhat misleading in that some of them are communicating with their classes in that way, updating course blogs and teacher Web sites. In spite of official discouragement from the National Education Association, some of the faculty also social network with their students. EST (Educational Support Team) meetings, convened so teachers can discuss students in academic jeopardy, are as likely to include mention of what a kid has posted on his Facebook page as what he's missing for homework. Teachers have always been aware of their students' existing in a world outside of school; the difference now is that there are multiple, mostly virtual worlds, and teachers move in them too.

So do bullies, which may be another reason, besides the generally friendly climate of the school, why one sees less evidence of hazing in the halls. You can always stick it to somebody online. What one does see (and always saw) are kids who can't seem to say anything that wins the approval of their peers, kids who've met some orthodox and perhaps disability-based criteria for "weird" or "annoying," and other kids too socially invisible to be either, who seem always to be alone. I try to seek these kids out when I walk, as other teachers do, and some begin seeking me. My after-lunch walks will be short-lived for that reason; there's a boy who starts coming to see me at that time, and I want him to find me "at home."

For now I have the young woman sitting on one of the benches in the main lobby to deal with. She's been testing me almost since the year began. Today she complains that our current writing assignment is a great trouble to her, which is why her first draft is late.

"I can help you if you'd like," I say, but she accuses me of not wanting to. She says that I "turned my back" on her the other day when I was preparing to leave class early for a medical test. Knowing I had an appointment to keep, with the sub already in my room, she'd repeatedly raised her hand to summon me to her desk to answer a series of bogus questions. They grew more insistent—nearly desperate—in tone as I began to put on my coat and glance nervously at the clock. I wound up rushing to my appointment precisely because I refused to do the very thing she's now claiming I did. I won't let her fluster me again.

Well, I can help you now, I tell her calmly. What's your subject? (Something she hates.) Well, what do you like? (Guys! Especially this new one.) Well, why don't you write about a guy then? (Yeah, but what about this illustrating a general thing with a specific thing that you want us to do?) Is the guy fun to be around? (He is.) Well, then give me an example . . . not now, in your essay.

"And one more thing," I add, walking back to her bench a few seconds after walking away. "If you really believe that I refused to help you the other day, I think you should complain about it. You might go see Mr. Messier or your guidance counselor. Both of them have a long-standing acquaintance with my notorious habit of turning my back on students who need my help. Tell them exactly what you've told me. And I'll make you a deal. If they don't smile when you say it"—as I'm careful to smile now—"you don't have to do your essay, and I'll give you an A for it besides. How's that?"

Mr. Messier will be easy enough for her to find; I just passed him down in the gym, shooting hoops with kids on their lunch hour. The guidance office is even closer. I'll make a visit there myself to find out what on earth might be eating this kid. It turns out to be a good deal more than anything I had to deal with at

unformed and vulnerable—your integrity depends in large part on holding your emotions in check, an object that the average human being is less likely to achieve through the exercise of self-discipline than through the ruthless cultivation of numbness.

I want to believe my students are better served by the actuality of a human being than by the impersonation of a robot. In the case of my own humanness, that means laughing when I'm amused, holding forth when I'm excited, crying out when I'm hurt, and apologizing when I'm wrong. Do these propensities make me a good teacher or a poor one? It is far too glib, if true enough, to say they make me both. What they make me most of all, at least in my private hours, is a wreck.

On a morning shortly before Halloween I unlock my classroom and find that a digital projector has been installed on my ceiling, the kind that allows one to make presentations off of a laptop, the kind that most teachers have and that I don't want. *Trick or treat.*

Now I have even more wires running up my wall, a mess of debris on the desks and floors, and a remote control device lying in the center of my desk. The effect is like that of a red cape waved in front of a bull. I know this is not my room beyond this year, though I sense that my chalkboard-retaining predecessor did not want one of these machines, and I resent what feels like an implication that I should or that my temporary watch should form an acceptable pretext for doing an end run around him.

Ungenerously, I suspect that someone—the librarian perhaps or one of the "techs," a man who enters an occupied classroom with all the insouciance of a shop foreman who needn't knock to inspect the work on "his" floor—has presumptuously made the suggestion that Mr. Keizer ought to have (i.e., ought to be coaxed into using) a digital projector. I regard the machine as no more than an upgrade of the old overhead projector, one more excuse for a teacher to hide in the dark, a telltale accessory of the most inept of my college and high school instructors, something I am proud never to have used in my life. The culprit cannot possibly be my department head and is probably not my principal, neither of whom is a technological evangelist. And what about this mess on the seats and floor, left here like coal dust in a one-room schoolhouse for the schoolmarm to sweep up after she's finished breaking the ice on the water bucket?

A gentle knock interrupts the fury of my reverie, and one of the students employed part-time on the school's custodial staff, a soft-spoken junior who's taking tenth-grade English for the second time, pokes his head in and asks if he might come in. Mr. Messier has asked him to clean up the mess left from the installation. He goes about his business, asking me if I had a good weekend. Listening to jazz records after we read the short story "Sonny's Blues" was a cool idea, he says. He used to play the trumpet, but eventually it got to be too much with everything else he had going on. He still loves Louis Armstrong, though. Not like Sonny in the story, who's more of a Charlie Parker guy. He's glad I played a song by Louis. Did I know that because of the music I played for "Sonny's Blues" and the music I've been playing before class Jenny Martin has downloaded a bunch of John Coltrane songs onto her iPod? She plays the tenor sax in band. She's pretty good too. "I'll see you later in class, Mr. Keizer," he says, and then he and his broom are gone.

He's blessed my morning, left me his peace. Those were supposedly my offices in the days when I supplemented my teaching income by working as a part-time (ordained but untrained) Episcopal priest. I don't do that work anymore, and if any students at the school know I did it once, they make no mention of it to me. I'm glad. It was over the hills, in another county, and they'd have been no older than ten when I took my last service. It could have no meaning for them beyond a few cautionary tales, and I can make those points with other examples, including those in books.

But there are a few advantages that come of having been a jack of all trades and a master of none, some little more than the motor memory of a useful gesture. I move my hand through the air in a pattern I have not made for a long time, placing the slide projector in the crosshairs of my benediction. Pinned to the ceiling like a fish-eyed bat and twice as ugly, the machine is nevertheless the sign of someone's good intention, the fruit of someone's careful work. The kids will like it, as they do anything that blinks and hums. Churches bait their hooks with bingo, why shouldn't I bait a few of mine with digital bling? I can show my students the possibilities of their own sentences; I can fiddle for their edification with a few sentences of my own. At the very least I can give them a few laughs as I press the buttons with all the wincing apprehension of a man detonating dynamite. And if an old dog can be taught a new trick, what possible excuse can a young dog have not to learn a few old ones? *Let's watch the screen, please, gentlemen. And our language.*

5

NOVEMBER

When chill November's surly blast
Made fields and forests bare.

—Robert Burns

I tried never to miss the annual school musical in my earlier years of teaching, and I'm sure to be on hand for the one this year, a spirited vaudeville review. The school has gone in for ensemble pieces of late, one of the faculty directors tells me, a measure intended to prevent performances from being held hostage to the whims of one or another indispensable star. Like its antecedents, the show is performed in the Orleans town auditorium, the school having no such place. The idea of adding one to the school was rejected as a fiscal extravagance, first when the high school was constructed and again, many years later, when one of Mr. Messier's precursors allowed his dreams to soar too far above the terra firma of level funding.

My suspicion is that nostalgia figured in these defeats no less than parsimony. It wells up in me now as Kathy and I mount the steps beyond the barred light of the ticket booth and find a white-shirted usher to take us down the aisle (amid whispers of "his wife") and point us to our assigned places in two of the orchestra section's wooden fold-up seats. Think art deco without much art but with hints of the early twentieth century seeping through the bricks, just as the Jazz Age must have seeped north-ward in its heyday, though mostly it came in the form of Quebec whiskey smuggled south. My imagination doesn't go back that far, but I do see ghostly showstoppers from twenty years ago—a waggish performer yanking up his trousers to produce those castrato high notes, a model student and future drama major transformed into such a credible witch that she almost needed to sing to keep the little ones from running in terror out of the theater, a boy in the audience so overcome with admiration that he let loose the most lifelike rendition of a bawling heifer I've ever heard, and I've heard some of the best.

I find the same magic I remember from previous shows—and some of the same teachers, still playing in the orchestra and doing makeup backstage, most of them gray-headed now—the magic of kids stepping out of their daytime roles and into new ones, the latter sometimes closer to their most authentic selves. Not always recognizable in their costumes, still less so when they sing, they seem charmed and immortal, happily lost in that thin place that is both school and not-school because it exists outside the scheduled day. The student elite are well represented among the cast, but there are also a few surprises, kids you never would have expected to see in a play, kids you never imagined could sing, kids whose mere attendance at rehearsals seems little short of miraculous. Moving in shadow are those who work the lights, change the sets, hand out the programs—the crew of "cast and crew," and an even more motley crew than the cast. Kathy recognizes kids she knew in preschool, including some who came to her for speech therapy—now delivering flawless lines in deeper voices—and others more severely disabled but also matured and in their carefully cued movements no less splendid than the leads. "From each according to his ability, to each according to his need"—if I didn't know better, I'd swear that Marx jotted the line on the back of a program at a high school play.

At the end of the last ovation, as the audience files out of the theater, mothers of actresses identifiable by the bouquets in their hands, the vice principal calls me aside and says that the principal wants to speak to all the faculty in the basement under the stage. When we gather, Mr. Messier announces that Frank Smith, a thirty-nine-year-old teacher and a former student of mine, has died suddenly at home from heart failure. Visibly shaken, Mr. Messier wants us prepared for the next school day. Smith taught some of his social studies classes in an alternative, hands-on program at the school, gathering his students around a woodworking table in the shop area downstairs. A special education aide who works with many of the same kids begins to wail. "He was so young. He'd just gotten married."

Veterans on the staff might breathe a guilty sigh of relief that we have been spared a suicide, a disastrous auto accident, the death of someone not yet kissed, all occasions they have seen before. There is no mourning like mourning in a school. It's another kind of theater, another ensemble piece. Every conceivable human response to death, from the heartrending outburst to the opportunistic excuse, struts and frets its hour upon the stage. Adults are fond of saying that kids are too young to comprehend death, which may be true, though high school kids are at least old enough to grasp their own incomprehension. They're at sixes and sevens to know what they should feel. Outside counselors join the guidance staff to handle the overflow of referrals. The main office hands out round blue buttons with Smith's initials written in the script of the New York Yankees logo, a tribute to him and his favorite team. School is canceled for half a day to fill the Orleans Catholic church to standing-room-only capacity, the standers spilling to the outside steps and sidewalk. The eulogies are long and tender, spiced with jokes; but for the setting, one would think the deceased had retired with decades of golf on his horizon. Perhaps because I distrust sentimentality, something in me tends to harden at a funeral, something of which I've never been proud. Where better people hold back tears, I am often holding back bile.

But what is my job about if not holding back? On the day of the funeral a girl in one of my classes asks me if I could "use a hug." Of course it is she who could use one, bereaved as she is, not so much by the death of a teacher she scarcely knew as by the recent absence of a father who keeps in touch mainly through disparaging remarks about her falling grades and increasing weight. I would gladly oblige, but what might her classmates say about her if I do, and how many of them will assume that hugging their teacher is either the ticket to his good graces or a likely risk of coming to see him for extra help? "You've already hugged me by offering to," I say, only to see the disappointment of yet another rejection on her face. Once again I yield to my recurring fantasy of receiving a phone call from her father, a demand to know why she's failing my course and a chance to see if my way with words is sufficient to throttle a human being long distance or, failing that, to dupe one into hastening my retirement. ("I'm afraid we can no longer employ a teacher who would address a parent as 'you philandering piece of shit.'") I'll hug you then, my sad darling, and everybody else I pass on my way out the door, but for now you don't want to put your arms around anyone like me. It'd take you another year at least to get warm again.

My heart begins to thaw when a knock comes at the door

and one of "Mr. Smith's kids" appears, someone I can't recall seeing before today, though it may be the forlorn expression on his face that makes him unrecognizable. He is holding a yard-square wooden cross. I assume he made it in the shop where Mr. Smith held his classes. When he hands me a pen, I notice that the cross is covered with signatures. As soon as I've added my name, he turns and trudges out of the room, a towheaded little Christ from the invisible downstairs world, carrying our names and who knows how many of our sins through the halls.

Even in the absence of an unexpected death there is nothing like a school to make one aware of mortality. You may be thinking of other professions where this is more the case, medicine or ministry for example, but I buried the dead and visited the dying for many years and do not recall ever leaving a hospital or a grave with a heightened awareness that I must die. Mostly what I felt was relief at being alive. But the relentless experience of finitude that is teaching, the Angelus that rings—not three times a day, as in a monastery, but every forty-five minutes—remorselessly drives home one's sense of limited time, of diminishing chances to do the work and get it right. The kids are probably too young to feel it this way, and one hopes so, but they know what a deadline is and they can hear the word *dead* when we give them one.

If the bell schedule and the calendar are the body of a school, transcendence often comes as an out-of-body experience. Whenever a classroom teacher can manage to get kids "out of school," either physically or psychologically, then school can begin. Sometimes that happens simply by inviting students to stay beyond the scheduled day, which can be difficult, though it helps if you have refreshments and a few students with nothing better to do at home. I have both. Sometimes it happens through a special project, the more hands-on the better. Since our culture increasingly regards manual work as the domain of toddlers and dolts, transcendence just as often translates to shedding the chrysalis of false sophistication—which if you're an American teenager is probably better described by the metaphor of a straitjacket. Simply put, learning is sometimes abetted by giving self-conscious young adults permission to remember what it means to play.

I hand out markers and invite students to deface enlarged photographs of my face (taken with perverse pleasure from the jacket of my last book), awarding one blacked-out tooth or booger per part of speech accurately identified, and everybody wants to find a passive-voice verb. At the close of our unit on the American short story, I ask my students to make a museumlike display of projects based on the literature we have studied. Though I encourage the use of technology, their overwhelming preference is for projects made with tangible stuff, perhaps because more than one person can touch it at a time. The more macabre stories seem to inspire the most projects: there's more than one black lottery box loaded for Shirley Jackson's famous tale and even an edible diorama of the lottery itself. (Instead of stoning a single villager, we get to eat them all.) Among several references to Poe's "The Black Cat" are an ambitious short film and a high-decibel dramatic monologue that brings the principal rushing to the classroom door in the expectation of preventing bloody murder. Flannery O'Connor's racially charged "Everything That Rises Must Converge" inspires two depictions of the purple hat that Julian's mother and her black antagonist both wear, one of them perched atop a Styrofoam head symbolically painted half white and half black. A boy with a passion for computer games builds one based on Hemingway's "The Killers" that allows a player to search for doomed Ole Andreson through several rooms, including the diner where Nick Adams and his coworkers are taken hostage. Other games are in the conventional mode, with playing pieces and question cards—good review for our upcoming unit test, assuming the information on the cards is correct, which it mostly is except for spelling.

We invite other members of the school to visit our display, treating them to baked goods and asking them to sign a guest book and leave their comments. I like to think we're giving them a chance to play as well—if only to pretend that the established order has been shaken for a day. "Honors" students are our spectators for a change; the office secretaries and cafeteria cooks seem touched that we've gone out of our way to invite them upstairs. The vice principal gets to ask his hot-seat regulars a different sort of question than "Where were you second period?"

"Had you read any other stories by Poe before?"

The students seem to have as much fun as I do, though mine is counterbalanced by the bother involved, no small part of which entails finding vacant rooms for the classes displaced by the activity. The cleanup is protracted—many of the kids seem equally indisposed to taking their projects home or chucking them out— and the productions are going to be a devil to grade. Effort has to count for a lot, the quality of the materials for relatively little. To do otherwise comes down to grading the resources available in a student's household (though I'd like to know what manner of grading *doesn't* come down to that in the end).

On top of this, I've allowed students to do their preapproved projects (without the requirement of preapproval, special projects amount to whatever quasi-relevant artifact can be yanked off a living room wall on the morning of the due date) in preapproved groups. So I need to take into account what one student did on her own versus what three students did together, which in the latter case can come down to what one student did on her own and two other students tried to take a free ride on. "If you're going to team up," I tell my classes, "make sure you hold up your end of the deal and make sure you choose somebody who's capable of doing the same. Have a reason for working together besides your fear of being alone." I wonder if, for some kids, this is the most valuable takeaway of the whole assignment. To drive home the point, I grant few divorces once the groups are formed and none after the projects come in.

What a complicated mess it all can be—I don't wonder that some teachers fall in love with the illusory precision of standardized tests, the tidiness of a daily worksheet, the radical individuation of the report card. The little clay figurines that topple over after a day or two, the glue that gives way along crookedly folded seams, the cardboard pieces that go sliding onto the floor, so lovely for bearing our human thumbprints, turn out to be sad for the same reason.

I have no illusions about the retro nature of some of my methods, but it takes a special faculty meeting devoted to swapping ideas for "using technology in our classrooms" to make me understand just how retro I am.

"We've just about eliminated class discussions," one colleague notes, as though class discussions were a rare strain of malaria. In lieu of verbal exchanges, his students record their comments on something called Moodle, sitting shoulder to shoulder at their screens like mute commuters on a crosstown bus. Since everyone seems to know what Moodle is, I decide not to waste the group's time by asking. I couldn't trust myself not to ask what's wrong with a class discussion. My colleague also notes that his students like to vote in class polls using their cell phones, which requires a waiver of the rule prohibiting cell phone use in class and also, needless to say, possession of a cell phone. The matter of possession surely accounts for the "mere four students" who opt to keep a paper journal for another teacher's class, in which the majority do their journals online. Thus a paper journal takes on the stigma once attached to patched pants. Recently I took a confidential classroom poll to see what I could conscionably expect of my students in terms of online research at home, and I could easily have predicted which of the kids had the equipment and which did not, based on their clothing, their attendance, and the sadder narrative details of the paper journals I require all of them to keep.

Fairness is not the only basis for my requirement. As the months go by, I come to recognize the extent of my naiveté in regard to the brave new world of digital cheating. It is not uncommon, I'm told, for students to photograph exams on their smartphones and send the photos to classmates who will take the same exam later in the day or on the day following an absence. I find that some of my practices are in woeful need of an upgrade. It has always been my policy, for example, this year and in the past, to permit students to use their notes on any pop quiz based on their reading assignments. My aim is to see that conscientious application gets its wages, with no penalties for poor retention. "So if you're worried about forgetting what you read, jot down a few notes. And if you're still worried after you take the quiz, then pass your notes in with it. If I can find something accurate—or, better still, something insightful—in your notes, I'll see you get credit for that too." Surprisingly, many of the students with the most expansive notes elect not to pass them in. Just as surprisingly, a number of students phrase their answers with identical wording, even though the wording is not from the text and even though none of them appear to be glancing at one another's quizzes.

What they're doing, though it takes me a little while to catch on, is downloading plot summaries from online sites like

SparkNotes and using them in lieu of the notes I've encouraged them to take on their own. The sharper kids cut and paste the information into what appear to be their own word-processed documents; the duller ones don't even bother to do that. An orderly society could hardly exist but for the natural affinity of dishonesty and laziness: thieves steal because thievery is easier than work, and they get caught because it's too much work to be a good thief. In that regard at least, technology fosters order.

As for discouraging the use of SparkNotes and its ilk, that is done easily enough, as in the following quiz, which derives its rationale from the folk remedy for dissuading children from smoking cigarettes by having them smoke cigars:

> Printed below is the text of a summary of chapters 6 and 7 for *The Secret Life of Bees* as found on a sleazy Internet rip-off site specially designed for students who have more important things to do in their lives than read books. I apologize for making you even *look* at such a thing, but I'm hoping we'll have some fun with it.

> Read over the summary and then, based on your own reading of the chapters, list 7 details, events, exchanges, or other information that the summary misses or waters down. Your 7 items can include details of description, the narrator's thoughts, a character's words, or anything else, however small, that is not found in the synopsis below. A full page of hints follows the summaries, but feel free to use your own material.

It takes but a few such stratagems and counterstratagems before teachers and students alike are missing the point of reading literature in the first place. To say nothing of missing some glaring ironies: the likelihood that the same companies producing the crib notes are marketing all kinds of expensive software to address illiteracy, the fact that educators who can't speak three consecutive sentences without using the phrase *critical thinking* almost never encourage, much less model, critical thinking in the adoption of technological tools. And this irony too: that in my tortuous efforts to get my students to enjoy reading, I am making it less than enjoyable for them and me alike. This is what kills me more than anything: the loss of pleasure as an admissible reason for doing anything, its utter insignificance in the ethos of Get-R-Done.

Nevertheless, a strange poetic justice can occur when disadvantaged students who lack the tools for online cheating turn to their books and almost by default begin to shine on their quizzes and in our class discussions, however anachronistic the latter may be. Still, it's cold comfort: even the principled refusal to cheat winds up belonging to the technologically entitled. How can we have allowed so much of *public* education to rely on *private* property? Perhaps because our whole conception of public education, originally intended to prepare students for the obligations of democratic citizenship, is to foster the acquisition of private property. You need a laptop to get a good education, so you can get a good job, so you can buy each of your children a laptop.

The young librarian, whom I've gotten to know well enough to find a number of affinities in our politics but not yet well enough to broach the subject of restoring the Library of America to the library of Lake Region Union High School, asks me what I think of the idea of writing a grant that would provide every student with a laptop. She's full of energy and commitment, and the last thing I want to do is slam a good idea. At least she recognizes the educational inequality that exists when every student doesn't have a laptop. I'm not sure this is a recognition shared in the school at large. I would indeed like to see every student with a laptop—or at least every student with equal access to one. But, I go on to say, how about starting with a grant that allows every student to do his or her homework in an adequately heated house? (A social agency rescued one of my students last winter from living with her boyfriend in an unheated trailer behind her grandparents' house, which, for all I know, might not have been any warmer than the trailer.) In fact, there are such things as fuel assistance grants, but they seldom cover the heating demands of a northern winter and are always subject to unanticipated spikes in the price of oil, in the numbers of eligible applicants (an additional ten thousand Vermonters will join the poverty rolls this year), and in the cost-cutting zeal of the Congress. By January, if not before, some residents will be spending their food money on fuel, hoping to make up the difference by scrounging at community food shelves. In such a context, "let them have laptops" comes dangerously close to "let them eat cake."

The librarian sees my point; I'm not sure she sees the writing on the digital wall. As an enrichment experience, I set up an after-school showing of Atom Egoyan's film of *The Sweet Hereafter*, the Russell Banks novel I wish were on the Popular Fiction syllabus in place of his *Rule of the Bone*, though I admire them both. I require parental permission slips (the film is rated R) and send out for pizzas. At one point in the story, what is arguably its thematic climax, a lawyer who's come to an Adirondack town to litigate in the aftermath of a tragic school bus accident stands in the snow next to the demolished bus and soliloquizes that "something has happened to the children." He doesn't mean just the victims of the accident, one of whom was a victim of father-daughter incest before she lost the use of her legs. He means the children of America, his own drug-addicted daughter not least of all.

"What has happened to the children?" he demands of the dark winter sky. What indeed? I look up from the papers I'm correcting at the back of the room to see what effect this bleak soliloquy might be having on my students. All but one are staring at their cell phones.

After the film is over, the leftover pizza is distributed, and the students are dispersed (not before they've thanked me and said how much they enjoyed the movie), I go down to the locked main office to sign myself out of the building. I find two girls seated on the bench in the lobby, not my students, just kids waiting for a ride. As I approach they ask if they might be allowed to come into the main office and use the secretary's phone to call home. This is somewhat irregular, but since I'm able to stand outside in plain view, I see no harm in granting the request. It should take no more than a minute.

But it takes much longer, and not because the girls are taking advantage of my time. It takes longer because the person they've called, a father, I assume, or someone else in the house who goes by the name of Dad, is proving doggedly reluctant to come to school and drive them home. From the girls' responses coming to me through the glass, I can infer his list of suggested alternatives, which seem to stop short of hitchhiking in the dark but veer close enough. "Can't a friend drive you?" "What about a teacher?" All the options that any parent with even the slightest capacities for worry would jump off a moving train to avoid. "Come on, Dad," the girl on the phone implores, shifting from one foot to another, grimacing at her friend. She's at school too late to have stayed for a detention; my guess is that she's just gotten out of a sports practice or perhaps been seeking extra help from a teacher. In other words, she's been trying to make the most of her school

day. If there's any supper waiting on the other side of the phone
line, it's likely to be cold by now. If there's homework to be done,
the girls will get a late start. But the negotiations continue, as if
in a hostage crisis, except the hostages are negotiating for themselves. *Why not? Please! Just come, will you?* Finally, it seems a
ride is on its way. The girls come out of the office and thank me
for letting them use the phone. Am I mistaken to think they're
ashamed at what I have overheard—could not help but overhear,
given my responsibility to keep them in view—or am I the one
who's feeling ashamed for their sake?

I don't need to teach to know this feeling; I need only go to
the supermarket, need only wait in line for a stamp. I seem to
have become more sensitive to it over the years: the spectacle of
parents without a single kind word to say to their kids. But what
was that stat that went with the 30-million-word gap, the one
about the class differences in what children hear by way of praise
or blame? *Quit it, cut it out, smarten up, you're gonna be sorry*—
the soundtrack of my world. Sometimes it's pure display: Look
at me, I'm a strict parent; I make my kids mind. Other times, it's
probably little more than a grudge against life. Even when there's
no apparent annoyance, the sheer inattention can be staggering.
I will never forget my daughter's elementary school science fair,
all the little scientists standing by their rabbits and soil-filled
soda bottles, their eyes fishing for the slightest notice, the alac-
rity with which they seized on the briefest show of interest, while
their parents, the ones who'd even bothered to come, yakked
and flirted among themselves like attendees at a junior high
dance. The children and all their paraphernalia could have vanished without a trace and hardly been missed.

With report cards come parent-teacher conferences, and a
corrective to my dismay. True, there are many more parents who
stay away than come, not untypical for high school (as opposed

to the younger grades) or for the midlevel classes—or, it ought to be said, for a school in which parents have a passing level of confidence. If all is well, there's no need to check things out. But enough parents come to keep me busy for most of the night. A handful show up the next day, which has been set aside for the same purpose. Some of these are former students of mine. One of them, a freshman in the first year I taught, hobbles into my room on crutches, the result of her playing King of the Hill with her athletic teenaged son. She's impressed that I can recall the position of her desk on my 1979 classroom seating chart (which I could also do for the boy's father, but he is out of the picture now) and quote the first line of an essay she wrote that same year. My remarks about her son are more guarded. He's making progress, academically and behaviorally, but not without bumps. She's been keeping close track of those. So strange for me to see the teenaged girl's face superimposed on the mother's, a few wrinkles now and a great deal more worry, but not without that indefatigable smile. "Keep me informed," she asks, the devoted parent's perpetual refrain.

I can give a more stellar report to the next mother who comes through the door. She, too, is a former student, one so quiet I might have forgotten her by now, or at least her name, except for her memorable parting years ago—when she took my hands at the end of her senior year and tearfully thanked me for "everything you did." I wondered for years thereafter what on earth I might have done out of the ordinary for this conscientious student who took a one-semester course in which I gave her no extra help I can remember, not even a letter of recommendation. Long before I realized I had her daughter in my class, she had come to occupy a symbolic place in my mind—the little Goddess of Unaccountable Thanks. Now here she is a good twenty years later, wife, mother, coach, community pillar, taking my hand again and saying how glad she is her daughter has me in class. And how glad I am to have her daughter—I can say so without reservation. And what a wonderful movie she and her friends made about "The Black Cat" for our museum project. "I hope they didn't leave you to clean up all the blood."

Other conferences are more fretful—one boy hurries upstairs ahead of his parents and asks if I intend to tell them about "that stupid thing with the SparkNotes I did today." I assure him the thought never crossed my mind; it runs entirely counter to my code. No cheap shots on parent-conference night, no ingratiating bullshit either, but no cheap shots, especially with a kid who I'm almost positive has learned an important lesson. Not a few of the tenser exchanges involve mothers who are at wits' end to know what to do with the surly young men who've suddenly emerged in their hitherto man-free houses. Without their sons in tow, they're at liberty to confess. This may have something to do with my age, but I don't recall many times in my first years teaching when a lone parent came out and said, "I don't know what to do with him. What should I do?" I venture no advice beyond urging them not to give up on the question, "which you're obviously not going to do if you bothered to come here tonight."

Parent conferences help to remind me that good parenting defies all ideologically based predictors. Social conservatives, I'm sure, would like to see a better correlation between "intact [heterosexual] family" and happy child, just as my socialistic convictions would rest easier with a stronger correlation between class deprivation and family strife. No doubt, we each have ample evidence for making our case. But the exceptions make mischief with our best arguments: the illiterate parent who sees to it that the homework gets done, the village brawler who never once strikes his kids, the mother who shows up at school looking like a refugee from Cold Comfort Farm but who will get her daughter, and eventually herself, through college, whatever it takes. Kathy brings me more than one of these stories home from her work at Dartmouth, my favorite having to do with a mentally impaired divorced father with a menial job and a sympathetic boss who gives him the day off so he can drive all night across four state lines every time his child has a school conference or a doctor's appointment. He may or may not grasp what it means to have a kid "on the autism spectrum" or an advanced degree in pediatric neurology, but he knows enough to grasp his child's hand and not to let it go.

The matter of "how much to say" comes easier to me in parent conferences than it sometimes does in individual exchanges with kids. With the parents, there's an etiquette, a scripted agenda: the grades, the behavior, the things that are causing difficulty, the potential I see that I hope the parent sees with me and that we want the child to see as well. "Call me anytime" takes the place of a formal bow among the Japanese: the parent says it, I repeat it, we go back to our respective sides of the teahouse, me to my desk and the parent to the door. With the kids, it's a dicier proposition, and *dicey* provides the right metaphor, because often the exchange takes the form of a game.

For instance, the game of "Do you believe me?" The student makes the first move by pretending not to have understood the difference between taking notes while reading an assignment and downloading prepackaged notes off the Internet. "You said we could use notes." Or the student pretends to have believed that "you wouldn't mind" if she went AWOL for half a class period. The apparent object here is to place the teacher in the position of losing no matter how he responds. Refuse my excuse, and you're calling me a liar. Accept my excuse, and you've as much as called one of us an idiot, since it would take an idiot to believe what I've just told you. Or, worse, you've shown that you're much more concerned about smooth relations than you are about an honest student-teacher relationship.

Too often this amounts to an accurate depiction of a school's priorities. Behind a pretext of "mutuality" and "giving students the benefit of the doubt," the institution winds up convincing any student with half a brain that he scarcely matters at all. It's the pretense of rectitude we care about, the idol of ourselves as "caring people" that we worship instead of the latent god in the living kid. So we allow a kid to negotiate his way to functional illiteracy, then congratulate ourselves on our fair dealing. For the moment, the kid believes that he has conned us, but I fear he often grows up to understand that we have conned him. A bitter epiphany if he does.

I try to explain that to my students when I disallow certain dodges. "I don't want you looking back ten years from now and saying to yourself, Mr. Keizer seemed like a pretty nice guy at the time, but he was just going through the motions and picking up a paycheck and laughing at me all the way to the bank. In fact, he must have thought I was pretty stupid." Sometimes this connects. Sometimes it doesn't. The problem of how much to say is complicated further by the problem of how much is likely to be heard. A teacher should never underestimate the factor of selective listening. Simply to use the word *stupid* risks having a kid believe, or claim to believe, that you've called him stupid. He hears the word and nothing else. A failure in auditory processing, as much as any willful recalcitrance, lies at the root of more than a few classroom conflicts.

Many of these are innocuous enough, even comical, but others play out in more disturbing ways. In fulfillment of an ice-breaking assignment I inherited years ago from my department head—"Talk to a Chair" (that is, to someone you imagine sitting in it)—a girl talks to her father's new wife. I've explicitly warned the students at the outset and in writing that they should not use the assignment as a therapy session or to violate anyone's confidentiality, including their own. Use your imagination, keep it light, be discreet. But the girl who steps to the front of the room has either not heard what I said (a real possibility given that she's often running to the nurse's office or her guidance counselor at the start of class) or else has chosen to ignore me. She makes unflattering references to the new wife's ethnicity and her wiles in catching her husband. In a class with more than a few stepchildren, the girl's no-holds-barred attack plays like a battle cry. The kids seem thrilled, and I have to admit that the talk is strong. For the girl I imagine it represents a kind of catharsis. But in the midst of my praises for her diction, her dramatic delivery, her use of specific examples to illustrate general statements (a point of special emphasis for this class, notwithstanding the examples that made me squirm), I feel it necessary to caution her about matters of confidentiality and the real danger that certain kinds of remarks might be construed "by someone who doesn't know you as well as we do" as racist.

Later in the term a colleague tells me, "Deidre thinks you hate her. She says you think she's a racist." Should I have made my remarks to her privately? Would it have made any difference? And didn't the audience for her remarks oblige me to address my caveats—and my praises—in front of the same impressionable audience? I can't help but wonder if the wicked stepmother doesn't feel the same exasperation as I do. *Say what I will, the child never hears me.*

The best I can do is to make the points I think need to be made as clearly as I know how to make them and, no less important, to be as keen to listen as I am to talk. In other words, I need to be as ready to learn as I am to teach. I'm presented with an opportunity to do both in an exchange with a trumpet player who hails me from the band teacher's office. He's overheard some of the jazz I played for my sophomores in connection with "Sonny's Blues" and thinks it was cool stuff. With an eye to his trumpet, I ask if he knows Miles Davis. He doesn't, and so I offer to lend him *Kind of Blue*. Pointing to the name and face on the front of his T-shirt, I ask if he'd care to requite my Davis with a bit of Dr. Dre. If he's willing, I wouldn't mind a lesson or two in hip-hop, a genre about which I know little and would like to learn more. Would he be willing to teach me, in other words. He would.

"You made Mike's day by asking about Dr. Dre," the student's English teacher tells me. But my request remains in limbo for a while. Eventually, I'm given to understand that the delay owes to Mike's difficulty in finding tracks suitable for a teacher's ears. The problem of selective hearing works both ways, you see, and he's fearful that I'll hear "the rough parts" and nothing else. I tell him he should give me what I asked for and not worry about offending me; his only concern should be with giving me a good introduction to the music.

That he does, and it's no strain to find some songs that I like and some well-turned lines that I admire. But how far should I go in tackling the misogyny in some of the lyrics? The last thing I want to do as a white teacher talking to an African American student is to play the dozens with his music—especially when he has fewer than a dozen schoolmates, and no instructors, of his color. But I'm playing the same game with his intelligence if I simply nod my head in bland approval, adopting that tolerant mien Emerson so memorably describes as "the gentlest asinine expression." I have to say the word *women* at the least. I have to speak to what disturbs me.

Mike knows what I'm talking about, and it disturbs him too. He tries to give the issue some historical context, parts of which I find more convincing than others, but I don't need to tell him so. Perhaps the best antidote against selective listening is selective talking: say no more than what's most important to say. In this case, that includes "thank you," and not just for teaching me. He has also trusted me.

So has the girl who comes to me to tell me why she's been missing so many classes. How without saying too much do I suggest that she may be revealing too much? The word *medical* is quite sufficient, I want to tell her, all I need in order to understand why I ought to cut her some slack. I'm quite willing to do so without any reference to her ovaries. But there's a thin, thin line here between helping her to understand that she doesn't have to barter intimate details of health history in exchange for some compassion and driving her back to that zone of misogyny in which women are supposed to regard their bodies as unmentionable. It would take a self-defeating number of words to make the first point while disclaiming the second, so I say less than I could.

I wish I'd said more when I overhear—when everyone in class overhears—several girls gabbing that the reason Rhonda is out of class again is that she's got gross things growing on her ovaries. "Let's let our classmates' medical matters be their own business," I say, though I can tell from the ensuing facial expressions that what I meant to say and what was heard are at considerable variance. *Let's let our classmates die of ovarian cancer and not give a damn about them because our homework is all that counts around here*—that's likely to be what got heard, not merely or even primarily because the kids are not listening but because so much of what I say is filtered through the larger culture, in which knowing the details of other people's pain increasingly becomes the substitute for relieving it. "Knowledge is power,"

gossip is compassion, attitude is protest, doing nothing whatsoever is doing everything imaginable so long as you're well-
informed. But you can't say that to a bunch of sophomores, and
they'd miss the irony even if you did.

Stick to the curriculum, focus on the task at hand, that's what
you tell yourself, but even that bumps up against certain cultural
norms that you either swallow or push back on. I have a student
who comes to school every day after only a few hours of sleep.
He sometimes dozes off sitting upright in his desk. In addition
to doing chores on his family's farm, he reports to another barn
at 2:00 a.m. and milks for several hours there. "Your studies
need to come first"—that's what I want to say, but the matter is
more complicated than that. I know from talking to him, as I
will learn again on a deeper level when I have him in a second-
semester Composition class, that his sole vocational goal is to
become a farmer. In that light, his time in the barn *is* his "studies." In fact, his father has purchased the farm—a perilous step
at best in the current agricultural economy—with the plan of
giving him the training he desires and a place to put that training to profitable use once the farm passes from father to son.
What to do, then, but talk to a guidance counselor and talk ever
so gingerly to the student, lauding his work ethic and sense of
vocation while reminding him of his need for sleep and for the
literature that is no less his inheritance than the farm, no less
nourishing than milk.

A girl in another class explains to me, not without frustration, why her grades have fallen from best in class to failing. I
know something of her background, and so I have no reason to
disbelieve her when she says, "I've been raised to believe that
your family and your friends come first." In other words, when a
parent tells you to involve yourself in some ridiculous kinship
drama as opposed to reading a book about someone else's kin-

ship drama, you don't disobey. How does a teacher question a value so irreproachable as "family loyalty"? Perhaps by expanding it. "I agree with what you've been brought up to believe," I tell her, "but only if you include your future family in the mix. It's possible to let down your yet-to-be-born children by being too afraid to let down your parents. A mother with a good education is less likely to be forced to choose between caring for her kids and earning a living." As feminism this is pretty thin gruel—what about the young woman's obligation to herself?—but it's the message she's likeliest to digest. It is her future welfare, not my ideological purity, that's at stake. I cite my wife as an example; her education has allowed her some options that other women, other mothers, don't enjoy.

If I'm dangerously close to undermining a parent's authority, I'm even closer to undermining my own argument. It's the same sad paradox that every teacher faces: "Get a good education—so you can be more like me." Are teachers the happiest, most esteemed and prosperous people that a kid is likely to meet? We are certainly among the best educated, at least in a community like mine. At times I try for a better exhortation, spicing it with a bit of sardonic humor: "Get a good education—or else you could end up like me." I'm telling them to lay hold of every educational opportunity at hand. *Surpass your teacher.* But is that what they hear? Quickly, lest they draw the wrong conclusion, I add that I consider myself very fortunate, as indeed I do, to serve as their teacher and to spend time with them every day.

Finally, I make time to drive to Burlington for dinner with my grown-up daughter, a biweekly custom in my freelance life but increasingly rare in my schedule now. I look forward to it all day. For one thing, I'll be on the road in daylight, out of work early—I've asked for and been granted permission to leave school when the students do—and for another, I can count on being a better conversationalist than usual. Often I find myself casting about for topics beyond the usual paternal remarks about maintaining tire pressures and keeping the door open for graduate school. A writer's regimen provides little in the way of anecdote. Today, though, I'll be coming to the table full of stories; both of us are teaching now.

Within moments after driving out of the busy school lot, I find myself in the middle of an ominous caravan snaking along the winding, damaged road that goes past the school toward Irasburg. Two cars ahead of me, at the head of the line, is a school bus. Directly behind me, practically in my backseat, is a car driven by a student who appears to be tripping on some drug. He is gesticulating crazily—at me, at another car, to his music, who knows? I could read his lips in my rearview mirror if I took my eyes off the road long enough. Behind him, swerving frequently into the oncoming lane, is another car with a student sitting with his body outside the passenger side window and his hands on the car roof. Should the driver brake abruptly, his buddy's as good as airborne. A third car behind those two is also jockeying for position, driving the others up against my back. The thought flashes through my mind that at fifty-seven years old, with a salary of less than fifty thousand dollars per year and very little to leave my loved ones in the way of wealth, I am going to be killed in a wilding incident on a secondary road in Podunk. That the car threatening a head-on collision with any vehicle coming the other way has the grille of a late-model Volvo only makes the thought more bitter. I am going to be sideswiped or run off the road by a seventeen-year-old kid whose parents can afford to send him to school in a Volvo. I am going to be eulogized in spray paint on a bridge abutment as people weep their eyes out for the poor teacher who lost his life in the unfortunate "accident," to say nothing of the damage to the goddamn Volvo.

I'm out of my car almost before the school bus has come to a full stop at the next T intersection. I tap the driver's side of the car behind me until the driver, who does not look at me at first, rolls down his window. I shout out to the other drivers behind him, all of whom are looking at me now and who seem surprised to see me. Some kids have just gotten off the school bus and they're watching too. I ask what anyone would like to bet me that any of these cars is going to be allowed a parking space at school tomorrow. I have no takers. I have at least one apology—I don't remain long enough to hear any others.

Instead I drive back to the school. On the way into the lot, I nearly collide with another teacher approaching on my right; neither of us sees the other till we hit our brakes just in time. This shakes me up further, though I'm already pretty shaken. I doubt Mr. Messier has ever seen me this upset. "I don't mind not having a life for a year," I say melodramatically, "but I draw the line at *losing* my life." He smiles when I add "to a Volvo no less." He knows which student drives a Volvo, along with the names of the others who fit my descriptions. Within fifteen minutes he has spoken by phone to every parent connected with the incident. He doesn't get any blowback. He says he intends to speak to all of the students tomorrow, informing them that although his jurisdiction does not extend beyond the school grounds, the sheriff's does, and he will notify the sheriff. When he gently voices his concern about my driving so many miles in such a bad state of mind, I say that I will probably abort my trip.

"If you still would like to have dinner with your daughter, and you want a driver, you've got one." He is talking about a round trip of 180 miles, six hours out of his day at the least. And he means what he's said—I almost can't bear to register how sincerely he means it. He also offers me his phone and the privacy of his office to call my daughter.

The next day passes without incident. Mr. Messier has told me he will not order the drivers to apologize; wisely he intends to "see what they do." He probably knows how little a forced apology would mean to me: less than none at all. One of my students does ask what was happening behind the school bus yesterday, which he saw when he'd gotten off at his stop, tactfully adding "Are you okay?" I'm fine, I tell him. "I just don't like being crowded." I can't help recalling a character in the novella we're reading, Howard Frank Mosher's *Where the Rivers Flow North*, who shares a similar dislike. "Don't crowd him, you," says his common-law wife, before he drives a cant hook through the hand of a man who ought to have heeded her warning. Perhaps my favorite scene in the book.

At the close of the day, three penitent young men appear at my door and ask if they can speak to me. I'm listening. When one of them swears that he'd never have tailgated my car had he known a teacher was driving it, I have the cue I need to say what matters most. Though my own safety was uppermost in my mind at the time, I urge them to think of how much more was at stake in the case of their own lives. I do not want to die, I tell them, and yet if I died now, I'd die in the satisfactions of a happy marriage, of having watched a child of mine grow to adulthood, of having seen most of my ambitions fulfilled. All of these satisfactions came to me when I was older than they are now. To die before one is even fully conscious of his own capacities for happiness—and to die stupidly into the bargain, what a terrible waste that would be. "Your friend, the guy leaning out the window—what if he'd lost his balance?" and so on. They've heard all of this a hundred times, I'm sure, but there is always the chance it will sink in on the 101st try.

I impart no other life lessons before shaking their hands and telling them we're square. All in all, not without the help of my principal and probably of some parents too, I've managed to bring the whole business to a satisfactory close. I've seized what educators are fond of calling the teachable moment and used it to good effect. I should be feeling better about things than I do.

For the truth is that the slowest learner to have entered this classroom at the end of the day is the one left standing in it. Maintaining professional detachment, setting boundaries between work life and personal life—a time to punch in, and a time to punch out—at these I'm still an apprentice. A decade and a half since my previous year of teaching I remain stuck in the same rut on the near side of wisdom. I'm still ready to grasp the teachable moment even as I lose the livable one. I should have waited for the school bus to make its turn and made mine in the opposite direction. I should have shaken my head in disgust and driven on to Burlington. *But someone might have died*—to hell with that. We're all dying. *I'm* dying. The daughter who once wished aloud that she could make two daddies, one to grade the kids' papers and one to play pirates with her, ate dinner without her father last night, just as she did so many nights in the past when his body was at the kitchen table and his mind still at school. Who am I to lecture anyone on the subject of a terrible waste?

6

DECEMBER

There is nothing like tempting the boy to want to study and to love it: otherwise you simply produce donkeys laden with books. . . . If it is to do any good, Learning must not only lodge with us: we must marry her.

—Montaigne, "On Educating Children"

Not long before the Thanksgiving recess I begin what will prove the most arduous task of the year: teaching my three tenth-grade classes how to write a research paper. Another member of the department, no shirker and perhaps the best trained of any of us in the art of teaching students how to write, insists that tenth graders are still too young to handle such an assignment. He may well be right about that, though there are precedents that might refute him.

At one time, roughly concurrent with my last tenure at the school, a research paper was a standard requirement in the tenth grade for both English and social studies. Attempts to coordinate between the departments and allow students to write a single paper for both classes probably did as much as any factor to discourage the assignment in subsequent years. Naturally enough, social studies teachers tended to see "content" as their prerogative, which greatly restricted the range of acceptable subjects, and "form" as belonging to their colleagues across the hall, which prompted English teachers to feel they were being asked to run an editorial laundry service. In retrospect, the disagreement was probably no more than the inevitable outcome of any team teaching effort involving more than one team.

Many things have changed since then, not least of all the emphasis on writing across the curriculum. These days it's not unusual for me to be invited to admire a piece of student writing generated by a phys ed class. Sara has said the time has come to revive the requirement of a tenth-grade research paper. She has asked if I will help. Her wishes are enough to get me going, though I have my own inducements. I've recently written an intensively researched book, so I feel up to speed on the process. I'm also vain enough to want a crack at anything deemed too difficult to teach.

Not to say I ever found the unit easy. Research writing is the decathlon of the language arts, requiring a range of skills that most teachers can hardly claim to possess themselves, let alone know how to teach anyone else. The simple act of defining a topic can amount to a procrustean bed of adjustments, either because the topic is too broad for adequate treatment in a short paper or too narrow for the limited resources of a high school library. The Internet goes a ways toward helping with the latter, but only as far as a teacher's willingness to allow students to rely exclusively on Internet sources—in my case, not very far. The topic should ideally be of interest to the student (a toughie with students who claim to have no interests whatsoever or to be interested "only in sports," which as often as not means only in the statistical profile of a favorite player or team) and covered by at least one source that might plausibly be deemed reliable. Not least of all, the topic should be within the student's conceptual grasp.

Beyond that hurdle, which includes the ability to work one's way not only through the library catalog but also through the indices of books with no more than a tangential relation to the topic, lies the formidable matter of learning how to take notes. This, too, has its component parts: learning the difference between paraphrasing and direct quotation and when to opt for one or the other, learning to construct note cards in such a way as to be able to document the information accurately. In the past I used to tell my classes that research writing was mainly about telling the truth. It's also about constructing a usable memory of one's work, taking notes in such as way as to permit their flexible organization once the student reaches the outlining stage, which is yet another skill, another lesson plan, another potential pitfall.

Still, I agree with Sara in thinking the assignment worth the trouble. The reasons go far beyond that of "getting students ready for college." Not all of mine will go to college, and some will probably wind up in colleges where writing research papers is as much the exception as the rule. All the more reason for initiating students now. Learning how to write a research paper is the educational equivalent of a Bar Mitzvah or First Communion, the rite of passage when students make the giant leap from passive learning to aggressive learning, from the familial cave of the classroom to a larger assembly of scholars. And "form" is not the least part of it, in spite of the understandable temptation for the creatively minded teacher to play down form as persnickety and pedantic. Few people would see writing a research paper as an artistic endeavor—I certainly wouldn't—yet it has this much in common with many works of art: the struggle to find self-expression within the confines of material limits and traditional conventions. The need to make *this thing*—this canvas, this chorus, this genre—*mine*. And the need to follow incremental steps, the recognition shared by Darwin and Moses alike that few things worth our wonder are constructed in a day.

But that has never stopped us from looking for ways to abridge a process. There are computer programs that allow you to build Rome in an hour. I know that some of my younger colleagues have their students use a Web site called Noodle Tools to enter information and have it automatically arranged on the screen on virtual note cards, which can then be formatted and sequenced. The program also arranges bibliographical data—authors, titles, publishers, etc.—into one or another standardized format for footnotes and bibliography. It acts something like a magical hopper: you throw the raw materials in and the desired product emerges on the other side fully assembled. To the chagrin of a few students—and probably to the puzzlement of some of my colleagues—I announce that we are not going to be using Noodle Tools. We're going to learn how to take notes the old-fashioned way, on 3×5 note cards. I precede the announcement with the first of several raids on the school supply closet, knowing better than to require students to go foraging in the nearest convenience store, and pass out the booty as I speak.

I spare them an account of my complete rationale, including my distaste for anything so absurdly named as a Noodle Tool. I tell them I'm teaching them how to be chefs, which is not to my way of thinking the same thing as teaching them to preheat an oven to 350 degrees and peel back the foil on the peach-cobbler side of an aluminum tray. Cooking involves knowing how to choose ingredients, how to prepare and combine them, how to exercise the judgments of one's eyes, tongue, and nose. You need to blow on your noodle and put it in your mouth to know when it's done. I want them to learn the actual process for which Noodle Tools is merely the metaphor. Indeed, how would a kid fully comprehend such a program who hadn't first performed the process in three dimensions?

I have other unspoken reasons beyond that spiel. I want students to feel that *they* achieved the work, that they were more than acolytes of their digital tools. I want students without Internet access or computers at home to be on the same footing with their better-equipped peers. I want students with learning disabilities to have the advantage of being able to manipulate their information in three dimensions. I want them to be able to lay it out and turn it over in such as way as to see it all at any given time.

Finally, I want to preempt another Web wonder: a bogus research paper delivered whole cloth for a fee. The opportunities are legion. Given my approach, with its step-by-step benchmarks along the way, a student determined to cheat would need to construct by hand an entire counterfeit "preparation" of his research paper backwards from the one he obtained online. I don't rule out the possibility that a student might try to do just that—cheating has other motivations besides the avoidance of work—though I doubt he could do so without learning something along the way.

In the faculty workroom, the head of the social studies department watches me tape two handwritten sample note cards to a sheet of paper that I will then lay on the photocopier to make yet another handout. I ink in arrows to various parts of each card and write in labels: "topic heading," "author's last name," "page number for where the material was taken," "quotation marks for direct quotation," "slash to indicate that quotation continues on a new page of the source," "note from source, one per card," "your comment about the note (optional)," etc.

"So you're teaching them to do it with actual note cards," he says.

"I am." My ears are tuned for a note of disapproval. I know he has a Web site for each of his classes and posts all of his assignments online. I doubt he thinks very highly of my approach.

"I'm so glad to see that," he says. "I think the kids do much better when they can actually hold the cards in their hands."

I'm slightly surprised—though I shouldn't be; good sense was always his trademark—and more than slightly gratified by his warm approval. Something else occurs to me, which must have occurred to him first since he obviously tolerates the use of Noodle Tools in his own department. With physical note cards on my side of the hall and virtual note cards on the other, our students will have the best of both worlds—like having a hip younger aunt and a stubbornly opinionated grandpa both living on your street. What fun to be adored by them both, even as you tell tales about each in order to scandalize the other.

All in all the range of topics that the students choose to research is not disappointing. Neither is the number who choose topics of particular relevance to their own interests and plans: a paper on depression by a student whose uncle committed suicide; a paper on the life of John Deere by a self-described "redneck"; several papers on occupations that students hope to pursue, from real estate agent to obstetrician; a history of one of the oldest farm families in the region, including an account of why they stopped farming. The suggestions I provide at the outset run the gamut from the Matewan coal strike to the revival of farmers' markets, from Somali pirates to surrogate motherhood. In three classes I have only two takers: a girl who may be my most consistent high performer, who chooses the rescue of Jews in the French village of Le Chambon during the Second World War; and a student who's retaking tenth-grade English after failing it the year before, who chooses the giant squid. The rest of my topics go unexplored, quite possibly because some would require preliminary investigation to be understood, though others would seem like easy sells, especially given the brief oral teasers I provide as I go over the list after handing it out. But if the main reason has to do with students wanting as much ownership of the assignment as possible, then we're off to a good start.

In any case, the topics students choose on their own are often as intriguing as the ones I've suggested: traditional clothing in India, the early Negro baseball leagues, the bubonic plague. Sometimes the topic comes out of a dialogue between a student and me; the student supplies an area of general interest, I supply some avenues for further investigation. These hybrids are my favorites and make me feel as though I'm really teaching, though one of them leads me to worry if I've forgotten the age level I teach.

A girl tells me she is interested in the subject of self-mutilation. "People who do weird things to their bodies." Her interest seems more anthropological than psychological. I doubt the topic is in any way personal—she's definitely not a cutter; as far as I'm aware, she doesn't even have a tattoo. I feel I have the perfect suggestion for her, at once topical and relevant to her interests. Taking care to see that another female student is with us and employing the most tactful, nonexplicit language I can muster, ready at the slightest show of discomfort to segue to another topic, I suggest she examine the subject of female circumcision, or female genital mutilation, as it's also called. She's immediately enthusiastic, though I'm not sure if this is mainly in response to the subject itself or to the implication that she's mature enough to handle it. In any case, I seem not to have offended or shocked her. I feel I've taken an appropriate risk, one that might pay dividends beyond a decent five-page paper. *I*

trace the roots of my work with Egyptian women's groups to a
project I did for a high school English class . . .

But after school lets out for the day, I begin to wonder if I've
assessed the risks from the right perspective. My spontaneous
thoughts during class were focused almost exclusively on gauging
current standards of propriety and the girl's level of maturity,
which I'd rated as fairly loose and fairly advanced, respectively. On
those criteria, I've probably managed to stay abreast of the times
and to take an accurate measure of my kids. Where I have surely
been more clueless, as usual, is in the area of technology, where my
imaginative grasp continues to be perilously weak. More to the
point, it does not conjure the high-resolution image of a raw,
infected, newly mutilated vulva thrown up on a fifteen-year-old's
computer screen by the simplest combination of keystrokes—to
say nothing of the variety of sadomasochistic monstrosities that
might be harvested by a comparable number of clicks.

Not yet panicked but beginning to perspire, I go to the guidance office and look up a phone number for the girl's house. I
know her mother works at another school in the district, so it's
likely she'll be home by this hour. I decide I'll start with the
mother if I can, though I also decide that I'll need to speak to the
student herself if she answers. I'll only create needless anxieties
if I say "I need to talk to your mother." Sure enough, the girl
answers and is home by herself. I keep my tone light and my message brief. I'm calling, I tell her, because I want to ask that she wait
to begin her online research until our school librarian can help. I
hadn't given enough thought to the likelihood of such a topic
leading her to inappropriate sites, which the librarian will know
best how to avoid. I also tell her that I hope she realizes she's free
to change her topic if she comes to have any doubts about it. "I
know that whatever you do is going to be thoughtful and well
done; it doesn't have to be this one."

The girl takes my call in stride. I get off the phone thinking I've done the right thing—and making a mental note to inform the librarian of my recommendation tomorrow morning at the latest—though I also have the sensation that I keep digging myself into an ever deeper hole. *Male teacher suggests lurid topic to teenage girl, then phones her at home the same day.* I wonder if I have ever had a proper appreciation of the fact that I'm teaching *kids*.

This perpetual need—not only to interpret every manner of adolescent grunt, grimace, and gesture but to anticipate how my most carefully articulated sentences might be *mis*interpreted—it makes me tired, and after a while it makes me sick. The work I can do, the misbehaviors I can handle, but the self-imposed prohibition against thinking clearly, speaking frankly, and reacting honestly—that, most of all, is what's beginning to wear me down. Plus the nagging insinuation that conscientiousness may be my worst liability. In terms of professional survival, upping the intellectual ante is almost always less advisable than keeping your head down and letting the students find their own way.

Well, a few class periods of doing research in the library are enough to qualify that notion. Letting students "find their own way" is just a euphemism for abandonment. Small wonder it's the lazy teacher's favorite cliché. The deadbeat parent's too. With the help of our excellent librarian, my student finds a number of good sources, along with a tidy abbreviation for her subject: "I'm doing my paper on FGM," she'll say with a touch of archness, though she has no qualms about identifying the letters and she exhibits not the slightest inclination toward sensationalizing the subject matter for her peers. I'm proud of her. And for the most part I'm proud of the way my students commit to their subjects and to the deadlines ahead, of their attention to detail when they show me their first note cards, and, not least, of the assistance they offer to one another.

I suppose I shouldn't be surprised, though I am, at the reluctance of many students to consult books. I expected that *locating* books might be an issue for some of them, but the unwillingness even to *open* the books I help them locate still puzzles me. I recall times in past years when a student stumped over a research paper would take a newfound source from a teacher's hands as if it were a rich uncle's will. Not so much now. I bring in books from my personal library, naively warning students not to let even an excellent source—or any single source, for that matter—take over their paper. I needn't worry. In one case—when I bring in an article about computers that beat chess champions for a boy who wants to do research in the area of computer games—the source is refused outright. "Thanks, but I think I'm okay."

I'm even more surprised when some of my few overtly bookish students resist looking beyond some book they already know. I'm happy to learn that one of my students wants to do a paper on chakras, a topic that seems right down her New Age alley while also offering plenty of interesting side streets. But I can't seem to get her interested in any sources having to do with Hinduism, including one with an ornate diagram of kundalini rising through the chakras of a yogi's spine. Instead she wants to rely almost exclusively on a chiropractic manual that contains not a single footnote for its several glib assertions about "ancient traditions of the East." Another student, who reads assiduously if not widely, takes meticulous notes from a single online source describing the esoteric meanings of mythical Chinese animals but shows no interest in a lavishly illustrated book on Chinese mythology that I find for her on the library shelves.

At bottom I'm seeing a truth too easy for teachers to forget. Learning something new—especially about a subject you already know something about—can be a terrifying thing. Research is not for the lazy, our teachers and professors tell us, but it might be more pertinent to say that above all else it is not for the timid. No less than discipline, it takes courage to reconfigure your view of the world. If you're perfectly satisfied that the earth is flat, you're not in any great hurry to sail beyond the horizon. And falling off the edge of the earth is not the worst thing you fear.

Not for the first time I organize an after-school workshop, this one devoted to the research paper. Adhering to the principle that failure is not an option, I make the session mandatory for students who've failed to keep pace with the various deadlines in the process and optional for those who'd simply like some extra help. Or perhaps what they'd like is an after-school snack. No matter, they come, volunteers and conscripts alike. At the end of the year one of my colleagues will inquire how I managed to motivate so many students to stay after school, to which I will reply, "I fed them." Never all they could eat, though. Any messiah who took it upon himself to feed five thousand of these guys wouldn't have had twelve baskets left over, I can tell you that. It seems they are always ravenous. On a whim I've gotten into the habit of hanging a bunch of green bananas over the blackboard and there's as much interest in their status of ripeness as in anything written underneath. For the after-school workshop, I bring extra bananas, potato chips, cookies, apples, whatever I can grab out of our household cupboards or off the shelves of the mini-mart on my drive to work. A few of the students add provisions of their own. One girl will almost always bring in a tray of home-baked goodies whether she herself is staying or not.

I sign laptops out of the library for kids who will need them. I ask if they'd like music, and when they say they would, I put on Bach's *Well-Tempered Klavier* (highly rated by one conspicuously pierced and purple-haired underachiever in my study hall who said she liked working to it). And Herbie Hancock gets a turn at the piano too.

I park myself next to an empty desk and take customers as they come. I open my laptop next to theirs for some "floor time." My wife's old friend and preschool teaching colleague says that she hardly ever sees preschool teachers on the floor with their kids anymore. In her work as a college instructor of novice practitioners she's just as likely to see a teacher, even a mentoring teacher, recording data. In our case, two open laptops side by side count for a floor. So does the after-hours library. I take the students down in relays, unlocking the doors and helping them to canvass the stacks. Back in the classroom, I write a few note cards "for free."

It's easy to underestimate how much these small steps can mean, especially when they're *first* steps. One boy with more than adequate ability to perform the assignment but lacking a single of the twenty-five note cards he was supposed to have completed by the end of last week, slides in beside me and sighs with frustration and self-disgust. "You know what I wish, Mr. Keizer?" he says. "I wish I could stack your firewood for you and get out of doing this paper." Well, bud, I won't say that isn't a tempting offer, though it wouldn't be all that good for your education or my waistline. Let's try a stack of note cards instead. May I do the first one? How long did that take me? Watch this. Here's number two. And keep your eye on three because it's going to be finished before you know it happened. Now your turn. Look at this: card number four. One more and you're 20 percent done. How many do you think you can do before your ride shows up or we run out of food?

It's that invisible net of helplessness that perplexes me, though I am no stranger to it. I'm simply old enough to have learned how to extricate myself from procrastination, how to rip it open with one decisive swipe. A girl whose recently changed topic has to do with her intention of becoming an obstetrician tells me that she's "looked" but there's "nothing on the Internet" about obstetricians. I assume she means that there is *so much* on the Internet that she has no idea where to begin. She stands beside my desk in an absurd pose of languorous disaffection: Why must life be so impossibly cruel? Here's where a book or a magazine might have served her better, something definite she could hold in her hand, but I put that aside for the moment and give her some hints on refining her search. As with the boy and the note cards, I find her a first link and telegraph the article to the teachers' room printer. I also suggest that she interview an obstetrician as one of her sources, which at the least might give her some idea of the radical change she'll have to make in her work habits if she hopes to get into, to say nothing of finish, medical school.

Not that I would say such a thing, and I'm not exactly pleased with myself for thinking it. Even in this funky little tutorial I am reminded of how hard it is to predict when and how a girl or boy is going to catch fire. I'd as soon predict the weather on a day thirty years from now as predict the achievements of any student walking into his ten-year class reunion. I'm reminded as well of how hard-won an achievement a kid's mere attendance can be relative to the forces keeping her down. Another girl who's also way behind on her research paper—and in fact will never hand one in—stops in the middle of our conference to receive the first of several importunate text messages . . . "from my father's new girlfriend." If you want to talk to me, you need to turn that thing off, I tell her. And if you want to accomplish almost anything else—I don't tell her that. After all, she's *here*, she showed up, with everything she has on her plate. And perhaps, who knows, my greatest contribution to her life may be the remembrance of a single late afternoon when she glimpsed what it means to be part of a community of scholars. It will be my fondest remembrance too: I know even as I'm sitting here that the year will hold nothing better than this.

I make sure the door stays open. Students not in my classes also drop by to visit—and munch—always welcome so long as they don't interfere with our work. They rarely do. Nor do the kids in the workshop seem to waste much time. Of course, the compulsory attendees are eager to get themselves caught up and out from under their obligation. "Am I done now?" But even the volunteers stay pretty much on task. The socializing is quiet, convivial, proportionate—*natural*. We're at our ease. Ever mindful of the ways in which any given classroom approach models a type of society, I find in these workshops what may be the best case for anarchism. How wonderful if the formalities of my assignment were to wither away like the nation-state, leaving us to learn and write without coercion. Yet it is partly coercion that has brought us here.

Not entirely, though. Nor is it entirely vanity that brings me to this paragraph. A forgivable vanity if it is. A passerby sticks his head in the door, momentarily dumbfounded by what he sees, a gathering too late to be class, too loose to be school, too full of books and paper to be a club. "What are you doing?" he mouths to the girl sitting nearest the door, the girl who baked the cupcakes. "We have Mr. Keizer with us," she says. "Otherwise it would be detention."

My impromptu workshop isn't the only school activity that takes place after hours and off the activities pages of the yearbook. This is not a school where teachers hit the parking lot running at the end of day. I'm invited to a poetry reading organized by a couple of seniors in collaboration with our librarian. I doubt many of my students will attend—the big draw will come from the honors classes and the upper grades—but I'm happy for two or three of my sophomores who've professed artistic aspirations. This will be a good venue for them to showcase their talents and, perhaps even more important, to find their community. At the very least, it might encourage them, as I have been gently encouraging them, to consider taking a crack at the honors-level electives next year.

Two of them drop by my room before the reading. The less friendly of them, a girl who seems to believe that creativity is most reliably authenticated by an air of haughty disdain, though I would guess she's a sensitive kid who lives in daily fear of being found out as less intellectual than she appears, asks if I would be willing to read three of her poems. She wants to read two of them this evening, and she wants my opinion as to which of the three she should choose. I've read enough of her class assignments to know she is talented, and she's read enough of my comments to know that I think so, but this tentative overture outside of class is something new between us. A younger teacher would likely be more inclined to see it as a breakthrough. For my part, I think she may be seeking my judgment only to have an opportunity to overrule it. But even that would mark some progress.

I read the poems. Unlike her precocious short fiction, her poetry is on a par with what you'd expect from an adolescent with literary aspirations. That probably means no more than that she's read more fiction than poetry. One of the poems has for its subject how bored she is in my English class, a theme belied by her attention and participation, though probably truthful enough in the area of certain assignments she deems beneath her. Fortunately the poem about her boredom in my class is one of the stronger of the three, so rendering my judgment is a simple task. "These two," I say, and hand them back to her without further comment.

When I go to the library, I find it set up like a coffeehouse, separate tables, intimate lamps. One of the English teachers has brought his guitar. I hope no one expects me to sing. I can't stay long; I have a ton to do this evening. I'm putting in an appearance mainly as a show of support. It's a good half hour before anyone stands to read, most of it taken up by eating and fraternal chitchat among the college-bound. My two sophomores must feel out of place, yet they may have a better claim on the activity than the kids for whom this is at best an evening's diversion, another kind of dress-up event, like Spirit Week or the prom. I'm not surprised that the girls have gravitated to our young librarian, who wants her library to be a hub of cultural activity at the school, a gathering place for kids who might not find an appropriate gathering elsewhere. I laud her objectives. They might even provide me with a jumping-off place when I work up the nerve to suggest reinstating those exiled volumes from the Library of America.

I expect the event to stir some nostalgia. I always participated in the poetry readings at my state commuter college and always looked forward to them, but in retrospect they seem like sad affairs. Imitating their Beat idols, the readers frequently showed up stoned. Halfway through my freshman year, I already knew most of the repertoire; new material was in short supply. Yet there were a few bright lights among us, and I wonder where they are now. Possibly in situations similar to mine: teaching high school English and waiting for their nostalgia to kick in at a student poetry slam. The thought doesn't cheer me.

I'm sure my mood has been tainted by having read the girl's disparaging poem. I suppose that in some ways she's done me a favor: without the in-your-face preview, I might have been tempted to hang around long enough to hear her read, which is to say, long enough to be late for dinner. I have no intention of making such a sacrifice now. Are my feelings hurt? A little, I suppose. But I've taught long enough to know that these affronts are almost never personal in the strictest sense. They have to do with needs and grievances way beyond any teacher's powers of interpretation. And I know as well that if little irritations can still irk me, then breakthroughs just as little can elate me too.

The next day one of my tenth graders tells me that someone may have stolen her English binder. She suspects it was tossed into the garbage by one of her enemies. This is especially worrisome because midyear exams are just around the corner and because all the materials about doing the research paper were in the binder. The loss is also worrisome because her grades have been falling, the reason she's now required to spend her free period in one of my lunchtime study halls. In the beginning of the year she seemed flippant at times, certainly not very motivated for school and evidently not much taken with me. Lately, though, we have enjoyed a better rapport. Today we'll seal it.

I tell her that we are going to reconstruct her binder. We're going to do it in study hall, she and I, and we're going to finish it in one period. We won't be able to restore any of her homework papers, but there were too few of those to begin with. At least now she'll have a clearer idea of the assignments she needs to make up.

I clear my desk and lay out labels for the different categories: literature, vocabulary, composition, etc. I cut out and tape together some makeshift dividers. I go through my promiscuous bundle of handouts and have the student sort them into the appropriate piles as I give them to her one by one. We discuss the best placement for pieces that might go in more than one category. We make use of scissors, paper clips, markers. This is floor time, high school style, and the most fun I've had all day. Does the student notice? All she seems to see is the "extra trouble" she's given me. But what I see is the slow eureka dawning in her eyes: *With something this pulled together, I might actually be able to pass.*

I can't resist adding a didactic note when I hand her the finished notebook, neat as a freshly barbered head. Like all my didactic notes, it's one I need to hear as much as any student does. "I'm willing to wager this notebook is in way better shape than the one you lost or had stolen ever was." She doesn't deny it.

"If somebody did steal your notebook, then you and I just turned their theft into an advantage, didn't we? That's the best way I know to deal with crap like that." I choose a verb I know she'll understand. "*Defy* it."

Soon it will be the winter solstice. For weeks now I've been driving home after dark, enjoying the Christmas lights as I go. Many of them have been up since Halloween and some will stay lit for months into the bleak New Year. I drink them in as I drive through Barton and along Crystal Lake, where there are additional lights glistening across the ice from the fancier digs on the opposite shore. "Santa Claus is coming to town," Springsteen sings on my car radio, one of the few popular Christmas songs I'll endure, though I'll probably warm up to "Little Saint Nick" in another week. What's coming to town for me is a recess, neither fat nor particularly jolly but welcome just the same.

We have some Christmas lights at school as well, mostly in the main office, though by rights we're not supposed to have any. The superintendent decreed several years ago that as a public school district we were not to pay homage even to secularized religious holidays. The ruling seems to be honored more in the breach than in the observance, at least beyond the confines of the central office. Since the central office is located in the same building as the preschool (which used to make a point of teaching the region's mostly gentile children about Hanukkah), this essentially means that the only students in the district lacking tokens of holiday cheer are three and four years old. For my part, I tack a string of unadorned white lights around my blackboard, hoping they'll do for my students what the lights in Barton do for me. Hang on, kids, your break is coming.

The Christmas spirit at school does seem more subdued than I recall from years past. I get a few small presents—homemade cookies and handmade ornaments to hang on my tree at home— some very touching cards, including one or two from boys, though fewer of the edible presents that used to come my way. I'm just as glad; I could hardly bear with the sugary largesse of the old days, when the girls presented me with tins and trays and tinfoil pouches of fudge, peanut brittle, cookies, brownies— enough to keep my family and our guests flush with desserts for a week. By the close of the last day of school, I'd go down to the gym for Christmas assembly (still allowed in those days), vaguely nauseated and probably several pounds heavier than when I walked in the door that morning. But the parting good wishes are as frequent and amiable as they ever were, including a few from students who are not even in my classes but stick their heads in my door on the way to the buses to wish me the joy of the season.

I know it will be a sad holiday for some. Their parents will have split up earlier in the year or lost their jobs or both. Some asked-for presents will not be under the tree or else will materialize in spite of all expectation, not miracles so much as dire omens, the reckless parental generosity that can take a child's breath away. Low men on the retail totem pole, some students will spend their holidays minding the store, tending the drive-up window at the fast food joints on Christmas Eve. Friends whose parents have more money will decamp to Orlando and Cancun; their poorer counterparts will lack transportation to come over and hang out. Younger siblings will be home and require babysitting, the decoration-deprived three- and four-year-olds making up for lost time with a vengeance. Parties will be happening all over the county, with some kids invited to all and many invited to none. A girl might get engaged, most likely because her older beau is on his way to Afghanistan. Some houses will be less than warm. A few will be less than safe, mistletoe hanging like a noose when a certain uncle is lurking about. Some-where in some hollow, like a lottery number waiting to be called, a trailer is going to catch fire. People will "lose everything." All their presents. Maybe even their pets. There will be a coffee can with their name on it in the mini-marts, next to the chocolate Santas, a day past season and priced to go.

For weeks now I've been haunted by the memory of walking to the faculty parking lot one late autumn afternoon to find an uncomfortably obese woman wedged behind the steering wheel of her wreck of a car jabbering into her cell phone. It would appear she doesn't have a pot to piss in, but of course she has a cell phone. In the back seat are two filthy, bedraggled children, a boy and a girl looking for all the world like Ignorance and Want under the green robe of the Ghost of Christmas Present. They are not dressed warmly enough for the cold. They stare at me as if I might have food to give them, a blanket—a word—anything to acknowledge their existence on earth. I catch myself growing angry at their mother, only to recognize she is merely the same neglected child under the robe of Christmas Past.

I read somewhere that the Puritans had a crier go through the streets on Christmas Eve and cry "No Christmas tonight."

This was to prevent any backsliders from reverting to "popish" calendars and pagan entertainments. The most sterile of all carolers, he made his way through the song-starved lanes. I've always imagined him with a handbell, though perhaps I've misappropriated that detail from the Salvation Army. I'd want to knock him down if I met him; I look forward to my turkey and my tree, to our daughter coming home for the holidays, and to the gifts I know I am going to like because I always do. Still there is something in me—the memory of those children in the car, the sad faces of some of my students as they trudge with their token candy canes to the school bus—that wants to borrow a page from the Puritans and from the superintendent too and walk through the streets of the Orleans Central Supervisory Union on the twenty-fourth of December crying, "No Christmas tonight!" No Christmas, no Hanukkah, no Kwanzaa, no New Year's Day . . . "nor shall my sword sleep in my hand, till we have built Jerusalem in [New] England's green and pleasant land."

7

JANUARY

But the more he thinks of educating them . . . the more he has
to ask himself: by what right do I do this? It is not certain that
it will make them socially happier.

—John Berger, *A Fortunate Man*

As I was at Thanksgiving, I was sick for most of the Christmas
vacation, for a few days almost too sick to move. Except to take
meals or stoke the furnace, now and then tossing a grocery bag
of spent Kleenex onto the fire, I rarely rose from my living room
chair. My condition was familiar from past years of teaching—
the way vacations give a stressed mind and body permission to
ail. On more than one Christmas my wife and I would drive to
visit our families in New Jersey, only to have me spend a feverish
week in bed. I wasn't hit that hard this time but hard enough to
keep me from returning to school as refreshed as I'd hoped to be.

Fortunately, I don't have anything to make me dread my
return. Just as I know from experience that a school vacation is a
likely time to get sick, I also know from experience that the mel-
ancholy of a Monday morning will probably not last beyond the
arrival of the first bus. I have two boys in my first-period class
who come into my room early and visit, often finishing the last

bits of their outrageously nonnutritious breakfasts as they dribble boy talk and lob the rolled-up greasy wrappers into my trash can. They're not my best students by any stretch, and they're not brownnosers either, but they seem to enjoy my company. I certainly enjoy theirs, and I'm happy when I learn that I'll have them next semester in a Composition course. I've already gleaned a few of the topics they might write about—metal bands and football teams, fathers and cows, cars and tattoos. Later on, in my third-period class, there's a girl who always returns my "good morning" to the students with a rousing "Good morning, Mr. Keizer!" that seems intended and is definitely received in the spirit of a cheerleader's hurrah. I think that on some level the students sense that I'm trying my best and often tried to my limits, that I can use every little boost I can get. I get plenty of boosts, in any case.

Lately they take the form of a few wistful queries as to the possibility of my returning to teach again next September. I've only been hired for the current year, I say. As I'm sure they know, I'm filling in for a teacher on leave, a teacher that none of my sophomores have had in the past. They have no basis for comparison and thus no more than a provisional reason for wishing me back.

"But what if he decides not to come back?" one of them says, adding that she and a few of her pals might be willing to make "the other guy" an offer he can't refuse. I'm touched by this, though I'm careful to appear no more than amused. And they're only asking what others at school have asked—including a custodian who I imagine is missing his after-school chats with my more garrulous predecessor—something I've lately been asking myself. What if the other guy doesn't come back? What if I'm invited to apply for the position and, as some of my colleagues have assured me would happen, I get it?

My official response is that I'm going back to my desk to resume my work as a writer. On most days that is also the sincere response. But it weighs on me—how could I conscionably turn down the stability of a job with salary and benefits, including retirement benefits, in order to return to the precariousness of my previous work? If a permanent position were to open here and I were hired to fill it, Kathy would be free to explore more adventurous options than the part-time elementary school speech position she's taken to cover our health insurance next year, including a possible expansion of her consulting work at Dartmouth, where she continues to thrive. The catch-as-catch-can, hand-to-mouth nature of freelance work would be behind me. No more humiliating queries to newspapers about delayed payments, no more rug-merchant negotiations with libraries and academic departments looking for ornamental talks. How many of the writers I admire most have shored themselves up with teaching work—admittedly in cushier places than the one I'm toiling in now—and who am I to imagine I can sustain myself another way? As for the writing itself, no doubt my output would be radically curtailed to what I could churn out during the summer, but might its quality improve just as radically? "Having time to write" is not always an unqualified advantage. I have sometimes thought that I was a better writer, or at least a more socially useful one, when my daily life was pushed up against harsher realities. I'd never want for those here.

Nor would I be without teaching's less dubious perks, not the least of which is being loved or, failing that, being "on." I have to admit that I like an audience. No less do I like the one-to-one instruction, the narcotic high of coaching a skill. I like my gratuitous exchanges with students not in my classes, who have nothing to gain by seeking me out. Though I am and always was a solitary teacher, a shut-the-door and get-on-with-the-work teacher, eating alone and rarely devoting much time to off-duty gab with my colleagues, I enjoy having colleagues. I feel a mutual respect with most of them. And I find the presence of youth invigorating—sometimes, yes, in the way that youth reverts to childhood and to childlike delight in simple discoveries and small surprises, but more often in flickering revelations of adulthood. I apologize to a girl for having been short with her about her failure to complete an assignment when I ought to have been more sensitive—how could I have forgotten she has just lost her grand-mother? "I accept your apology," she says, "but I ought to have been more responsible than I was. And I shouldn't have been so snotty to you." This from a kid, and a kid who's grieving besides.

At times I begin to be gripped by a sense of destiny closing in. I've come here for a reason, and the reason is that I am meant to stay. This is where I belong, this is where I can do my best work. I've had a good run with my books and articles, more than most late bloomers get to accomplish. I've proved whatever it was I had to prove, and if I had any aptitude to achieve great-ness, surely I would have realized it by now. There is no shame in the fact that I haven't. My little trophies are honorable enough and will remain so; time now to put them on an attic shelf and resume the work that will see me through to a solvent old age.

I almost can't believe what I'm thinking. When I broach the possibility to my wife, she refuses to see it as anything but a delu-sion. It would be a mistake, she insists, and I would wind up very unhappy. *She* would be unhappy. "This is *not* your real work."

Fortunately, any thoughts of continuing past the current year are hypothetical and sporadic, little more than passing moods and possibly nothing more than my ego's infantile predilection for regular feedings. All it takes is a class of unprepared kids— half of whom are clambering for a third copy of an assignment sheet to replace the loss of the previous two, for a book to replace the one that's been left behind in a locker, for permission to use the restroom, for a Band-Aid, for an extra day to complete the homework, for the repetition of directions I've already given twice—to make me ask myself if I'm out of my mind. Do I really think I could enjoy spending the rest of my working life like this? And would I have the staying power to devote myself to the work with the intensity it requires? To say nothing of the patience. I make up detailed syllabi for several of my classes, a day-by-day roster to help my students plan the time remaining till the end of the semester—only to have it knocked askew by an unanticipated school closing when the temperature dips to 30 below. These disruptions happen all the time. Teaching, which grants few successes without careful planning, hates nothing so much as a planner.

When I'm most conscious, most on top of my game, I can appreciate my moments of frustration and my most exasperating kids as aids to clarity. The pains in the ass are in fact my muses and angels, sent to deliver me from temptation, sent to remind me that the work I most want to do is elsewhere. And in the semester to come I will meet my share of angels.

Surprisingly, the high point of my enthusiasm for teaching comes at one of the least likely junctures, the time of midyear exams. Normally, this would be just the time when a teacher would have the wind taken out of his sails. But I've trimmed my sails to avoid that.

I no longer see midyear exams as a confirmation of "mastery"—as if mastery of any meaningful kind were the provenance of sixteen-year-olds, as if mastery could be ascertained so soon after imparting the material. Instead, I see the exams as a chance to instill the hope that mastery is *possible*, that whatever slow progress we've made has been worth the effort. On the crasser level of "the data," I see the exam process as a chance for my foundering students to redeem their grades. This doesn't mean that I intend to give easy exams or to weigh them too heavily in computing my semester grades. It means that I plan to do a fair amount of review and to construct my exams more than I ever have in the past out of the review exercises. In a few cases, I will write pages of the exams from the review sheets with virtually no alteration. I've taught long enough to know that even this will fall short of a complete giveaway: some students won't do the review work either. But those with their chins still above deep water may sense the life preserver I've tossed within their reach—and take hold of it.

As I've been doing with the research paper (still in progress), I hold some additional preparation periods after school. To those students who attend, I'm especially generous, though I still hold my cards close to my chest. "Here's something I'd especially want to study if I were in your shoes." I'm somewhat surprised by the makeup of these sessions. I'm not surprised that some of the kids who show up hardly need the help; I'm surprised that they're not, in the usual way these things go, in the majority. Most of those who come are underachievers who've taken a sober measure of what they need to pass. I credit at least some of their sobriety to the work of the tutors in the academic support areas, who encourage this kind of self-assessment and strategy. I'm especially moved by the earnestness of a few of my sophomores and amazed, as ever, by their appetites for food, which might in this case be partially attributable to nerves. Only four show up at one of the sessions, but they demolish a whole tin of cookies within the first half hour. What they don't know yet is that they've also devoured most of what my exam is going to contain within a half hour after that.

To my satisfaction no one in any of my five classes fails his or her exam. Among the juniors and seniors taking half-year electives, I have only one student who fails the course, a bright senior with a history of standing as close as he can to the precipice. His exam performance is good but not good enough to cover weeks of missed work, even with the bonus points I always add to any major test as a cover for possible mistakes I might have made in correction. The boy takes his F with an attitude that another generation would have called "manful"; I only wish he'd taken his studies in the same way. In that regard, I'm glad he failed. A passing grade would have insulted his intelligence, which is to say, it would have affirmed his overreliance on intelligence at the expense of hard work.

His peers who drop by to learn their grades are not so stoical. More than a few receive the news of a C or even a D by pumping their fists with a vocal rendition of Meg Ryan's orgasmic *yes!* I'm sad to note the survival of a shortcoming that always dismayed me in years past: the school provides no class day in the schedule for teachers to go over midyear exams with juniors and seniors in semester-long courses. There's no feedback beyond the giving of a grade, no chance to clarify mistakes for students who don't bother to pick up their tests. After such an investment of time and labor, the exercise winds up feeling like a sham.

It's a different story with my sophomores, who are back in the classroom after the conclusion of exam week and with whom I'm able not only to go over the test results but even to have some fun. I can't resist teasing them just a bit before rejoicing over their good performance. In my most somber tone, and with an unwavering deadpan expression, I say, "Well, I have finished grading your exams." No one dares to ask, though some faces do: "Were they bad?" "There's much I could say about the class's overall performance, but I find that the words don't come easily." Uh-oh.

"Therefore, I thought it might be advisable to have someone else speak for me, more particularly one Mr. Marvin Gaye."

Still stone-faced I depress the button on my boom box and detonate the opening piano notes, pointing to the class on "You" and not allowing myself to smile until the words "pride and joy," at which point, with a flick of my wrist I send the pulled-down projection screen snapping upward to reveal the tally I've written on the blackboard behind it: many As and even more Bs, a few Cs, and no Ds or Fs. I'm not quite dancing as I go up and down the aisles handing back the tests, though I may be as close as a middle-aged white man with weak arches and work boots ever gets to a "groove." I hold the standout performances briefly in front of some noses before slapping them down on the desks and "movin' on down the line." There's laughter, most of it in relief, the rest occasioned by the sight of me so animated and happy. There's no instance where "the first are last"—the world is not overthrown so easily, and I hardly want my highest achievers to be overthrown—but there are at least a few where the last are first, or damned close to it, and the pride and joy on their faces speaks even more eloquently than Mr. Gaye or his superb backup chorus to what I feel.

When things settle down, we go over the tests, item by item, with special emphasis on those tasks that required more attention to the directions than they sometimes got and on the distinguishing features of the better essays. I note the places where students supplied correct answers I did not anticipate when I made up the test, and other places where a bit of logic on their part could have prevented some goofs. Inspired by the Mosaic prohibition against picking up any stray sheaves dropped in the act of harvest, I instruct students not to tell me about any correction errors I've made in their favor. The gleanings must be left on the ground for "the poor and the stranger." But the poor and the stranger are still inclined to ask if you're sure you want to let the errors slide. For every cheater a teacher might have in a given class, there are usually half a dozen students who'd rather take a hit than an unfair advantage. Perhaps a few can't resist telling me that I'm less than perfect, but I'll go with the more generous interpretation.

That doesn't come hard, given the generosity of some of their remarks. For one of the "constructed responses" that made up the written section of the exam, I called for a journal entry of the type we've been doing on a regular basis throughout the semester. Above a photocopy of a ruled page from a paper journal, I wrote the following: "This exam is based on material you have learned in class. But in most classes, students learn things that were not taught, not intended, or not noticed by the teacher. On the journal page below, write a thoughtful entry on something 'extra' you have learned in class. It might be about your own study habits or learning style, about getting along with others, about your own pleasure or displeasure, or about the effects of literature."

The answers I receive are not all on point—some address central elements of the school curriculum—but few miss the point entirely, and many suggest that there is indeed some "extra" learning going on here:

I have not ever studied too hard but the tests we have been given this year have made me change that. For a reading quiz I actually have to read the book and can't just scim it. This class has tought me better studying techniques I will use for other classes as well.

When different types of music is played that most teenagers do not listen to it exposes them to new music. While listening to the various songs played I've learned that I like some of the different types that I never thought I would like.

"Can you give an example of a piece of music you enjoyed?" I write at the bottom of the page, illustrating by example being one of the skills I've tried to emphasize during the semester. If I don't subtract at least one point, the comment won't carry any weight, so I do. Other students show a better knack for following the general with the specific, though not always with the best syntax:

> Something I have learned in class this semester is I learned new studying methods. I was introduced to 3 × 5 note cards and I found it to be much easer to gather info I didn't know and place them on a card. I found I could study myself this way and it was a convient way to learn things. Next semester I will probally do this in many other classes because I think it benefited me on this exam!

> I don't really like writing but when you write about something you like it is much more enjoyable. An example would be when we had to write a journal entry of our own topic, I had writen about my horse and that was the easest thing I had to write.

> This class has opened some doors for me. As an example, I've started reading more, I look for similare authors like the ones we have read in this class because I find their book/short stories intreaging. I learned that a lot of literature can be touching, especially about the black History and what they went through, not only that but some of the fiction stories were interesting and I didn't find them boring because they always kept me on edge.

Much to my delight, others echo the last sentiment. "I have learned that reading really isn't that bad," one student writes, while another goes so far as to claim that reading has led her to a major recognition: "I now believe that the teachers don't assign books to torture us and they do it because it may have been something they enjoyed that they want to share with us"—to which I can't resist writing, "Of course we do like to torture you too!" Obviously, I have to be open to the possibility that some students are telling me what they think I want to hear. But when I weigh their remarks against my own daily observations and the reports that come to me through other teachers, I feel entitled to accept much of what they say at face value.

That's especially true in the case of several students who write about the pleasures of learning in an environment of camaraderie and mutual respect, something the teacher certainly intends though sometimes fails to fully appreciate. "I have learned how a class of students could become more like a familly. . . . We can joke around with each other and have fun but we still manage to get all of are work done." One entry that begins "This semester in english has been a blast" goes on to elaborate on "blast" in terms that might surprise adults with little or no acquaintance with young people:

> The class has been very smooth, with no interruptions, everyone's respectful and kind to one another, and we all work as one to always have a productive day in class. That makes learning easier for me and others. Some of my classes are so wild that we never learn anything. That makes tests and quizzes harder because you don't learn anything. With that being said, I learned that a good class with manners, respect, and kindness to one another, you learn more and respect the subject more.

That the reality is somewhat less ideal is noted by another student, whose basis of comparison is several years of being schooled at home:

> I used to want to be a teacher. But now I am not so sure. I realized that teaching is not so simple. Teachers can't just say what they have to say and get on with it. First they have to fight for the class's attention, then they have to tell the class what they need to tell them in a way that relates to teenagers. It's not so easy.

No, it isn't—and it's an indication of how touched I am by some of the paragraphs that this student's frank appraisal of the realities comes to me as a corrective reminder. She's right, I do sometimes have to fight for the students' attention, don't I? But it's easy to gloss over the difficulties when a student who's given you some of your worst times to date, who even acknowledges that he's "been a pain" in his opening sentence, goes on to refer to you as "a real man" who "showed me that with respect and random acts of kindness life is a whole lot better. Also with hard work and someone to guid you, nothing is imposible." We weigh our praises according to their source—according to whether it's Machiavelli who's calling us a prince or Thomas Paine. For this kid, I know, "real man" is the highest accolade, and there is no irony here—at least none coming from him. For my part, I doubt a "real man" would allow himself to be as moved by this as I am, but it is the way his words are proved by his recent behavior that moves me most. That and the fact that this kid sucks up to nobody.

I'm taken down a peg, though, by another of the short-answer sections of the test, which asks students to construct a single formatted note card from a short passage of information. The task ought to be an easy ten points for anyone who's been doing his or her research and noting my comments through successive reviews of the cards the kids have been been handing in, but grading it is like watching artillery mow down a cavalry charge. Few riders emerge from the smoke unscathed.

Exams provide an opportunity for students to reflect more broadly on the literature they've been reading and for the teacher to do the same in regard to what he's been assigning and to what purpose. I don't have many students who ask, "Why do we have to read this?"—in fact, I don't think I have one. Perhaps by this age they've gotten tired of asking. Perhaps they'd be surprised to learn that I haven't.

Young people tend naturally toward a didactic appraisal of literature, and English teachers are supposed to discourage the tendency. Literature has "themes," not morals, we're supposed to tell them, though I find that formulation itself didactic and rather prissy to boot. Ditto for talking ad nauseam about irony. Why shouldn't students—or adults—read literature in the hope of clarifying their own moral understanding? The problem is not that young people search literature for "a moral"; the problem is rather that they come to it with a set of moral preconceptions that impede them in their search. Their approach to James Baldwin's "Sonny's Blues" is typical. Sonny is a heroin addict, drugs are bad, and so the point of the story—almost all of them insist—is that doing drugs will wreck your life. Drugs will surely do that, though Baldwin and his narrator seem to have other concerns.

A similar superimposed reading occurs with another short story on the syllabus, Toni Cade Bambara's "The Lesson," in which a self-appointed neighborhood teacher takes some black children on a tour of the city that concludes at the FAO Schwarz toy store. There they see expensive sailboats and other baubles their parents could never afford. The teacher seems intent on goading her charges—and the author on goading us—toward an awareness of the "savage inequalities" that stack the deck against minorities and the poor. By the close of the story, the recalcitrant young protagonist, Sylvie, outwardly resentful of her day's instruction, shows that she has taken it to heart. We would say her consciousness has been raised. But for many of my students, Bambara's story amounts to a Horatio Alger tale in hip-hop idiom. Rather than see a swindle—a swindle not without implications for poor, working-class, and even middle-class kids growing up in rural America during a period marked by the greatest income disparity since the Great Depression—they perceive "a lesson" on the need to work hard in order to get ahead. Any sense that society may be at fault seems missing from their consciousness.

Even among my older students this seems to be the case. The last reading assignment I give in my Popular Fiction class, which I have decided to center on the theme of young people in search of self-knowledge, is Tim O'Brien's short story "On the Rainy River." After being called up to military duty in Vietnam, a young man comes close to running away to Canada but decides that he is simply not courageous enough to buck the social pressures compelling him to serve. With bitter irony he concludes that he is too cowardly to be a draft dodger, an epiphany my students strongly resist. The girls in class are the most adamant. The narrator needs to be a man, they say. He needs to do his patriotic duty and stop whining about it. Though no one uses the phrase, the implication is that he needs to "get real." Which means what exactly? To bow to the world as it is.

The same resignation informs the majority response to the actions of a black housekeeper named Rosaleen in Sue Monk

Kidd's novel *The Secret Life of Bees*. After swallowing all the degradation she can gag down, Rosaline pours tobacco juice from
her snuff cup on the shoes of some white men who are verbally
abusing her and is beaten and thrown into jail as a result. "Stupid," say more than one of my students, meaning Rosaleen's defiance. This does not mean that the students are racists. In their
eyes they are merely being realists, which is to say, what we're
often urging them to be. Peer pressure we would like them to
resist; aside from that, resistance is seldom held up to them as a
virtue. The essentially political question John Berger raises about
a country doctor in his classic essay *A Fortunate Man* applies to a
teacher too: "How far should one help a patient to accept conditions which are at least as unjust and wrong as the patient is
sick?" More to the point, how far should one help a patient—or a
student—not to accept them? The best I do in the case of Rosaleen
is to turn my students' assertion back to them as a question: "But
is she stupid?"

I know enough not to ask "Is she wrong?" Interestingly
enough, the moralistic preconceptions that students bring to
their reading of literature also include the notion that all morality is relative, or as they would put it, "a person's own opinion."
Their relativism is not confined to morality. At the start of my
Popular Fiction course, which I teach both semesters, I break
the class into groups and ask them to parse the course title by
coming up with a definition of *fiction* and a tentative list of what
ingredients might make a work of fiction *popular*. Though the
students have no problem with making an absolutist assertion
that fiction is "not true," they balk at the notion that popularity
can be analyzed. Popularity, they argue, is purely "a matter of
opinion." It is no such thing. As they, of all people, ought to know,
a person is popular or he isn't; he has friends or he doesn't. Books
sell in the millions or they wind up in remainder bins. The

students are confusing popularity with the right of an individual to his or her tastes, including tastes that are decidedly unpopular. Well, clarifying these sorts of distinctions is what teaching literature is all about. We're "helping kids to think." I know that—but I also suspect that some of the confusions originate in the haphazard teaching of that very subject.

Fortunately, we also read with our hearts, where "what it means to you" has a valid claim. In that category my favorite exam comment comes from a looming giant of a boy who writes that the young protagonist in *The Secret Life of Bees* "has experienced more pain in her little body that I ever have in my life." Not a bad thing for a big man to ponder—the capacities for pain in a little body.

A less sophisticated emotional connection, one based on similarity rather than difference, probably explains the perennial popularity of John Steinbeck's *Of Mice and Men*. I imagine kids are drawn to Lennie for some of the same reasons they were drawn to *Curious George* when they were small. Like them, Lennie and the monkey mean no harm but can't seem to stay out of trouble. Oh, for some Man in a Yellow Hat or someone like Lennie's smarter sidekick, who may not always be nice to Lennie but who sticks by him through the worst, to believe in your good intentions and to make your dreams seem real and, not least of all, to shoot you in the back of the head before you can embarrass yourself to death. I recall from years past one particular student in another teacher's English class, a large boy who raised rabbits, as Lennie dreamed of doing, who became almost obsessed with the story. The book did not necessarily change his life, but it seemed to reflect his life in a powerful way—which in the end may be just as important.

Literature will give my students a larger frame of reference, I keep telling myself, a better understanding of human complexity, of all that shouldn't but often does go wrong in a human life. It may help them to a more compassionate heart. At the least it may give them some diversion from what is going wrong in *their* lives. So can beer—as the poet A. E. Housman put it, "Malt does more than Milton can / To justify God's ways to man"—but knowing some lines from Housman gives you an extra option, something you didn't even know you could order at the bar. That's what I want my students to have: all the options on the menu, all the songs in the catalog, every last word on the privileged side of the 30-million-word gap.

The paltriness of what they do have can be stunning at times. In one of my sophomore classes I'm asked what the word *woo* means. It's a simple enough question, I suppose, but it catches me off guard. I would not need to define *rape* for my students, would I? Or *hick* or *dyke* or *loser*. To woo is to pay court to someone, I say, still short of the mark. It's what you do to win a person's love; it's how you say they're worth the trouble. And so I add one more thing to the list of what I want my students to have along with the 30 million words and a sweet, long life: a sense of themselves as worth the wooing.

It will take more than wooing to get my sophomores to read Edith Wharton. *Ethan Frome* is probably the hardest slog of the year. Vocabulary is a large part of the problem, that and a certain reverse naiveté in sexual matters that is probably best encapsulated in their ignorance of *woo*. Why can't Ethan and Mattie just fuck? The novel is so close to their experience on so many levels—but it also belongs to another universe, another language, a language with all kinds of big words. To say nothing of a lot of little words that I did not realize are big ones to my kids.

I try enticing them with a project I call "The *Ethan Frome* Vocabulary Face-Off." I divide each class into several teams and assign them to master their own customized list of unfamiliar words from the novel. Eventually they'll compete in a three-day bowl for prizes, including grades for their team's performance and bonus "tickets" entitling the bearers to postpone due dates and cut class, plus animal crackers, coconuts, and other edible novelties (a fairly broad term in a region where teenage supermarket cashiers routinely ask me "What are these things?" when ringing up eggplants and Brussels sprouts). Each team member is required to contribute to the team's list and to devise practice exercises for his or her teammates. Homework assignments are to be generated, completed, and corrected by each team.

The project has other intentions besides vocabulary building and honing their cooperative skills. I'm also trying to buy more class time for individual conferences on the second drafts of their research papers. Exams were a brief hiatus; now we're back to the grind, aiming to have papers completed by the beginning of February. I need to have the students working on something while I conference with individuals. The activity needs enough bustle to preserve the confidentiality of the editing sessions and to keep my own whispering from disturbing the class's concentration. The "face-off" seems to fit the bill.

As I ought to have anticipated but didn't, I'm also going to need to stay in close touch with the teams if I want solid results. Even the lists will require some feedback since the words in the text will as often as not be different parts of speech from the forms defined in the dictionary. I'll accept words in any form, I tell the students, so long as some variant appears in the novel and so long as definition, part of speech, and usage align in the materials they prepare. I grumble to myself that students ought to have learned these concepts in middle school—only to imagine some professor saying the same thing about me, several years hence, as she shakes her head over a student's research paper. What were his high school English teachers doing for four years, pray tell?

The difficulties are compounded whenever a student copies a word incorrectly or confuses one word with another. Thus the definition of *intricate* might be given as "a secret or underhand scheme" (the definition of *intrigue*). The last person to claim that he knows the entire English lexicon or the text of *Ethan Frome* by heart, I wonder for a moment if one of my students is teaching me a new word: *malise*, "a piece of hand." In what context would one need to denote a piece of hand? Medicine? It takes a few beats before I realize that I'm missing a piece of definition, "luggage," and the correct spelling of *valise*. Suffice it to say, the vocabulary project does not buy me the time for writing conferences that I hoped it would.

Certainly it would have bought me more if most of my students were willing to consult the meticulous instructions I've written up for them. They'd rather ask me a question as it occurs to them than search for the answer on a printed sheet—or listen carefully when I answer the same question for the third time. My refrain becomes "What does the sheet say?" I wouldn't want to give the impression that my students are too lazy to read the sheets, though some of them are. A better explanation is that they trust what comes straight from the horse's mouth more than what is mediated by the horse's handout sheet, or—to get closer to the crux—more than their ability *to read and comprehend* the horse's handout sheet. Flattering as this might be to a teacher, it is less than reassuring to a teacher who hopes to live out his remaining years in a democracy.

I try to give the matter a political slant. When a rule is written down, I tell the students, then the writer is bound by it no less than the reader. That is why we have a constitution. In an autocratic state the king's whim is the law. Maybe one day he feels like reading a six-hundred-word essay; the next day he feels like a six-line poem. But in this case, I can't hold you accountable for any requirement that isn't spelled out on the sheet. You can wave that sheet in my face as evidence, and I can't win the argument simply by saying "I wrote the sheet." I have to win by referring to what the words actually say. I seem to be getting through— somebody's raising his hand.

"Do you want us to write down the parts of speech?"

They're doing the best they can, I tell myself, and I need to remember they're just kids. Still, it troubles me to think that these kids are only two years away from voting.

I'm similarly troubled by the dubious responsibility students feel toward other members of their teams. Although I allowed optional partnerships for the museum project in the fall, I almost never allow students to form their own groups for in-class assignments where teams are mandatory, competition is expected, and cliquishness is always a risk. I try to mix boys and girls, good students and poor students, strong personalities and more passive personalities, but a class of twenty kids in four or five groups only allows for so many combinations. In spite of my best efforts, some groups jell and others don't. Just getting them to arrange their desks in a propitious formation can be frustrating. As I explain at the start, the best arrangement is a circle or a neat square, with every member having easy access to every other. A few teams get right to it; others have different plans. Some students try to form subgroups within the group, me and my friend versus everyone else. Some isolate themselves by literally turning their backs to their teams. Some cozy up to the borders of other groups in order to facilitate over-the-fence gab. A

few seem to find the simple act of moving a desk an inexpress-
ible agony, every inch a station of the cross.

As interesting as they are to observe, the social dynamics fall
into predictable types. Familiar to anyone who's ever tried to
foster "cooperative learning" is the bossy overachiever, often a
girl, who realizes at once that her grade is dependent on the collective efforts of several real or perceived nincompoops and is
therefore in serious jeopardy unless she whips them into shape
or does all the work herself. Just as often there's someone on her
team who recognizes the anxiety and is quite willing to exploit
it. Most exasperating are the do-nothing Tobacco Road boys,
who lean back in their chairs and grin, so evidently pleased with
themselves one would think they'd just invented grinning. Only
the most unimaginative teacher would see them as the future
failures of America. A fair number of them will go on to own or
manage businesses, with a female clerical staff doing most of
the work. For the present, I tell them to set all four chair legs on
the floor and get busy. I suppose that if I really wanted to "prepare them for the future," I'd urge them to put their feet up on
the desks and scratch themselves while holding forth about welfare cheats and all the other deadbeats living off the taxpayer's
hard-earned dime.

What's exciting are the groups that manage to come together,
calling forth the best qualities of their members. Invariably,
they're not only the most productive but also appear to have the
most fun. They *socialize* in the deepest sense of the word. The
work is fairly divided, with the weaker members doing their best
to pull their weight and the more capable doing all they can to
enable their more-challenged partners to make a respectable contribution. Occasionally, a notorious slacker surprises everyone
by doing yeoman's service on behalf of his group. Sinking yourself and sinking everybody else: two completely different things,

dude. He's praised by his teammates—what's more, he feels entitled to praise them. You see, says the collectivist half of my heart,
cooperation works. To which the other half replies: It certainly
does—in the rarest of cases. Whether it's individual cream or
collective cream, it's still cream that rises to the top.

Sometimes when I'm walking the halls between classes I become
aware of Mr. Messier walking beside me. On certain days and in
certain fragile states of mind, the experience feels almost numi-
nous. I sense I'm not as alone as I've been feeling, and then I see
Mr. Messier alongside me or just to the rear of my shoulder. How
long has he been there? He smiles and asks how my day is going.
The way he puts the question enables me to answer "good" with
honesty. Right now, yes, it's a good day. How could it be otherwise with his support?

I feel it from others as well. I'm not sure I've ever had a stronger sense of being "taken care of" by my coworkers, not even forty
years ago when I found my first full-time job in an accident-ridden
glue factory. Back then I was "the kid" or "the youngblood," as the
foreman liked to call me, and now I'm one of the old-timers, out
of mothballs and quite possibly out of my depth. I wonder sometimes if I look more fragile than I feel, as if I'm a stumble away
from a broken hip or from a more comprehensive breakdown.
The cold I developed over Christmas has proved hard to shake.
Over the years one of my eyelids has dropped down lower than
the other, so I imagine I often look tired. People routinely say that
I do. Certainly no one but the most hyperactive kid could regard
me as less than energetic—my stride is still brisk, and I teach on
my feet with a full dose of adrenaline—but that too might be
cause for concern.

Occasionally I sense a tension in my colleagues between a

wish to warn me and a reluctance to prejudice my perceptions. I can tell they want to say more than they do. Just as the new semester was about to start, for example, a group of junior and senior girls accosted me in the hall, smiling, and informed me that they'd be in the spring section of my Popular Fiction class. A sparkly bunch they were, a flashing feminine constellation of white teeth and diamond studs, with large buckled purses in place of the customary tote bags and backpacks. They asked the usual questions about what we'd be doing in class (Popular Fiction tends to be the default reading elective for midlevel students, who sign up with vaguer expectations than, say, a student might have signing up for Mythology) and whether I was "a hard teacher." They didn't seem to be much worried; in fact, they seemed rather keen. They had heard I was "nice." After I told them not to believe everything they heard and thanked them for introducing themselves, they moved on. A passing teacher offered this cryptic aside: "I see you've met the posse."

8

FEBRUARY

To expect too much is to have a sentimental view of life and
this is a softness that ends in bitterness. Charity is hard and
endures.

—Flannery O'Connor, in a letter

I used to say that if anyone asked a new teacher which of the
three week-long vacations on the school calendar she could
most easily do without—December's, February's, or April's—
she would probably choose February, if only by default. Losing
December would make short work of Christmas, here today,
gone tomorrow, while forfeiting spring break would make the
spring seem, well, less like spring, and life depressingly less like
college.

In contrast, February break has no nostalgia to recommend
it, no holiday to sanctify its claims. It falls too late for Valentine's
Day, usually late enough to run through Vermont's annual town
meeting on the first Tuesday in March, which is to say, just in
time to jog the memory of any voter who may have forgotten
how cushy teachers have it. Ask us to jettison one vacation, and
anybody in her right mind will toss February over the side.

That is what I used to say, all by way of underscoring the

irony that the February break was always the one that found me in the most enervated state. The closer it got, the more indispensable it seemed. It appeared in my imagination like a lifeboat on the open sea. This year finds me yearning for it no less than before.

The research paper is killing me. With an eye toward teaching the process and leaving no child behind, I've let it go on for too long. In the hopes of allowing for more depth, I've sacrificed too much momentum. Papers are due at the beginning of the month—with all pieces handed in, including notes, drafts, an outline, an e-mailed list of electronic links from students with online sources, and physical books for students who've consulted books—which at the maximum means over fifty papers to correct before the break and countless pieces of documentation to review. A few students have barely started.

As I knew would happen, some students are attempting to catch up by circumventing steps in the process. A teacher insists on such steps in order to keep students from falling through the cracks—they respond by searching with all their might for some cracks. I close every fissure I see opening, if only to remain true to the promise I made at the start of the unit: I'm willing to accept any piece as late as it comes, but I won't accept any piece without the piece that was supposed to precede it.

What ought to be a learning process becomes a chess game, a series of calculated moves. Kids are smart enough to figure out that a teacher is far less likely to cry foul on one of their maneuvers if they use another teaching colleague for a shield. I find a rough draft and note cards for a topic that was never vetted with me, a biography of Winston Churchill, in my office mailbox. This is the first substantial piece of work I see on a paper that was supposed to be about mental telepathy. The student includes a note that he has been working on this paper with one of the tutors in the academic support areas. In short, he has used his tutor to make my requirements of no effect, and he's counting on professional etiquette to sanction an end run around them. That he knows it's an end run is clear from the fact that he won't even put the materials into my hand.

As I will eventually learn when the student and I finally sit down to sort out what happened, he and his father pretty much cobbled together the draft from some books they happened to have lying about the house. The documentation, what there was of it, alternated between inept and fudged. Then he turned to his conscientious, hardworking tutor and had her help him construct the preliminary pieces, in effect walking backward from the finished product, though she had every reason to believe they were moving forward. But all I feel holding the largely bogus materials in my hand is that I've been played a fool. I'm also annoyed that the tutor never thought to keep me in the loop. It's possible I'm also feeling jealous: why didn't the student come to me?

I ought to be happy he turned to someone. He's a palpably unhappy kid with what I've been given to understand is a home life marred by mental instability and parental domination. I've seen him smile only once in almost six months—it was that remarkable, and it lasted but an instant. A research paper is the least of his troubles. Still, I can't help but think that in our zeal to see that failure is not an option, we have unwittingly created an array of options for avoiding *the work assigned*. The ideal is an instructional program tailored to meet student needs; the reality, I fear, often devolves to teachers working at cross-purposes and students working the system to their own (dis)advantage.

The reality also includes the fact that, in spite of its innovations, our school remains a traditional competitive system of grades and rankings, the fair and consistent management of which falls to classroom teachers like me. Our remedial colleagues can focus on coaching the individual players, but it's left to us to maintain the decorum of the playing field and the integrity of the scoreboard. Small wonder if we occasionally wind up butting heads.

At my best, I'm able to see that the friction of competing interests is as indispensable to an effective school as it is to a viable democracy. God save us from the harmonious operations of a more totalitarian model. But I'm not at my best right now. I vent my frustrations over the paper with the tutor. She frustrates me further by suggesting we look at the episode as a teachable moment. I offend her by saying how much I'm coming to hate cant expressions like "teachable moment." That's unfair, and I apologize. As is typical of her—and fully consistent with her approach to students—she pays less attention to my apology, which she accepts warmly and without hesitation, than to the stress she feels I'm under. She's worried about me.

In fact, the unspoken litany of my daily complaints often begins with "I'm tired." My wife says that I've gotten into the habit of exclaiming the words aloud when I'm home. "Why are you tired?" she asks gently, as much to call me back to the present moment as to know the reasons. Well, I'm tired of giving instructions to the wind. I'm tired of working with classes when I'd much prefer to work with individuals. I'm tired of the social and economic conditions that weigh on some of my students, making a mockery of my most reasonable expectations. Here is tonight's homework—which some of my students must try to complete in what no one but an imbecile would call a home.

At the same time, I'm tired of the constant negotiations among teachers, tutors, and counselors, of what I sometimes perceive as advocacy run amok. I'm sick of "intervention strategies" that involve three adults spending up to a half hour on an issue that would not even exist had one perfectly capable student devoted fifteen minutes to doing a simple assignment. Or fifteen seconds to addressing the issue directly.

A colleague approaches me in the hall. She tells me that one of the students in her study hall came up to my room to hand in a completed late assignment but that when I saw him through the glass beside the closed door of the classroom—I was teaching at the time—I gave him "a dirty look." Or that's what he told her anyway. I have no recollection of seeing this student outside my door, much less of giving him a dirty look. I'm certainly not ungrateful to my colleague for taking the time and energy to nip a grievance in the bud, but I also feel exasperated at having to offer the same explanation twice, once to the colleague and again to the student when, with my full consent, she brings him upstairs (her second trip up, mind you) to meet with me.

First of all, I explain, I have no reason to be giving dirty looks to this boy, whom I happen to like and who often comes to check in with me during my preparation period, never without my giving him a warm welcome and seldom without a word of praise for his shaky efforts at keeping up with his assignments. Couldn't any of that history have figured into his hasty interpretation of my look?

Second, I've gotten into the habit of taking off my glasses when I teach in order to permit my middle-aged eyes to read whatever papers I happen to be holding in my hand, which may explain why I don't recall seeing him outside my classroom. Probably I *couldn't* see him.

And finally, the clincher, which I find both satisfying (because even the student acknowledges it as the clincher) and demoralizing (because after six months in my classroom the clincher ought to go without saying):

"Donald, have you ever once known me to communicate my

displeasure about anything or anyone by any means other than saying exactly what's on my mind? Can you think of a single instance where you had to guess whether I was happy with your performance or dissatisfied with your behavior?"

He can't.

"There's a simple reason for that. I don't speak Dirty Looks, and I don't speak Body Language either. I speak English. As in the following sentences: You are a good kid. I'm happy to accept your assignment. In the future, if ever I seem to be annoyed with you or if you are annoyed with me, come to me right away and we'll straighten it out in five minutes."

But will he come? Always an open question, and not just for the students. I arrive promptly at the announced time and place for a morning meeting between a parent and all of her child's teachers, first scribbling my whereabouts on the blackboard for the benefit of those students who might come to see me before their first class. I discover the meeting's nowhere near ready to begin, dash back to the room for some work to do in the meantime, dash back—still no mom.

When the parent does arrive, I find I'm quickly tired by the sense of charade, what strikes me as dramatic pretense on both sides: *I only want my child to succeed. We only want to help your child reach her full potential.* Such lovely words, so full of virtue and rectitude, but is that really what we want? More than once I sense that the student is asking herself the same question. I used to wonder if my daughter asked it too in the days when her mother and I attended school meetings on her behalf. Is it caring, or projecting the appearance of caring, that matters most to us? Adults are no different from adolescents: what we most desire is the approval of our peers. I include myself in "we." I won't risk this parent's disapproval in order to ask the most pertinent questions. You say that reading comes hard for your daughter. Have you ever given her anything to read? She has a cell phone, a snowmobile, and a horse. Does she have a book? Does she have a place to read where she doesn't hear the blaring of a television set? Does she have a decent place to work?

And if she does, do you think I could come over some morning around second period and borrow it? Because I'm also getting tired of going to the teachers' room and finding it filthy, the sink full of unwashed dishes and floating bits of food, the table grimy and littered with crumbs. Four times now (but who's counting?) I've held my dangling tie to my chest with one hand and wiped that table down with soap and water with the other, just so I could correct papers without picking up grease spots, so I could eat my own midmorning snack without contracting some disease. I want to leave a note of complaint but know I will regret it afterward. Crumbs on the table, teachers on Facebook, Walt Whitman and Willa Cather no longer on the library shelves. Yes, I'm still brooding over the Library of America. You would think that at the least I'd have gotten tired of that.

For any complaints I have, the kids themselves remain my best antidote. The implicit paradox is one that a parent will readily understand: the kids are much of what's driving you crazy and most of what's keeping you sane. Their good humor and almost daily displays of decency buoy my spirits. Still, there are certain patterns of behavior that are beginning to wear my patience thin. Among these are the attention-getting antics of the neediest kids. Antics like interrupting an explanation to ask questions that the explanation will answer in a minute. Raising a hand and then, when acknowledged, saying "No, that's okay." (Translation: You didn't acknowledge me right away so I'm obviously not important.) Like flashbulbs discharged in your face, the interruptions can wreak havoc on your concentration. Sometimes that seems to be their intent.

Finally, after trying private appeals in vain, I call out one of my worst offenders, giving the annoyance its proper name. "This is attention-getting behavior and it needs to stop," I tell her in front of the entire class. Even as I say the words, I feel them cut into her like a knife, because she knows they're true and because we both know why they're true. Attention is exactly what she's starving for. She gets almost none of it at home.

Distracting as they are, attention-getting behaviors do not weary me as much as acts of insolent inattention. My second-semester Popular Fiction class is periodically disturbed by gab, often instigated by but not always restricted to the claque of girls that was identified for me as "the posse." A few zeroes for talking during test periods cool their jets somewhat, but it's a fire I can't entirely put out. I'm told that at least one of my colleagues has given up with this crowd. "I just let them talk in the back of the room and go on teaching." But does such an approach allow the other students, including those most prone to distraction, to go on learning? Often the most neglected kids in a school system are not the so-called troubled children; they're the struggling but mostly cooperative children whom no one troubles to give a second thought.

With just such students in mind, I insist on the decorum of my classroom. But I grow tired of having to repeat myself—and of the strain of keeping my annoyance in check when I do. At an orientation session for new teachers at the beginning of the year, the superintendent told us "Never raise your voice," an equivocal directive given the type of student for whom anything close to a reprimand counts as "yelling." But I hold to the principle that a polite request that can't be heard at conversational volume needs to be repeated at a more audible volume, "audible" to be determined by compliance. Unlike the Temptations, I *am* too proud to beg, but if "yelling" is what it takes to permit a kid with learning disabilities to take a test under the most favorable conditions, I ain't too proud to yell.

In general, though, I'm more amazed than miffed at the amount of communicativeness that saturates the school day, not only among the kids but among adults as well. I'm still not used to it. I'm sure that some of my reaction derives from having worked so many years alone in my house. I try to factor in my own eccentricity. Even so, I find myself wondering if people in past generations felt, or people in other cultures feel, such a compulsive need to gab as I witness all around me. I'm astounded that people have so much to talk about. I sit down with my dearest at the close of the day and find that I'm incapable of more than a few sentences. What exactly is there to say? The food is great. I love your company. I'll be glad when it's February break.

Undoubtedly, some of my students are no less weary of the endless chatter than I. Mostly to give them a leg up on their assignments but also to provide a taste of something different, I devote the last half of a few class periods to silent reading. I'm immediately impressed by the number of students who take to it. One can almost feel them settling into the silence, as into the breathing of deep meditation. I take an empty seat in the middle of the room and read with them. I wish I could hook us all to heart monitors. I can feel the rhythms even out. Perhaps when the February break does come, they'll find occasion to repeat the experience. I certainly intend to.

Hardly a day goes by, no matter how tiring, when I don't feel thankful for my study hall, not a thing many teachers can say. Its sparse population allows me to seat the students at a distance from one another, though we've gotten closer in other ways. I sense a common understanding between us. On more than one occasion a faculty member has walked into my room, paying me no more mind than if I were one of my potted plants, and begun talking aloud—practically yelling!—to one of my study hall students. I'm tempted to protest, but I don't. I assume this must be the way some other study halls work, and I draw satisfaction from the sense that some of the students seem to find these intrusions embarrassing.

This is nothing compared to the satisfaction that comes of an unthinkable request. Unlike freshmen, who are assigned to study halls during any period when they do not have a class or lunch, upperclassmen with acceptable grades are permitted to forgo study halls for what is called earned time. So, in addition to my freshmen regulars, I have a transient population of sophomores, juniors, and seniors who enter and leave as their marking period grades fall and rise. The unthinkable request comes when several of these upperclassmen, newly sprung from study hall for having brought up their grades, ask if they might stay there anyway. They can get their work done, they tell me, and it gives them more free time at night. I find this gratifying, to say the least, including the part about the night.

I have no doubt that some of the attraction of my study hall is the ease with which I grant passes to visit other rooms and especially other teachers. Here too there's an understanding among my regulars: be worthy of the trust. They know that once in a while I'm going to step out of the room and check up on their whereabouts. On one of these forays I find a senior boy hanging out in the school store when he told me he was going to be working in the computer room. I'm pissed, and I tell him as much. Had he asked to go to the school store, I'd have let him. I've long been a believer in a student's need to stretch his legs now and again, a need I exercised quite frequently in my own student days. But there's a matter of accountability here: I need to know

where my students are in case of an emergency. If I don't, it's my
tail in the wringer, and I don't take kindly to people who take
frivolous risks with my livelihood or my reputation.

The boy's contrite. He tells me that he knows we've had a good
relationship up until now, and he's loath to think he's ruined it.
I tell him he hasn't, though it may be a while before I give him
permission to leave my study hall. I know the test will come
sooner than I'll find appropriate. And I know what I'll need to do
to see that both of us pass. "Do you think you could let me go to
the computer room?" he asks, meekly enough, a mere week later.
"I do, but we have one piece of unfinished business to settle before
I can let that happen."

I peel two dollars from my wallet and tell him to go to the
school store and buy two bags of chips, "for me and for thee."
When he smiles, I know everything is back where it belongs.
Like my earlier dustup with the tutor, the episode ends on a note
of reconciliation, though I could also call it rest. To be at odds
with anyone right now is simply too exhausting.

Having a wife and daughter working in the public schools saves
me from self-pity, though it can add to my sense of weariness.
Both women work in special education, a term that supposedly
refers to the disabilities of their students though it might just as
easily refer to the disabling requirements that go along with "special funding." Every year, for example, they and their colleagues
are absorbed in the completion of the "time studies" required of
all special education teachers in the state. In its disingenuous zeal
for accountability, the Department of Education wants teachers to
account for all of their day's activities in fifteen-minute incre-
ments. What the department doesn't want, and explicitly states it
doesn't want, is any accounting for hours spent before and after

the contracted hours of the school day. This strikes me as similar to asking for a description of a centaur that makes no mention of a horse.

Also inadmissible are the daily exigencies—calming a child's tantrum, waiting to meet with a parent who doesn't show up for a scheduled meeting, having a postmeeting heart-to-heart with the parent who does show up only to break down sobbing partway through—anything that can't be assigned a code and logged in with a keystroke.

So if scheduling conflicts (yours or the parent's) compel you to deliver services to a child before the school day begins, you can't count that as service. On the other hand, not counting the morning session as service risks showing you in default of your obligations to the student as spelled out in his or her Individualized Education Program. (An IEP is required for each student served under the umbrella of special ed.) Meetings with parents count only if you schedule them during the times when working parents are least likely to attend. If you work while you eat lunch, you must still indicate that you take a lunch: you can't enter two codes in one space, nor can you show yourself lacking a lunch. (By law every full-time worker in the United States gets a lunch whether she gets one or not.) If you suffer an attack of diarrhea from wolfing down your lunch, you can't note that on the form, since there is no code for using the toilet. You can either fudge the entry or leave the fifteen minutes blank and have the form rejected.

The time study must be recorded on a perpetually revised electronic document that may or may not cooperate in storing your information. (If public education has any current trends, this is at the very top of the list: the rate at which pedagogical conundrums are being replaced by technological ones. A close second is the alarming rate at which educators are losing their ability to tell the two apart.) Needless to say, the time taken to do the time study is not a permissible entry.

In short, under the pretext of wanting to know what its special education teachers are doing, the state wants proof positive that they *are* doing what the state itself inhibits them from getting done.

One might gather from the way I'm carrying on here that I have to do a time study myself or that my wife and daughter are furious at having to do theirs. I don't; they're not. I am alternately touched and amazed by their dedication and resilience—another reason I find the time studies so demeaning. Our daughter comes home for a weekend; she and her mother begin talking shop almost as soon as she gets through the door. I doze off in the living room to the sound of their kitchen-table conspiring—their inexhaustible zeal to find the best approach for this kid and that kid . . . *from each according to his ability, to each according to his need.*

I love them, of course, and they love each other; they also love their work, dispassionately, intellectually—they are no sentimentalists. But another love is at play in their banter, hinted at whenever my daughter says, "I like the bad ones best" or when her mother refers to one of her own baddies as "this little guy," a phrase that tends to dress the three-year-old it summons in a racketeer's necktie and fedora. There was a time when I thought that the weakest reason a person could give for wanting to be a teacher was "I love kids." The declaration of an airhead, I used to think. To some extent I still do—I am no sentimentalist either. But as a primary motivation, I now see it as indispensable, especially if one adds, "I love their parents too." Ditto for any reformist movement in school or out, let alone anything that dares call itself a revolution. "At the risk of sounding ridiculous," Che Guevara said, "let me say that the true revolutionary is guided by a great feeling of love." That goes double for the true teacher. It has become a kind of mantra with me over the past weeks: *I need to love*. I hope my episodic bouts of sickness have not begun to soften my brain. But the greater danger by far is that my midwinter weariness will begin to harden my heart.

For Valentine's Day I buy several bags of bite-sized chocolate hearts and give one to each of my students as Frank Sinatra and Barbra Streisand sing "I've got a crush on you, sweetie pie." With more forethought, I'd have bought some candy that was sugar-free. Childhood diabetes: yet another reason Valentine's Day can be the most depressing day on a kid's calendar. Or morbid obesity. Or you don't have a girlfriend. Or your father just found another one. Or you're the only gay marcher in the dominant culture's annual Straight Pride Parade. I might have done better to ignore the occasion altogether, but for that the school gives too little support. I'd have had an easier time ignoring Christmas.

As in past years the school's business club is selling carnations for a dollar apiece. The purchase price used to include delivery at any time: a knock would come on your classroom door (or else it would fly open minus the knock) and a club member would enter and present the resident sweetie pie with her fifteenth red carnation of the day (or one of less flamboyant hue if the sender was "just a friend"). The deliveries, at least, have become a bit more discreet. But the rest remains as it was. By afternoon the most popular girls are sashaying down the halls like beauty pageant winners while their less-favored sisters clutch a single stem or no stem at all. At least my kids can all clutch a candy, whether they choose to eat it or not. I put the hearts on a plate for the sake of elegance. I walk them up and down the rows in an effort to be courtly. Most of the kids say thanks or no thanks. A few say nothing but still take a heart.

Not long after dispensing the chocolates I have a nightmare in which I'm serving each of my third-period sophomores a splash of red wine. I'm not sure why I'm doing this, but it feels good to pour their allotments into the long-stemmed crystal glasses I must have handed out before the dream began. A teacher passing by my classroom—young and female, but no one I recognize—sticks her head through the doorway and insinuates that I'm violating the separation of church and state. "We're not allowed to give them bread either," she snaps. But I'm not giving them bread, I tell her, or talking about religion; it just happens that our little treat for today is some wine. *Wine!* Christ, I'm giving these kids wine!

"Everybody stop!" I shout. "Everybody put down their glasses right now. Mr. Keizer has made a big mistake." I manage to find a bucket into which I ask the students to empty their glasses. But I'm too late for Stevie, a gentle boy who sometimes comes into my room at the beginning of class and asks if I need any help erasing my boards or passing out papers. His glass is empty, his lolling face as green as a bell pepper. I'm overcome with remorse. *I've killed poor Stevie.*

My wife has an expression: "What would Dr. Freud say?" I wish I knew. Is my subconscious telling me that I need to remember I'm teaching minors? Do I expect too much of my students, discussing subjects or setting them tasks better suited to adults? I do my corrections with a green pen, and the boy who nearly drank himself to death has not had the smoothest sledding with his research paper. Does that explain his green face? Or is my dream symbolic of a deeper frustration, one that comes of acquainting my students with some of the headier delights of literature and culture only to feel thwarted by the constraints of a bell schedule and a grade book? Am I trying to achieve a deeper level of intellectual "communion" than I have a right to expect?

I discount the possible interpretation that my conscience is tender because I digress too often in class. I don't think I do. If anything I may be erring on the other side. In past years I was more likely to share a story, historical or even autobiographical, more willing to get off the subject and circle back around to it. Essentially I was trying to teach my students how to write, or rather how to look at the world like a writer. Then why do I do so little of that now? Is it because I'm overly driven by the various "standards," the Common Core curriculum, the ever-looming NECAPs, the need to hit the ground running because of the precious minutes lost by taking attendance on the computer? In other words, have I been too stingy, rather than too liberal, with the wine?

If I have, then I've been stingiest with my Popular Fiction class, where the omnipresent necessity of keeping order tends to discourage me from digression. I certainly feel the least at my ease with that group, which may mean that I'm keeping everyone at a distance for the sake of a relative few. I decide to strike a different note when my drive to work one morning fills me with an unusual elation. I pull off our dirt road onto the blacktop and look into my rearview mirror just in time to see my wife's red taillights winking at me through her car's exhaust as she turns in the opposite direction. No sooner have I redirected my smile to the road ahead than the biggest full moon I've ever seen begins following me to work, playing hide and seek along a range of mountains. I think I've finally lost it for good, and then it makes one dramatic curtain call just before I enter the village of Barton, so unreal in its diameter that I have to wonder if I'm dreaming.

Lesser lights accost me on the way, things almost as familiar as the moon but transfigured in its glow. An ornamental light-house beaming on the lawn in front of someone's mobile home seems preternaturally gratuitous, dares me to conjure the story behind it—this young working couple manages to get a week on the Maine coast, feels more alive than they have in ages, and decides nothing less than a five-foot lighthouse will do for a sou-venir. It's a challenge getting the thing into the car, wiring it to the house. It flashes a warning across their next electric bill—they don't care. To come home to that little lighthouse after a late night out or to wake up to it in the hours before sunrise lifts their spirits out of winter, wafts a smell of saltwater to their brains. A passing snowplow puts me on the same shore, splashing a wave of snowmelt against the side of my car, and I'm suddenly aware of every consolation of the man in the cab, how grand he must feel to ride so high above the road, a lighthouse keeper in his own right, his roof lights turning as he clears the way for milk trucks and school buses, pregnant women rushing to the hospi-tal, bread trucks coming up from the south. On no day can he question the importance of his work: it's as solid as a steering wheel in his hands. There's a thermos of coffee beside him on the seat, the memory of his wife's warm body when he rose at 3:00. He's going to tell her all about this giant moon when he gets home, while she lays on the bacon in her bathrobe and slippers, lighting the day's first cigarette at the stove. Maybe she won't have to go to work this morning, maybe they'll go back to bed after they eat. Maybe they'll make love.

By the time I'm in my Popular Fiction class, I've trimmed my narrative with an eye toward brevity and decorum. I've taken out the wife's warm body and the cigarettes. I don't know if the students are so quiet because I've captivated their imaginations or because they wonder if I've lost my mind. On another day I might have segued from the lunar to the etymology of *lunatic*.

But my lesson today is about art. "I'm a reader of history," I say to them. "I could tell you things that human beings have done to one another that would ruin your sleep for a week. But the world is full of beautiful things as well, and literature exists in part to help us perceive them. Literature helps us open our eyes."

It sounds glib, and I know it's reductive. It ought to have been better planned—what I really meant to say is that there's no way to assign pragmatic value to things of beauty. You can't do a cost-benefit analysis of a moon, a novel, a lighthouse on somebody's front lawn. There's no way to reduce these things to test results or data.

Only much later—now, in fact, as I write—does it occur to me that I may have given the cue, as well as permission, to a boy who decides one day to ignore the topic for that week's journal assignment and write about something else. He was up doing his barn chores on the morning the journal entry was due (but not yet attempted) when he caught sight of a coyote loping across the snow-covered cornfield. He ran for his deer rifle and got back in time to place the varmint in his crosshairs. He fired and saw it drop. He felt "so good" that he decided to write about the episode for his English homework. Did I inspire him to do so? It hardly matters. The important thing is that he was inspired—that he believed I would be capable of appreciating his inspiration. Never mind that a coyote might count as one of the world's beautiful things. Never mind the albatross that Coleridge hangs around the neck of the Ancient Mariner who shot it out of the sky. There's only one person in this room old enough to qualify as an ancient mariner. "Let that boy alone," quoth he.

The due date for the research papers arrives. Right up till the deadline I've been meeting with students both during and outside class to go over drafts, tidy up citations, coach concluding paragraphs. I highlight with a yellow marker any sentences that I suspect have been plagiarized and require students to review them with me before handing in their final drafts. For the few who go limp at the prospect of following the MLA style used by our department, I do the bibliographical citations with them, side by side. I know that in the academic support areas the tutors have been putting in lavish amounts of time to get some of their more challenged charges up to speed. The range of performance runs the full gamut from students who have taken their paper through multiple drafts to students who have still, even now, done nothing beyond choosing their topics. I'm already figuring out terms for a grace period following the due date.

With one eye on those students for whom staying organized is a particular challenge and the other on those adults (parents, tutors, etc.) trying to help them close the gap, I devise a detailed checklist to be handed in with the final product. This is hardly an innovation—I credit the IRS and the Guggenheim Foundation, both of which provided similar kinds of assistance to me— but I'm pleased with it nonetheless. I take pleasure in imagining my students, perhaps with the assistance of their friends, parents, or study hall teachers, methodically putting their various pieces together and checking off each item as it's added. Like packing for a trip, I tell them. I also take comfort from the thought that I'm not going to lose a lot of time or break a lot of hearts (including my own) by having to subtract points for missing pieces.

Grading for major assignments at the school is generally done by means of a rubric, with points awarded for each of a set of criteria and then totaled for the final grade. The way you build mercy into a rubric is to see that there's a "floor" of points awarded simply for coming through with the goods. The main plank in my floor is the last item of the rubric, a criterion labeled "completeness," which allows a student to earn up to twelve points, more than the point spread for a whole letter grade. My hope is that the checklist will enable students to gain a full complement of points for this category, as well as for another called "process," which acknowledges their diligence in following the required steps.

If I devote so much space to discussing the relatively humdrum matter of a checklist, that is because it eventually comes to encapsulate my frustrations and sense of failure. If you like your alliteration to come in threes, you can add a third "f" and say I'm floored by some of the results. Intended to strengthen the connection between my requirements and what the students actually deliver, the checklist comes to stand as the disconnect between us. The old saw about leading a horse to water could not be more apt.

Some students simply do not use the checklist. They lose it, ignore it—don't have it. Granted, if they have all the other pieces listed on the sheet, then for them the document was a superfluous nuisance and its absence of no consequence. Except there is almost no one who has all the items and no checklist. This is simply not how these things work.

Other students supply an accurate but unsatisfactory checklist: that is to say, they check off what they have completed, but what they hand in remains incomplete. The checklist has not prompted them to do anything more than what they would have done without it. Imagine asking your traveling companion, prior to driving to the airport, if he's remembered to bring his photo ID. "No," he says, "but I have all my luggage," and gets into the car. Yeah, but there's still time to go back in the house for the ID. "Nah. Let's go. If anybody asks, I'll say I don't have it." He's honest. He may not make it onto the aircraft, but he's honest.

A more bizarre variation is the student who checks off every

item on the list whether he has those items or not. The checklist
is a form, you see. You're supposed to fill it out. All those lines
need checks; here they are. At the other extreme is the student
who hands in the form, duly stapled to the paper, but has not
checked off any of the items. The Zen approach. I start fumbling
with a mental checklist of my own, some of it straight and some
of it bordering on the facetious. Was every kid present when I
explained the checklist? Was every kid paying attention? Did I
give a quiz to see if they understood? Did I spend three days
discussing it? Did I turn filling out the checklist into a lesson in
itself?

The checklist business is an irritant, the number of students
who hand in a late paper or no paper at all is a discouragement,
but the truly demoralizing thing for me is the number of students who completely ignore my edits and suggestions on their
rough drafts and hand in a "final" draft identical to the rough
one they handed in weeks ago. It's as if *draft* were merely a syn-
onym for *printout*. Had I not assigned other writing units prior
to this one I'd be wondering if I've mistakenly assumed an
understanding of the meanings of "edit," "rough draft," etc. I'm
inclined to wonder anyway. Is it possible I have students who still
don't grasp the *reason* one does a rough draft or who think that a
final draft exists only for the sake of neatness?

The lack of revision extends to some of the passages I've highlighted as likely plagiarisms. They remain as they were. The students did not come to see me, did not attempt to paraphrase and
document what I rightly suspected they'd simply copied verba-
tim from their sources. The same Internet that put the text at
their fingertips makes it easy for me to locate the lifted phrases. I
speak privately with the most egregious offender. Did she not
understand the sheet on plagiarism, the one that we went over in
class and that every student signed? No, she understood it. Why

didn't she come to see me about the passages I'd highlighted? She's not sure. "I guess I didn't have time." It's like a bout to see which of the two of us is the more clueless, and I'm the one winning. I simply cannot comprehend why anyone would be so careless of her own welfare.

I shouldn't neglect to say that any disappointments are offset by some wonderful results. Not surprisingly, the paper on Le Chambon is a splendid piece of work, preceded by enough conferencing to allow for no surprises. I'm simply able to enjoy it. Assigning the grade is a mere formality. A paper on the Ashanti people of Africa and another on the traditional clothing worn in India both exhibit not only some of the cross-cultural perspective one hopes to gain through research but also the writers' ability to snap back after a prolonged absence from school. A hockey enthusiast relieves the monotony of statistics that characterizes the typical paper on sports with piquant commentary from members of her hockey-loving clan: Grandma weighs in on this year's prospects for the Maple Leafs and gets a formatted citation for her trouble. My self-described redneck follows through with a respectable paper on John Deere; an art-loving student shows off her new knowledge of Fauvism. The writer on female genital mutilation earns the right to stand on the feminist soapbox of her concluding paragraph and gets some applause in green ink. The boy who wrestled until the very end with the giant squid survives the struggle and emerges with his head just above water, scarred by a few suckers but still glad to be alive. For a midlevel sophomore English class, the unit has hardly been a disaster.

But the results should have been better. I wasn't expecting perfection, but I should have seen a basic competence across the board. I don't. This is especially troublesome given the school administration's repeated reminder that the chief measure of success is not "what got taught" but rather "what got learned." I can hardly find fault with that. Doctors are judged by how many they heal, not by how many drugs they prescribe. But aren't there cases where medicine simply doesn't work, where the doctor's only consolation comes of knowing that he did everything he could?

What else should I have done? In some cases the answer takes the form of a regrettable omission on my part, an error I ought to have flagged on a student's rough draft or note cards but failed to catch in my scramble to return things on time and preserve our momentum. These goofs hurt but at the least I can see they don't hurt the student's grade. Other goofs I can't perceive; probably some of them have to do with the sheer limits of what one teacher can accomplish within the waking hours of a day.

Still others, like the case of plagiarism, have to do with deeply ingrained habits of passive resistance. When asked how he'd attained his mastery of Latin, Dr. Johnson famously replied, "My master whipt me very well. Without that, Sir, I should have done nothing." What a bleak view of human nature, I used to think, but after spending my first Saturday going over research papers, Johnson's reply strikes me as outlandishly optimistic, as if a beating were all it took to teach a kid Latin.

For someone who's spent much of his adult life trying to mine personal experience for "larger," often political implications, it's hard not to feel a stinging challenge to my politics. Most teachers are some variety of centrist liberal, if only because they rightly see their own livelihoods as dependent on a generous social contract. But it is only with a great leap of faith that they achieve even the most lukewarm progressivism, which by its very definition requires the belief that human beings can progress—or want to. It's in making that leap that I lose my footing. I have never doubted that many a disadvantaged kid was saved from the gallows by going to school. But to create a society in which gallows were permanently abolished—how many holdouts would first have to hang? At the risk of sounding impertinent, Comrade Guevara, how many people did your "great feeling of love" inspire you to execute? To reduce ignorance is one thing, but what remedy for inertia—for the tendency in many of us to find the demands of all but the most pedestrian forms of learning or liberation simply *too much work*? The question is way above my pay grade. I can't even find a remedy for plagiarism.

Late in the afternoon of the first Sunday of my February break, I drive up to school to record the research paper grades on Power-School. It has taken me two weeks and two complete weekends of correction to reach this point. It would have taken longer had every student handed in a paper. I'm ashamed at the gratitude I feel toward the kids who've lightened my load.

This semester the administration has enabled the feature that allows students and parents to check their grades online; I've promised to make the research paper grades visible by this date. The scores will make a positive difference for some students, who are my main reason for wanting to get the data into the system. We'll go over the papers themselves after vacation, after my disappointment has had time to mellow. For now it's enough to drive up to the empty school, deactivate the alarm, turn on the lights, and hope the Internet is up and running.

Can it really be no more than a month since I came off midyear exams feeling so elated? I keep asking myself if the results are really as dismal as I think they are or if I'm concentrating too exclusively on what was missing to the neglect of what was not. I know I must never sneeze at the fact that a great bulk of material got handed in. I sneeze all the same. Is it some insipient hypochondria that creates the impression of a disease laying hold of me even as I'm driving home? I was sick for Thanksgiving and sick for Christmas; surely I can't be getting sick for February break as well, not now when I've finally gotten through all those papers. My bottle of water is too cold and I drank from it too fast; probably that's the reason my ears ache when I swallow. A lingering residue of chalk dust might be all that's making me sneeze.

Ice fishing shanties dot the frozen surface of Crystal Lake like a forlorn tundra settlement, smoke rising from their chimneys. The ice will soon be thinning; every year someone waits too long and his shanty, sometimes along with his pickup, breaks through and sinks. Some of my kids took the same sort of risk with their papers. It's the local way, I tell myself, but no, it's the human way, the few degrees that separate any one of us from disaster. I take care not to speed, not to let my wheels hit the salt-softened slush on the shoulders. All I need now is to skid onto the lake and go through the ice. I'm not going to let anything put a crimp in my vacation. That includes obsession with the research papers, my fitful nights of correcting them in my sleep notwithstanding. I did the best I could with the unit. Perhaps with another two years I might have it down pat. *Another two years*—is that really a possibility? No word yet from my predecessor. Contracts will be going out next month, and he'll have to give an answer then. If a position opens up, I may have to give an answer too. I've got my heater blowing hard enough to muffle my music. I can't seem to get warm.

9

MARCH

The only bearable days I can remember in the course of many years were the few days of a sultry feverish attack of influenza.
　　　　　　—Louis-Ferdinand Céline, *Journey to the End of the Night*

Kathy says she can't remember ever seeing me as sick as I am now. We've been married for thirty-six years. I've had my flu shot—in fact, owing to a glitch in the paperwork at my doctor's office, it seems I've had two—but flu is what I have, what I had throughout the February break, and what has kept me out of school for the first six school days of March. It would have been eight, but school was called off for two days because of snow.

I don't wonder that the disease can be deadly. The spoon in my hand shakes so violently against my soup bowl that I sound like a wedding reception agitating for the newlyweds to kiss. I can't resist a joke about consumptive Russian poets, wheezing out the punch line as my wife looks on in alarm. In bed she holds me tight until I stop trembling. In the morning I wake so drenched that she has to strip the bed. I dream I'm still correcting research papers. I keep making mistakes. I recalibrate my grades only to have them disappear from my computer or float off the screen, curling like ashes above the keyboard. In about as many days I've lost nine pounds.

For as long as we've lived in Vermont I've done my snow removal by hand, a matter of fitness and a point of pride. Within a week I've gone from slow shoveling to being unable to shovel at all. As if the mere sight of me out of doors is a reproach to the neighborhood, men with tractors begin dredging out my driveway even before the sky clears. Kathy insists on shoveling the path to our door. I watch the activity from my window like a child who can't go out to play.

I'm too sick even to attend town meeting. Voting for the school budget is a point of pride more adamant for me than shoveling my own snow. When our daughter was young enough to attend the town elementary school, I acted with obvious self-interest—all the more reason to be a disinterested supporter of younger parents now. And since I don't live in the same school district as I teach, no one can accuse me of trying to pad my own paycheck when I speak in support of teachers. True, I'm not as given to verbal brawling as in years past, and I scarcely have the strength for it this year. Kathy will have to go without me. We're hoping for a quiet meeting. But even a level-funded budget won't pacify the skinflint contingent if they're in an ugly mood.

Past bones in its craw have included an all-school ski program (a "frill," notwithstanding the school's front-yard view of Burke Mountain, whose lodges and condominiums are routinely mucked out by parents who can't afford to buy their own kids a ski pass), a largely state-funded free breakfast program (based on the apparently outrageous proposition that children ought not to be punished for the poverty or neglect of their parents and opposed with the predictable perversity that prides itself on rejecting "state handouts"), and that perennial bugbear, special education. The last of these gripes has always struck me as the most deplorable, especially when the parents of handi-capped students endure the abuse in embarrassed silence. More than once I've had a moist-eyed parent approach me after a meeting and thank me for my remarks.

The air of masquerade can be almost as depressing as the sentiments themselves. Lavishly pensioned retirees step out of immaculate $35,000 pickups to bear witness to the tribulations of living on a "fixed income." Solidly middle-class landowners hold forth on the burdens of minuscule tax increases in the rhetorical overalls of Tom Joad. Countrified transplants who've sent their children to the best private colleges money can buy evoke the Vermont tradition of making do with less.

Not to say that there are no legitimate, or at the least under-standable, grievances with the school system. I've had a few of my own. And I've seldom left a town meeting as angry with my neighbors as I am with the social conditions that put us at one another's throats. Especially the people who speak from obvious poverty and even more obvious bitterness—are they wrong to wonder what school ever did for them? Or to assert that school costs are among the very few over which they have any control? Quite correctly they sense that in a class-bound society, education provides much of the basis for despising—and exploiting—those who lack it.

Even the obvious remedy seems to mock them: in a state (and lately a nation) where organized labor is more the exception than the rule, it's hard for unprotected workers not to resent the privi-leges obtained by unionized teachers, some of whom, I'd be the first to admit, are long on "organized" and short on "labor." Years ago the father of two of my students told me a story about working on the Crown Point bridge connecting Vermont and New York State. There was a crew from each side, and when they met in the middle, the Vermonters discovered they were making a third of the hourly wage of the workers from New York. "They had a union, you see. We didn't." What the father must have felt meeting his unionized counterparts is perhaps not unlike what some of my neighbors feel sitting at town meeting with the likes of me—the difference being that a teacher's union wages come out of their pockets. I try to remember that.

I'm glad to be spared the effort this year. I won't miss the sigh at the microphone or the grumble from the back of the room. I know that a few of my neighbors won't miss me. Vermonters love to speak of "our town meeting tradition" as "democracy in action," which is accurate enough, though not always the most stirring endorsement of democracy. To be the parent of a school-age child whose daily comfort and future prospects are at the mercy of a disgruntled electorate, half of whom are obstinately misinformed and several of whom, at ten in the morning no less, are stinking drunk, is not my idea of a spring tonic. Norman Rockwell does a good job with the tall fellow standing up as the personification of free speech, but he leaves out the dema-gogues and the dimwits waiting their turns behind him. He's a painter of miniatures, however big his canvas.

Kathy lifts me out of my funk when she returns at lunchtime to say that the budget passed by a good margin with hardly any dis-cussion. Rockwell probably wouldn't have been surprised. I guess I shouldn't be too surprised either. In other words, I shouldn't let the memory of a few benighted decisions make me cynical about democracy. I undermine my own position if I do. To lose all faith in the public's judgment, to forfeit what E. B. White calls "the recurrent suspicion that more than half of the people are right more than half of the time," is as good as conceding that human-kind is debased beyond remediation—in which case, why should I care one way or another if the school budget passes? What point is there in teaching those who will "never learn"?

But it's not democracy that gets me down so much as the surly kind of populism that likes to wear democracy's clothes. If in the name of the people we allow public education to be strangled in the tight-fisted mandates of "local control," if we're prepared to put the safety of a school building or the content of its textbooks to popular vote (at least Vermont does not do the latter), then we reduce democracy to what even our most optimistic founders feared it might become: mob rule. If for no other reason than to sharpen our sense that public education and responsible self-government go hand in hand, town meetings are a good idea.

Unlike the towns that make up the Lake Region School District, the town in which Kathy and I live has no designated high school. Most parents opt to send their children to the quasi-private academy in Lyndon, their closest option, though the town will also provide tuition to any other accredited high school at the academy rate. Like its counterparts elsewhere in Vermont, and according to a rationale I've never entirely understood, Lyndon Institute serves as a de facto public high school while retaining several of a private school's prerogatives. Its teachers need not be certified, for instance, and it sets its own tuition without the need for voter approval. For that reason, our discussions at town meeting rarely touch on secondary school expenditures. I have no doubt that the take-it-or-leave-it nature of the academy tuition accounts for the cost-cutting vengeance that some voters bring to the elementary school budget.

Other towns in our county also send their students to the Lyndon high school. Kathy is now working part-time in one of them. She uses what remains of Town Meeting Day, a day off for most teachers in Vermont, to practice further on her new iPad. In two years Lyndon Institute will eliminate all physical texts in favor of digital editions on such a device. That may be part of what's driving its adoption at the elementary school level. In the case of the special needs students Kathy serves, there's also a feeling that smart-book technology will foster the "accommodations" they require.

Kathy shares the hope, not without reservations. It sometimes seems that the accommodations are less to the student and more to the digital device. For example, Kathy fashions "communication boards" that allow nonverbal kids to make their needs and wishes known by pointing to a picture. A glass of water, say, or a favorite game. Up until now she has custommade these boards by hand with an eye to an individual child's skill set; now she's being urged to use a prepackaged app to do the same thing. But some of her students lack the sequencing skills necessary to make the app appear on their screens. When it does, it's likely to feature more pictures than a student is able to comprehend on a single visual field. Never mind, say the state consultants, stick with the iPad. "You can make this work." Kathy intends to do no less, though she has to wonder if putting a kid on an iPad is necessarily the same thing as putting a kid's needs first. In other words, what exactly is the *this* we are trying to make work?

In fairness it should be said that no one is forcing Kathy or her colleagues to go the iPad route, not yet anyway, but there is a definite sense of an imperative in the air. This is not the aberration of a single school system but part of a much wider trend— perhaps wider than most of us care to see. The institute's plan to have all student texts on iPads, for example, will be a blow to the local independent bookstore that has provided the school with texts at substantial discount for decades. It's also an oddly extravagant expenditure given the financial constraints that were cited only the year before to justify laying off a large portion of the school's unionized maintenance staff in order to outsource their responsibilities to a contracted firm.

Decisions such as these underscore the rarely acknowledged fact that all schools operate with at least two curricula: what the school teaches children through its academic programs and what it teaches through its administrative priorities. It may be that the institute is well aware of this. Surely no one can fault the school for failing to prepare the elite sector of its students to assume leadership positions in the "global marketplace." The lessons are apt and unequivocal: technology means everything, loyalty means nothing, local economy and organized labor mean less than nothing. More than any flu, the lessons make me sick.

But figurative sickness remains a luxury in my present state. The real variety is about all I can manage. As confirmed by a chest X-ray and a sample of the sputum I keep coughing up, my flu has become pneumonia. I'm given a strong antibiotic—what I've been asking for from the outset—one level of potency below what would require me to enter the hospital. I'm also given a doctor's note discouraging any quick return to work, not that those colleagues who've heard my voice on the phone would view that prospect with anything but horror.

I'm already at the stage where my lesson plans have shifted from those appropriate to a short-term absence to those appropriate to a last will and testament. I've always done thorough sub plans—to do otherwise is tantamount to throwing a substitute to the lions, even with a class of lambs—but the challenges of doing good plans increase the longer you're out, and there are certain limitations even at the start. Asking a substitute to present new material is at best a risk, at worst a guarantee that you'll have to repeat the presentation at a disadvantage later on. Busy work of the kind that a substitute can be entrusted to correct is immediately, and rightly, perceived by the students as an insult to their intelligence. Assignments that generate lots of material for the recovering teacher to correct might succeed in class but are not likely to work wonders for his recovery. Perhaps the only advantage of being a sick teacher is the chance to catch up on the paper load, an advantage I'm disinclined to surrender. There will be backlog enough without heaping it higher than it already is.

Either the night before an absence or early the next morning I type up my plans for the day, never less than several pages, and e-mail them to Sara and Mr. Messier. The duplication is not their requirement, but I think it's good for both of them to know what's going on in my classes. I suppose there's some display involved: *See, I'm still on the job.* So is poor Sara, who remains my chief mainstay at school, in sickness as in health. She'll print my plans for the sub along with any documents I attach in the form of student assignments. She'll also check in on my classes to see if things are going well. If an uncooperative student is ejected from my room, she's likely to be the first responder. She keeps encouraging me to take what time I need, but her health has not been perfect this year—she's been coughing almost continually since September—and I worry about the added strain I've placed on her.

I set up a relay. Another member of the department, who also commutes from a town outside the district, agrees to bring the sub's comments and any collected papers to the drugstore in Barton, which has agreed to hold the bag until Kathy can drive up after work and retrieve it. Once I resume the normal pace of correction, there's a daily exchange of incoming papers and outgoing papers. By this I hope to accomplish two things. The academic instruction can go forward, and by means of comments on the papers I can maintain some kind of connection to my kids. For my Composition class this exchange takes the form of editorial letters written in response to rough drafts. Were the class larger or on the whole more industrious, this might be too heavy a load. As it is, I can manage.

My greatest fear, the fear of every absent teacher, is that I'm going to lose my classes. The understandings we've forged together will gradually come undone. Nothing is more vulnerable to entropy than the climate of a classroom whose teacher is away— even for a few minutes, let alone three weeks. I'll soon be into my fourth. Every one of my classes has heard my September spiel about the gravity I assign to the mistreatment of a substitute. (I used to work with a teacher who made a point of professing his total indifference to how his classes treated substitutes. That was *their* problem, he used to say. I'm told he eventually became a veterinarian. Were he the only one on earth, I'd shoot my sick dog.) Every sub plan I type up includes a space for his or her report on the day. I'll give my classes an opportunity to tell me their version when I return.

The situation is critical with the juniors and seniors in my Popular Fiction class; I've not been with them long enough to bond at the most optimal levels. One of my sophomore classes contains a new student, or rather a return student who left school the previous year trailing an odor of trouble behind him. Even before my illness he was showing his potential as a catalyst for misbehavior with two other boys of a similar bent. I have no difficulty keeping them in line and in fact enjoy a tentative rapport with all three. The two were actually making some progress until the third arrived. In the cat's absence, however, the mice have begun to play. I hear this from the sub. I also hear it in more general terms from some of the students. "We need you back," writes one girl in her journal. Another sophomore, a poignantly introverted boy from whom I've scarcely heard ten words since the year began, writes: "This class is a waste right now."

I send some messages of warning to the frisky ones, and Sara also gives a few sharp yanks on the reins. There's a certain kind of boy—often, I suspect, the son of a certain kind of man—who has a hard time accepting female authority, but Sara's more than a match for the type, maternal Durga or fearsome Kali as the case requires. The sub is soon reporting improved behavior. But I know it is no more stable than the weather in March.

She also reports that my last-period sophomores are treating her with conspicuous courtesy, as I expected they would. We can't help enjoying some classes more than others, and these kids—some of whom gave me the most grief at the start of the year—have become the apple of my eye. "Do tell the lovies," I write in my sub plans for eighth period, "that I have received the news of their exemplary cooperation with particular pleasure, but no surprise. Tell them I wish I could build them an enormous beach house in Cancun where they could frolic away the rest of the winter while I hacked and coughed and read their papers beneath a distant—but not too distant—palm tree."

For the first time since school began, I find time to write something other than a letter or notes for my journal, a short op-ed on the Wisconsin governor's bid to deny public sector workers the right to collective bargaining. As output it's paltry enough, but when it appears in the *Los Angeles Times* I take it as proof I can still ring the bell. I do worry, though, about some local Internet surfer taking it as proof that I'm furthering the cause of international socialism at taxpayers' expense. Probably sipping a dry martini while I do it too. But I mustn't give a false impression: when one of the district secretaries routinely asks for the doctor's note required after a certain number of sick days, the superintendent is reportedly annoyed to learn of the request. It seems my stock remains high, at least as far as integrity goes. I worry about the op-ed all the same, like a monk who's just been caught winking at a milkmaid.

I take notes for another short piece but don't find time to finish. This one is about events closer to home. As part of the same beachhead launched in Wisconsin, the governor of Maine has judged the murals depicting the state's labor history to be anti-business propaganda and has ordered their removal from the statehouse. I have no doubt that if asked to explain himself he would hint at wanting to strike a blow at "socialistic" tendencies, even while ordering erasures of the historical record in the best Soviet tradition.

But governors have no patent on contradiction; we teachers are their equals at least. The Maine governor's initiative reminds me of a quotation I've heard attributed to a former Exeter teacher, according to whom there are only two legitimate "learning disabilities," one curable and the other not. The first is laziness, and the second is stupidity. I'd wager that the teacher was disabled by them both, too lazy to adapt his teaching style to the needs of his students, too stupid to realize why he had to. Like the governor, he became the very thing he hated. I should be careful not to do the same.

These musings and others like them are a feature of my sick days, products of my return to solitude and books. Which is to say that solitude and books are never an unqualified blessing. On some level I miss the unreflective luxury of a day's teaching, though I surely don't miss the need to be reactive. For better or for worse, I have more time for reflection now. It ranges over the usual ground—religion, politics, and literature. Inevitably, most of it comes round to school.

A William Trevor novel I've been reading leads me to consult some of his autobiographical essays, in one of which he reports that he was an indifferent student. I've already told my students that Hemingway couldn't spell to save his life; should I also tell them about Trevor, even though we're not reading him? More to the point, should I tell them that it was not until I'd entered graduate school that I began to approach reading assignments with the same conscientiousness that I demand of them? It comes as something of a jolt for me to remember this. I was not a conscientious reader. I always read, but I read as and when I felt moved to read, relying on my listening and writing skills to fudge my comprehension of assigned texts, including great texts, texts I was blessed to have put under my nose, *Billy Budd* and *The Return of the Native*. I was a procrastinator, a daydreamer, a faker. Well, it's not unusual for a hellion to grow up to be a strict father, but many is the strict father who bowdlerizes the history of what a hellion he was. His kids can sometimes read it anyway in his strictness. I wonder what my students are able to read in mine.

I reach further back into my earliest memories of school, trying to locate when the thought of becoming a teacher might first have occurred to me. It was probably in second grade, when Mrs. Davies would let me "teach the class" about my several interests. Second grade has always seemed like the Garden of Eden in the Genesis of my school career. I was probably never happier or more secure in school than I was then. No doubt much of this had to do with our teacher, though she has survived as a vague figure in my mind. I think of her as an old woman; it's possible she was no older than forty. Once she invited our entire class to a picnic at her house, an enchanted place as I remember, with a wonderful pile of dirt that I lost no time in excavating. I didn't take part in the baseball game organized by her sturdy, bald-headed husband, but I've preserved a distinct image of him catching up a classmate as the kid scrambled to first base like a harried piglet and whirling him around in jubilation because he was "safe." The next day Mrs. Davies laughed when she told us how Mr. Davies had fallen fast asleep in his chair that night. So had some of us.

It was also in Mrs. Davies's class that we made the wonderful kid-tall "Big Book" out of painted cardboard pages, each of them holding one of our original handwritten stories. With our teacher's gentle encouragement we read them aloud for our parents and for other classes at the school. Mine was an instant hit. Precocious in my authorial enthusiasm for discussing my work at length, I explained to one audience of admirers how I'd discovered my ingenious story in another book. I assumed that's what you did with stories: you heard them in one place and retold them in another. I can still feel the admiration dissipate like air from a punctured balloon—there may even have been an audible sigh that went with it—and my stomach turning at the sight of Mrs. Davies, so embarrassed and disappointed. Second grade may have been Eden but it was also where I fell from grace. I didn't learn the word *plagiarism* until much later, but it has always carried the implication of original sin.

Perhaps most adults are divided between those who knew the steady ache of never gaining their teachers' approval and those of us who knew the sharp, sudden pain of losing it. I remember accidentally knocking over my friend Tommy Gonzales's science experiment, which went crashing to the floor of our sixth-grade classroom when I opened a window too abruptly after school. Tommy was so knowledgeable in science and so talented in art that our teacher once compared him to Leonardo da

Vinci, which amused Tommy to no end, especially after he found a picture of Leonardo in the encyclopedia, "this wrinkly little geezer with long stringy hair." I still recall the sound of his glass vessels shattering on the floor, the nauseating splash of water. Tommy took it calmly, gifted even in his understanding of what it means to be a friend. As for Mrs. Spitzer, her bitter lamentation as she gathered up the broken glass began to sound as though my offense consisted less of wrecking Tommy's project than of not being Tommy, "such a creative boy, and so talented." I seem to have been some kind of walking disaster at age twelve, though that is probably a common experience of childhood, the sense that we are always, helplessly, screwing up.

It persists for some kids throughout their school careers, and for others till they die, this mysterious and inexhaustible capacity for letting people down. I reread a letter that one of my students handed to me at the beginning of the third quarter, shortly before I took ill:

Dear Mr. Keizer

I wanted to apologize for my lack of accomplishment in my previous term in your class. I started out okey, but then I got lazy and unfortunately it effected your class. I know how much hard work you put into grading my papers along with everyone elses. I know you see potential in maybe a pointless person. You deserve the up most respect. I'm very sorry for my disrespect. My distractions from home effected me in my work. Not that I'm using it as an excuse. Please just know, my work will get better. I will hand it all in. My greatest effort will be put back into your class. Thank you so much for not being upset, and being so kind and thoughtful.

For everything you have done for me.

I'm sorry I disappointed you.
Expect a great comeback
From me.

                                        Thanks always,
                                            [Name]
By the way . . . Im sorry about my misspelling. I am a horrid
speller.

Rereading the letter causes me to wonder if I give my students an exaggerated impression of disappointment, which must fall especially hard on anyone tempted to see herself as "a maybe pointless person." I also wonder how much weight I ought to give to such a letter, how much it grows from genuine remorse, how much it might be intended to make me feel remorseful. I can't remember ever writing one like it to any teacher of mine, not to say I wouldn't do so today if I had the chance. Perhaps to my seventh-grade teacher, Mr. Keeley, and perhaps only to tell him that I ought to have appreciated him more than I did. I recall the afternoon of an especially difficult day, when he dismissed his students one by one after the final bell and took a long time getting to me. "I'm disappointed in you," he said. The offense was not accidental. I had openly criticized him that day, almost to the point of outright defiance, though I can't recall the specific reason, only the cathartic release when the words left my mouth. Something he'd done had struck me as intolerably unjust, though the actual injustice probably had little to do with him. It had more to do with my emerging indignation at the idea that a "smart kid" wasn't allowed to rebel, wasn't supposed to get angry, shouldn't be popular enough to get a girl.

I doubt very much that Mr. Keeley had provoked me; he was not that sort of teacher. He advised a club for students who liked to assemble plastic model cars (I belonged) and let Bruce Cazazza play the Beatles' new *Rubber Soul* album at recess. Mr. Keeley was not married and had a little belly under his waist, proof positive according to one of the boys in class that he was a "fag." What Mr. Keeley was above all else, I think, was sensitive, a considerable liability for a junior high school teacher, so he must also have been brave. He seemed genuinely hurt by my defiance, though it's possible he rejoiced inwardly to see a sensitive boy coming into his own.

For a while now I have been asking my students to do their own reflections in paper journals, an exercise I find especially useful while I'm sick. The assignment keeps them writing and it keeps them and me in touch. Recent topics for my sophomores have included "What Is Something You Would Like to Change about Your World, Your Community, Your School, or Yourself?" and "Which Character Do You More Closely Resemble, Tom Sawyer or Huck Finn?" I also ask them to offer their thoughts on one of three current news stories: the revolution in Libya, the tsunami in Japan, and the union-busting initiative in Wisconsin. Not surprisingly, they are most familiar with the stories farthest from the geographical and political circumstances of their lives. I get a number of entries about Japan, fewer about Libya, none about Wisconsin. The governor of Maine may be wasting his energy: does anyone even remember what those labor murals are about?

The topic of a wished-for change brings the students closer to home. It also shakes my ideologically based tendency to see poverty as the worst thing they face. Though most of my students are not poor in the strictest sense—if I take the census figures for their county as the best indicator, then the label fits only between a tenth and a fifth of those sitting in my classes—I'm most inclined to cite economic disadvantage in any mental argument with an educational theorist or with myself. In the case of student journals, though, the most wrenching entries have to do not with material privation but with ruptures in the writers' families. I get a few like this one:

> If I could change one thing . . . it would probably be my parents . . . they are currently split up, and I haven't spoken to my mother in 4 weeks and it hurts. They don't get along very well anymore like they used to. Our family used to be <u>so</u> perfect and happy. We told eachother everything and all of ours problems were worked out. No secrets were kept hidden at all. It really hurts to know that the perfect couple I know as mom and dad, no longer love eacher.

I get only one like this, but it belongs to the type:

> I wish I could be enough of a reason for him [my father] to stay. I wish my heart was pure gold and that I couldn't disappoint anyone. . . . I wish I had the power to persuade someone who was about to jump, their reasons to stay. I wish I was the kindest, prettiest, smartest, most unselfish person around. Maybe then I wouldn't be such a disappointment.

I have been reading widely in this genre since the year began, regardless of the particular topic. "My Troubled Family"—it cuts across gender, age, and class. Even when students focus on their own social lives, I tend to suspect a domestic subtext. A frequent complaint is "all the drama." Ostensibly the writers are talking about school, the typical cliques and dustups of teenage life, but essentially they are talking about home, where adolescence never dies.

Given my empirically based conviction that a stable home

life is the single most reliable predictor of a student's success in school, I am surprised that the Republican Party, self-appointed champion of family values, takes no pains to press the point. Of course, to do so would undermine its agenda of weakening the very provisions that lend stability to family life, more specifically its agenda of dismantling public education, hamstringing teachers' unions, denying same-sex couples the benefits of marriage, preventing employed mothers from achieving income parity, curtailing reproductive rights, outsourcing manufacturing jobs, and filling the coffers of the various charlatans who sell education in the form of standardized tests. Not to mention the risk of offending constituents who'd rather harp on family values than value their own families.

But the Republican Party is not the only faction shouting down the question of what it means to be a responsible adult. That precious bourgeois squabble referred to as the "culture wars"—all it means to me now is two different ways of making war on children, two rival sects in the ancient religion of child-devouring Moloch: one that sacrificed and continues to sacrifice working-class children on the altar of American exceptionalism and the other that sacrifices them to the frivolous exceptionalism of the "transgressive" lifestyle. Winner take all, and children the losers no matter who wins.

"It has been vivid to me for many years that what we call a race problem here is not a race problem at all," James Baldwin wrote. "The problem is rooted in the question of how one treats one's flesh and blood, especially one's children." The race problem and just about every other problem that crosses a teacher's desk.

My repeated mistake, I've come to believe, is not so much to overemphasize the effects of poverty on my students as to define poverty too narrowly. The mechanisms that cause poverty are largely economic—the evidence for that is more compelling than the fossil record supporting evolution—but the poverty itself is breathtakingly diverse, as varied as the species evolution produced. Returning from a doctor's visit, I get gas next to an SUV at a mini-mart. There's a decal on one side depicting a woman bending over a fender and being fucked from behind above the caption "Only on a Jeep." In the back window is a sticker that reads, "Why should *I* have to press 1 for English?" In the front seat are two passengers, a young man and woman whose dull bloated faces belie any claim they might have as champions of erotic abandon, to say nothing of English. If there's no child car seat in the back it's less likely to mean the couple is childless than that their child rides without a child car seat. I don't bother to look—no more than they have bothered to consider what a child might make of the picture on their hatchback. There is more poverty in this vehicle than in any line at the social welfare office. I refuse either to condemn it or to make peace with it. Where a liberal might see an uneducated slob, where a conservative might see a potential vote (plus an uneducated slob), where certain progressives might see a subculture needing only a little more tolerance for bilingualism to earn an honored place in the Great Rainbow of Cultural Diversity, I see nothing but the waste and degradation of consumer capitalism. True to its progressive cast, the Vermont legislature has recently begun discussing a prohibitive tax on soda in order to prevent childhood obesity. As if soda were the reason children are obese! Who makes the soda? More to the point, what alienating social conditions make the soda—the Coke and the coke—so irresistible?

Once I'm cued in to the concept, this larger poverty dogs me wherever I go. Now some students have taken to complaining in their journals about the "sound quality" of the Ken Burns documentary on Mark Twain they've been watching in class. It's their excuse for not doing the journal assignment that asks them to

respond to the film. On one level, the complaint is valid enough
(the film is a copy and not the best); on another, it's a simple
dodge: most of the kids do the assignment, including the one
who complains most vociferously about the inaudibility of the
film. I'd lay a small fortune that the other with the biggest beef
was mostly impeded by the sound quality of her own incessant
chitchat during the film. On a deeper level, though, I can hardly
blame the kids. This fastidious obsession with visual resolution
and digital sound, irrespective of the quality of the *content
depicted*—what is it but the inevitable result of our gizmo-
hawking market? Vacuity with special effects. We inculcate in
our children the sensibilities of raccoons, a fascination with
shiny objects and an appetite for garbage, and then carp about
"the texting generation" as if thirteen- and fourteen-year-olds
who couldn't boil an egg are capable of creating a culture. They
grow on what we feed them. It has never been otherwise. The
only thing that changes is the food.

On the way back from the doctor's I stop at the state college
library to see if I can get a better copy of the video. I can also test
my strength by walking from the parking lot. I've gotten the red
ball to rise higher in the breath meter though there are still traces
of pneumonia in my lungs. After checking out the film and asking what happened to me, the reference librarian, a brilliant feature of this place for years, tells me of her plan to retire at the end
of the term. She's been helped to her decision by the recent initia-
tives to shrink the library. She and her colleagues have already
had to sacrifice some of their collection; now they are to lose their
entire periodical wing. The reason is to make room for an endowed
tutorial center just off the library. In a different mind-set I might
see this as a painful but necessary sacrifice; I'd recall the wonderful work done in the academic support areas at the high school.
But it's hard for me today, after six months of teaching and sev-

eral weeks of reflection, not to see the tutorial center and the decimated library as of a piece, not only with each other but with the economic system that contains them both. We sell the disease and we sell the cure, the carcinogenic chemical and the chemotherapy, the high-calorie soda and the exercise bike. We make kids illiterate by shrinking and/or wiring their libraries; then we build wired support centers to teach the illiterates how to read. An iPad for the one and an iPad for the other, twice the profit from the same slick deal. I make it sound more conspiratorial than it is. In fact, it is the absence of conspiracy, of anything approaching a plan or vision, that yields these absurd results. A crapshoot is not a conspiracy, but as social policy it's crap.

I know better than to spend much breath on saying this to the librarian. She doesn't need my homily and she doesn't need my germs, though I've been assured that I'm probably past the point of contagion. The important thing now is regaining my strength, including the physical ability to speak. But I can't stay out forever. I've already used up my fifteen allotted sick days; after using my few remaining personal days, I'll be on unpaid leave. I'm also missing my students, or some of them anyway. The eighth-period class I fantasized about taking to Cancun joins with my seventh-period study hall and sends me an endearing homemade card, a crayon-colored sad sack languishing in bed with an ice bag on his head and a thermometer in his mouth, surrounded by their greetings and signatures. It is possibly an indication of how much I've begun to fade in their memories that one of them can write: "We miss your wonderful face."

Sara includes the card in my relay sack of uncorrected papers. "I think your two morning guys are missing you too," she tells me over the phone. "If he's not back soon," one of them tells her, "we're going to have to go look for him." Perhaps to add emphasis but more probably to discourage her from assuming they've gone soft, his sidekick is quick to add, "Yeah, and we don't even *like* teachers."

Near the end of the month I get my doctor's approval to take my wonderful face back to school. Mr. Messier hires a substitute just the same. If I can't last the day, I'll have coverage; while I'm there, I'll have an aide. His choice of personnel could not be more to my liking: good old Mrs. L., mother of three former students of mine, all grown women now. Well liked by students and staff, she is proof against some bad behaviors, but not all. I've come to her rescue more than once this term when she's been in an adjoining room. My rap is always the same: this is the mother of three former students, and a fine human being, as I'm sure is also true of the students who are giving her a hard time, but they need to let her see their better side. Otherwise, they are going to see my uglier side, because I happen to take any mistreatment of Mrs. L. personally. Now it's her turn to save my bacon, not in the face of misbehavior but as a support to my tentative endurance. She helps me to hand out and collect papers, to monitor small-group discussions, to keep score during the several days of the long-delayed Vocabulary Face-Off. After three days of competition, she helps me tally scores and hand out prizes. I'm also able to do individual writing conferences in a quiet location while she proctors the class.

It's remarkable how much smoother things go with a competent assistant. Some teachers have the benefit of an aide, though strictly speaking the aide is often not the teacher's but a particular kid's. Which is to say that the need for an aide is usually predicated on a handicapping condition in a student, not by the limits of what one human being with two hands and two feet can accomplish in a room full of twenty to thirty kids. It might surprise you, though it shouldn't, that teachers are among the few professionals with no assistants. Think of a doctor without a nurse or a receptionist, a lawyer without a law clerk, a chef without a prep cook, even a clergyperson without an acolyte or deacon. Plumbers and electricians routinely have helpers. Rock musicians have guitar techs. Golfers have caddies. So much for the important professions. A teacher in charge of the educational development of fifty to a hundred diverse and needy human beings is routinely on his or her own.

Oh, to have the offices of a Mrs. L. when I'm running on all eight cylinders! But I know I'm very lucky to have her now. Together we make a whole creature, like the hind and front ends of a horse costume. (Should you be reading this, Mrs. L., be assured that I picture you as the end with ears.) Strictly speaking, a teacher should not leave his or her students unattended; the protocol for an unavoidable bathroom break or a rare summons to the main office is to open the door between adjoining classrooms and ask a neighboring colleague to keep an eye on both classes. With Mrs. L. in the room, I need take no such precautions. I'm able to scurry to the side door of the building, closer than the nearest restroom but still down half a flight of stairs, and spit the fluid I'm still coughing up onto the snow. Hot tea seems to give my voice more mileage (plus another fortifying dose of caffeine), and I can use a lull in the action to walk down the hall and make a cup. Mrs. L. offers to fetch it for me, but I tell her no thanks. I'm a public figure once again; I need to set the right example.

Is it good to be back? In terms of preparation and correction, I've not really been away—I've merely been home, still on the job, submitting my plans and corrected papers by the day. Returning to the bustle of the school day is certainly a shock to the system. But it's good to see the students, and for the most part they seem glad to see me. All but the most hopelessly egocentric make a touching effort not to tax my strength. My Popular Fiction class may prove to be the one exception. The class is too large, too diverse, too restless, too confirmed in habits that are one thing to break in a freshman or sophomore but quite another to break in a junior or senior. Even so, I sense that most of the students are trying to pull with me.

Among my tenth-grade classes, with whom my bonds are stronger, the results of my absence are still palpable. I don't mean that the kids give me grief, only that there is a sense of loss for which *grief* is not an inappropriate word. A parent will understand what I'm getting at; a parent who's lost touch with a child may understand it best. Children are growing all the time. They are not settled civilizations, they are nations coming into their own. The time you miss with them is never entirely recoverable in the way it is with an adult. Grown-ups can catch up; long-lost lovers can get reacquainted after time apart—their bodies may have aged or altered but are mostly the same flesh and fit together in their former ways. This is not to suggest that time lost with a child can't be redeemed; it just can't be recaptured. So I feel a certain sadness at coming back. To be sure, some of this is also about missing the tranquility of my days at home. The books I left unfinished by my living room chair are not likely to be finished any time soon. I pine for them. I'm already pining for the loss of Mrs. L., and she's still here. But mixed with that is the sadness of having missed a small increment of growth in my students' lives. It's like a secret we share, they and I, but are not going to tell each other. Yes, I was truly sick, I didn't cheat, yet somehow it feels as though I betrayed them. I left them in the hands of strangers. I assigned them tasks I couldn't help them do. The reasons are every bit as irrelevant as they are legit. The reasons don't change a thing. I wasn't there.

10

APRIL

If youth is the season of hope, it is often so only in the sense that our elders are hopeful about us.

—George Eliot, *Middlemarch*

Sara informs me that she's finally heard from my predecessor. He's been traveling in the Far East and touring with his band stateside as part of his unpaid leave of absence. For a while now no one seems to have heard from him, and the silence has generally been taken to mean that he's cut himself loose. Not so, Sara says. He's decided to sign his contract and return next year.

Since the end of August, I've kept his picture taped to the blackboard behind my desk along with my chalked best wishes ("Keep on rockin', Mr. H.") as a way of reminding the students—and me—that the room remains his. No need for such reminders now. There will be no opening in the department, no job for me to apply for on the strength of what I've accomplished this year, no sense of rash impracticality for choosing not to. I consider calling my wife at work to tell her the news, but I already know what she'll say. "You weren't going back there anyway. It was never a question." Maybe not for her.

I feel an extra spring in my step, though I'm still a ways from dancing. There's a quarter of the year yet to go and plenty to negotiate within it. At a department meeting Sara announces that we will be administering the Gates-MacGinitie reading test in our sophomore classes to assess the strengths and weaknesses of our curriculum. Another glitch in my lesson plans. In addition, she's asking that sophomore classes devote some time to practicing for the NECAP (New England Common Assessment Program) tests they'll take next year. Apparently, this has been a strategy for several years running, a preprep preparation for the work juniors will do before their NECAPs in October. The consensus of the department, which to its credit seldom moans about the burden of assessments, or any instructional burden for that matter, is that we ought to do five practice essays based on prompts from past tests. It's been the custom to award students a grade of 100 for every good-faith attempt. This will give my students up to five separate transfusions of fresh blood to their marking period grades, some of which are anemic to say the least. That's the good news.

The bad news, aside from the sudden addition of roughly four hundred pieces of repetitive prose to read and evaluate (everyone writes on the same topic for each practice), is that the NECAP practices amount to a broadside fired at my plans for May and June. I'd planned to finish out the year with a unit on American poetry. Now it seems that Whitman and Dickinson will be competing with such soul-stirring tasks as writing a process analysis paper on "How to Instruct a New Student at School to Use the Cafeteria," with the top scores on the grading rubric reserved for those writers cagey enough to include a "diagram" of the lunch room with their "essay."

I estimate the total liability at around ten days, two per practice: a day to write on each prompt, plus two additional half days apiece for preliminary coaching and postpractice review of the students' performance. I can cut my losses by assigning some of the writings for homework, but that will reduce both my options for assigning other homework and the likelihood that the NECAP work will be completed by all the students. Once again, the demands of standardized testing move to center stage. And once again, we're left to solve a planning puzzle that offers no easy solution.

I keep my complaints to myself. For one thing, my English-teaching colleagues are merely trying to rise to the challenges that originate with powers outside the school. For another, it feels in very poor taste to complain about chores that I am soon not to have. It would be like a prospective parolee grousing about the prison food in front of the lifers. Though I'd be loath to admit it even to myself, I may be relieved to have the formidable task of fostering the comprehension of poetry without ruining its enjoyment tempered by something a bit more flat-footed. Yes, we'd all prefer sitting down in a good restaurant to lining up in the company canteen, but if you're the one doing the cooking, sometimes it's easier just to sling hash.

I won't forgo poetry altogether, though I will have to scrap a tentative unit called "Teach the Geezer." I began working on plans for it over the summer, but I never completed them. The idea was to have students teach me something they knew and I didn't. Units included skills such as fly-casting, dancing, basic sewing, and dressing wild game and subjects such as NASCAR, country-western music, and social networking—all areas in which I have little knowledge or proficiency. Students would have been asked to make lesson plans, practice exercises, and tools for evaluation. Fall probably would have been a good time to try the unit, especially if I wanted to use it as an icebreaker, though a slot in fourth quarter would have made it feel like a culmination, a passing of the instructor's mantle from me to them.

But when I look over the preliminary lesson plans I did for the unit last August, I realize that the kids have already taught the geezer quite a lot. The draft description is wordy, ineffectually humorous, presumptuous (not every student has something he could comfortably teach), and an evaluator's nightmare. I could only have composed such a thing over the summer. There is no time to revise it this April. Still, I think I might have made some form of it work.

As if to confirm April's status as "the cruelest month," three stories appear on the front page of the same local newspaper: a twenty-eight-year-old man drowned after attempting to fly his snowmobile over the Connecticut River in a state of drunken delirium, a two-year-old boy accidentally shot to death by another child with a .22 caliber rifle, and a wretched holdout of a farmer charged with animal cruelty for housing his starving cows in a mire of their own excrement. How the farmer and his family were housed is not mentioned, but I doubt it will produce any arrests.

As far as I know, none of these stories directly involve any student of mine, though I would not be surprised if one did. All of them bespeak what happens to rural communities when small-scale farming and the way of life it supports (the *culture* in *agriculture*) start to fail. If you can imagine Silicon Valley with no silicon you have a fairly good picture of the Northeast Kingdom without a sustainable price for milk.

It has been a little over three years since a fifteen-year-old boy in my town shot and killed his mother's twenty-four-year-old boyfriend in a trailer located on a dirt lane called Freedom Road. The mother suffered from mental illness and her son felt she was being sexually exploited by the boyfriend. The boy ordered the man from the house at gunpoint, a struggle ensued, and the boy shot him. I alluded to the tragedy during a discussion of the school budget at a past town meeting. I said that the shooter and his victim were "both our sons." Give or take a few years and miles, they might both have been my students too. It's impossible that one of them doesn't have at least a distant cousin in a class of mine.

As the pastures turn emerald and the poplar trees take on the color that must have inspired Frost to write "Nature's first green is gold," it's hard to believe that any of these things could have happened here. If you saw the high school where I teach, its neat brickwork and parklike grounds, its position atop a hill, with woods to the west and a view of grazing fields to the east, you would never imagine the suffering and squalor it conceals. That is doubtless true of schools all across America, but it is not supposed to be true of Vermont, a state so evocative of wholesomeness that its mere name on a bag of potato chips or a pint of ice cream is what a Catholic cardinal's imprimatur used to be on a book. Nothing dirty here. But just as one is amazed by reports of panther scat discovered in woods where it is no longer possible to get lost, to realize that moose and bear still make their homes on narrow tracts of land along the interstate, one is repeatedly amazed by glimpses of "the other Vermont" in the newspaper or on the midways of county fairs, even in the aisles of supermarkets on the days when the assistance checks arrive. I am capable of believing that such a thing as Bigfoot lurks in the wilds of Montana or that there are plesiosaurs gliding under the surface of Loch Ness solely by analogy to the poverty and violence that lurk behind the deceiving façade of scenic Vermont.

I overhear two girls in my homeroom talking about a fight between two women in a bar this past weekend. One lost her husband. The other lost her teeth. An ex-boyfriend brutally beats up the older sister with whom another of my students lives. Moving in with her had seemed a better option than foster care or remaining with her parents, both of them addicts and one on his way to jail. Now the girl is missing school to nurse the battered sister. If I keep coming back to this stuff, it's because it keeps coming back to me.

But not without respite. We get our rations of pride and joy. Word passes like wildfire through the school that Mr. Messier has been selected Vermont's Principal of the Year. No one is surprised by the achievement itself; we are merely surprised to find that the larger world suddenly knows what it's doing. It seems that Mr. Messier's been trying to keep the news under wraps. We're about to unwrap it.

A surprise all-school assembly is organized for the afternoon. A faculty volunteer keeps the principal occupied in his office while over four hundred students and staff members slip as quietly as possible from their classes to the gym. Birnam Wood could not have marched more stealthily to Dunsinane. The happy-birthday mood of conspiracy registers like barometric pressure in the halls. I don't think I've ever seen so many students so expectant as the ones leaning forward from the bleachers. It was here not long ago that Mr. Messier addressed the girls' basketball team during the winter sports awards assembly. They'd come close enough to a state championship to be heartbroken when they didn't take the prize. "You have no reason to be hanging your heads," he had told them, and their heads seemed to lift appreciably as he did. When all the recognitions had been made, he asked the assembled body his familiar question, "Who are we?" There was an unmistakable James Brown vibe when we said it LOUD: "Lake Region!"

So I can anticipate the volume of the ecstatic cry that's coming in another moment, from my own throat as well as everyone else's. My heart sinks just a little when the vice principal calls into his pager—"Mr. Messier, I need you right now in the gym"—because I can imagine the principal's own heart racing as he hurries down from his office, a dozen possible catastrophes scrolling through his mind. He swims before coming to school some mornings and shoots baskets with the kids after lunch, so we can assume his heart is sound. If it survives the next few minutes, it's good for another twenty years at least.

After he has the microphone and the ear of the assembly he loses no time in cutting up his honor, like the slab of cake waiting for him at center court, handing a piece of the credit to every member of his school. *We* are the ones who have made Lake Region an outstanding school; *we* are the ones who put his name in the limelight. Is he also thinking that "we" includes those kids whose deprivations add luster to the school's impressive achievements, though the deprivations remain? That the Cinderella stories of places like ours neglect to mention all the stepchildren who never leave the cinders? "Who are we?"—this time he doesn't pose the question, not aloud, but it has to be on his mind, not least of all today as he sees how much he is loved and is reminded all the more poignantly how much of our welfare is out of his hands.

Mr. Messier is too modest (and, by his own admission, too much of "an emotional guy") to turn his few words of acknowledgment into an acceptance speech, too discreet to start thanking Mom, Dad, and the Virgin Mary (all of whom I imagine he credits), but he would be no more than honest if he offered a word of thanks to his tribe. His surname is generally pronounced like the comparative form of *messy*; other families with the same name say

"MAY-she," but there must have been a time when it was pronounced "May-see-AY," when the bearers, like their descendants
almost to the present day, cut hay and raised cows on well-
managed farms. The best-kept secret about northern New
England is that many of its "old Yankee farmers" were not Yankees at all; they were French Canadians, diaspora cousins of the
Cajuns farther south. But farmers for sure, at least for a time.
There are now fewer dairy farms in the entire state of Vermont
than there used to be in Orleans County alone.

Mr. Messier was raised in that culture of morning chores and
summer fairs, Mass on Sunday and dances on Friday night, once
a kind of norm at Lake Region, now more of an aberration—so
much so that even some kids give voice to agrarian nostalgia,
something you'd scarcely have heard even fifteen years ago.
Teachers are not immune: Not long ago I was talking to a veteran
teacher in northern New Hampshire who told me that his community had lost its last dairy farm several years ago, the final
installment in what he saw as a much greater catastrophe. "When
you had those kids in your class, you could tell them apart from
the others," he said. "Their values were different. The way they
spoke to you was different. You could count on them. And they
were smart too."

I knew what he was talking about, though I also knew enough
not to succumb to romanticism. My resistance is best explained
by the story of a man of my acquaintance, raised on a farm, who
when he was a small boy got it into his head to play an unannounced game of hide-and-seek with his parents. After breakfast
he filched their car keys and locked himself in the trunk of their
car, waiting to be amused by the sound of them calling his name,
anticipating the moment when, after telegraphing his location
through the trunk lid, he'd spring into the sunlight like a jack-
in-the-box. He spent all day in that trunk. He wore his hands

out pounding. No one even noticed he was gone—until it was time for evening chores.

Still, I felt no need to offer my story as a qualification to the New Hampshire teacher's elegy. For the most part my sentiments were in line with his. His words come to mind as I work with my students this year. One of my sophomores gives a talk about his animals. He no longer lives on a farm, but he belongs to a family that farmed for generations, and he has the advantage of a barn for his small menagerie. His unabashed affection for these animals, neither livestock nor pets in any usual sense, is only one vestige of his heritage. Another is his peculiar sense of humor. We've all heard of barnyard humor, but that is merely the subgenre of a broader type, what is commonly called "corny" by people who can't laugh without condescension and know nothing whatsoever about corn. The humor of farm kids grows in part out of working side by side with adults, who like animals have a funny way about them when you study them up close, and in part from the sense of irony derived from dependence on the weather. It's a humor that comes of dropping things and having them kicked over, of getting manure spattered on your clothes. I suppose I could keep it simple and say it's the humor of people who still have contact with the material—as opposed to the virtual—world.

Happily, farm kids are not the only ones who have that contact. I'm refreshed by the range of topics for the process analysis papers my juniors are doing in Composition class, and by the literal hands-on nature of the processes described: how to change the oil in a car, how to bake chocolate chip cookies, how to execute maneuvers in basketball and martial arts, how to sight in a new rifle, as well as how to do a morning round of barn chores. Our young people still know how to "do stuff."

They also know the meaning of work. That was always the

case. The only thing that's changed—a difference very much due to the decline in farms—is the number of kids who travel to their jobs. These days more kids work farther from home, which also means farther from their homework. I have no statistics, but it would not surprise me to learn that more local students are holding down jobs at present than in the heyday of my teaching years in the 1980s. I base my hunch on a tougher economy (albeit one with no shortage of minimum wage service jobs) and a significant increase in "necessities." Now the indispensable vehicle (the preferred term in a region where half the "cars" are trucks) is matched by an equally indispensable cell phone. Since parents are likely to have cell phones too, there are understandable limits on how many "plans" one household can afford. As was always the case with vehicles, if you want one of your own, you're going to have to go out and work for it. To say nothing of households that require an older child's paycheck to make up for a substandard income, a laid-off parent, a missing parent, or some combination of the three.

The idea that a student's main job is *to be a student* is always under stress in a hardscrabble place. It seems to have its best chance when being a student includes being an athlete—a strong argument against the notion that athletics and academics compete for a kid's attention. They often do, but at least the competition is taking place at school. It's probably easier to crack a book in a gym (or a barn) than to smuggle one behind the counter of a Pizza Hut.

I remember sitting at one town meeting next to a father who was clearly proud of his employed son and angry at the elementary school he attended. Not even a teenager, the boy had managed to snag an after-school job for eight dollars an hour, the father told me, which at the time was well above the minimum wage. As for the school and its ever-increasing budget, he had nothing but scorn. The worst of it all, he said, was that "they," the teachers, "teach kids not to work." A strange thing to say. What I think he meant is that the school was teaching his kid that there are things in life that matter at least as much as holding down a job. If that's what he meant, he was right. So was the school.

But I'm not willing to dismiss the father's sentiments out of hand. They come to mind more than once this year, especially when the laudable ideal of "Failure is not an option" begins to make it seem as though futility is. It strikes me that the school often fails to capitalize on the one strength our kids are able to claim in spite of any social and cultural disadvantages that might affect them: they know the meaning of work. Teachers who complain "These kids have no work ethic" couldn't be farther off the mark. The problem is not that these kids lack a work ethic; the problem is that some of them see no connection between a work ethic and school. None of them would think, for example, to say to a customer at the McDonald's drive-up window, "Do you think I could get you those Chicken McNuggets some time tomorrow?" Yet we give sanction to that sort of request when it comes to school assignments. I'm surely not the first teacher to wonder if we might in the long run have cheaper schools *and* higher math scores if we paid students by the hour or at least by the piece. In a society that holds "value" as synonymous with "price," you get what you pay for.

We can't pay, though, so we pander. At a faculty meeting a study hall teacher praises a colleague for hand-delivering duplicate homework assignments to a student who might otherwise fail to bring the originals to his study hall. The voluntary courier then picks up the completed assignments at the end of the period. What is more, the study hall teacher adds, thanks to her colleague's exceptional routine, the student is actually doing his homework in study hall! There's a round of applause such as might occur during an AA meeting, though the teacher sitting next to me rolls her eyes as if to say, "Are these people out of their minds?" The recipient is a decent man and a dedicated teacher; I'd be happy to stand up and applaud him any day of the week. But I have to wonder if his skills are best employed in the capacity of a messenger boy. As for the kid who receives the service, he will undoubtedly go on to be a great success in any field he chooses, so long as its perks include a manservant.

In moments like these I wonder if I've put the wrong spin on the story of the farm boy who locked himself in the trunk of his parents' car. Is it really a tale of parental neglect, of a child with no worth besides his labor? Only if the parents didn't know their son was hiding. What if instead they'd seen him from the kitchen window slip into the car trunk and pull it closed over his head? I happen not to believe they did—but for the sake of argument, what if they had? In that case might they have been trying to impress upon him the kinds of foolishness people living on the edge of subsistence can't afford? Might they have been saying to their son what I have on the tip of my tongue to say at this afternoon's faculty meeting: that a lost sheep and a sheep pretending to be lost are not the same animal? You search for the first one high and low. You're not much of a shepherd if you don't. But if you spend your time running down the pretenders, aren't you telling the rest of your flock that they'd get a sweeter deal if they were lost? Pretty soon lost sheep are the only sheep you've got.

Mark Twain's runaway slave, Jim, expresses something like my indignation when a lost Huckleberry Finn tries to trick him into believing that he was never lost at all. He'd been in a canoe when a combination of fog, swift current, and an unseen island put him some ways from Jim and the raft. But he regains the raft while Jim, exhausted from his frantic attempts to reconnect with his companion, has fallen asleep. When Jim awakes, Huck tries to persuade him that he's dreamed the whole episode.

"I hain't seen no fog, nor no islands, nor no troubles, nor nothing," Huck insists. "I been setting here talking with you all night till you went to sleep about ten minutes ago, and I reckon I done the same. You couldn't a got drunk in that time, so of course you've been dreaming."

To Huck and perhaps to Twain too, Jim is the stereotypically gullible Negro, but reading the episode in my sophomore classes this year, I see him as the archetype of the ever-gullible teacher, or if not gullible then overly prepared to believe that any mistakes must necessarily be his. Jim assumes he must have been dreaming and even begins to interpret the symbolism of his "dream," like a flummoxed teacher searching out the mistakes he must have made in constructing a test that few of his students studied for. But no sooner has Jim succeeded in cloaking Huck's fiction in his own enabling exegesis than Huck points to some very real "leaves and rubbish" on the raft, torn from a tree and gouged from the riverbank during Jim's frantic maneuvers to steer the raft, and slyly asks, "What does *these* things stand for?" What follows is a cri de coeur from Jim—closer than anything I know in literature to the bitterness of a teacher who comes to believe he's been had:

> "What do dey stan' for? I's gwyne to tell you. When I got all wore out wid work, en wid de callin' for you, en went to sleep, my heart wuz mos' broke bekase you wuz los', en I didn' k'yer no mo' what become er me en de raf'. En when I wake up en fine you back agin', all safe en soun', de tears come en I could a got down on my knees en kiss' yo' foot I's so thankful. En all

you wuz thinkin 'bout wuz how you could make a fool uv ole
Jim wid a lie. Dat truck dah is *trash*; en trash is what people is
dat puts dirt on de head er dey fren's en makes 'em ashamed."

Huck was mean; most students who try to trick their teachers are simply lazy, but there are cases when the two overlap. The
first time I felt like Jim was in my rookie year of teaching, when
a senior boy whom I'd painstakingly coaxed along and gener-
ously cut slack for bragged shamelessly in front of me and his
girlfriend, then a freshman of mine, about how he'd bamboozled me the semester before. "Remember when I used to tell you
how I needed more time to write my compositions?" As I recall
he also mocked my praise of work he now boasted of having
slapped together with the least possible effort. I don't regret
helping him and I don't bear him a grudge, though I can't resist
mentioning that he eventually wound up serving on a school
board. I learned some hard lessons that first year, as all fledgling
teachers do, but no teacher learns enough not to get some "dirt
on de head" now and then, and to feel ashamed when she does.

That said, you need to read a whole text to get its full meaning, and the passage about Huck and Jim's reunion is bursting
with further implications. Huck feels bad and apologizes to Jim,
vowing to be a better friend. "I didn't do him no more mean
tricks, and I wouldn't done that one if I'd a knowed it would
make him feel that way." In other words—words that any teacher
does well to adopt as a mantra—Huck is just a kid. He's not yet a
fully formed (or fully moral) human being. He has more growing up to do.

At the same time, Twain reveals the social conditioning that
contributed to Huck's duplicity. Even penitent, Huck remarks,
"It was fifteen minutes before I could work myself up to go and
humble myself to a nigger." Huck is a product of his upbring-

ing, as is the smart aleck raised in the slaphappy folklore of "the teacher we drove nuts," a vein that runs through American literature from Washington Irving to Garrison Keillor. I've known teachers who reminisced fondly in the same vein. *There was this nun . . .*

I'm not sure I ever grasped as fully as I do this year how important it is for an English teacher to see the relevance of a work of literature to his own life. My primary responsibility is to make that connection for my students, but I'll have a hard time making a book come alive for them if it isn't alive for me. *Huckleberry Finn* was never more so.

I begin our class discussions of the novel by asking what questions there were on last night's reading. Invariably we seem to pass from humdrum details of comprehension—not a few caused by Twain's overwrought rendering of dialects, matters best solved by reading the knottier dialogues aloud—to matters more profound: friendship, racism, what it means to be civilized, to be free, to have a conscience. Like Huck and Jim, we let out our fishing lines in the enormous muddy river of this book; every day we pull them in and see what we caught. Some days it's a great bewhiskered lunker, other days something better sized for the pan, but rare is the day we pull up an empty line. I'm sure there must be days when we imitate Huck and Jim in the most wrongheaded ways—they are hardly traveling in the right direction for a runaway slave, down to the Deep South— but I trust the book as they trust their river, notwithstanding the fact that either one can drown you if you're not paying attention.

Resistance to reading continues to dog us; it shows up with the same maddening frequency as those scoundrels the King and the Duke. But it doesn't show up with all the usual kids, so I know that at least a few of them have made a new friend. Others seem not even to try. I break the book into as many bite-sized assignments as the year allows, I set aside class time for reading, and I devise an insurance policy of guaranteed quiz points for every student who gets help with the book in an academic support area. One of the teachers there suggests that my assignments are perhaps heftier than the average of 6 pages per night that I've mentioned to her. In the self-doubting spirit of Jim, I take out my syllabus and break it down with a calculator. It turns out I was wrong about the average. It's 5.8 pages, not 6.

But even in the stagnant, scummy water of self-justification, Jim and Huck don't abandon me. At one point in the novel they come upon a wrecked steamboat and make off with a great trove of books and cigars. They devote several days to smoking the cigars and poring over the books. I needn't be reminded that I am in the hands of an author who made his living from books and spent a hefty portion of it on cigars. Naturally he projected his favorite enthusiasms onto his favorite characters. But Twain was also keen to create characters his readers would find credible—a necessity for any writer who needs to move units to keep himself in smokes—and he doesn't seem to find any lack of verisimilitude in a rough-and-tumble kid and an illiterate slave regarding a salvaged library as real booty. I point this out to my students. I even point it out to the tutor when I tell her, "It's 5.8."

Resistance to reading is hardly my only problem. I have a black student in one of my classes—a minority of one in that section—and I wonder how he'll feel about Jim and the word *nigger*. Before deciding to assign the book, I talk this over with Sara, who says that he needs to confront the issues that have caused the book to be banned in other schools, needs to find his own response, and might as well do that with the help of a teacher who at least realizes the issues are there. As it turns out, the student leaves school before he can see Jim freed. That means he's also spared the nearly unbearable final chapters of the book, when the narrative sinks to the level of sadistic minstrelsy, with Huck and Tom Sawyer subjecting Jim to every conceivable indignity in order to make his emancipation more suitably romantic. Tom has derived these fancies from books, so Twain might be the first person to line up with his critics and say, "Be careful what you read and how you read it."

Even those insufferable chapters speak to my situation as a teacher. If Huck and Jim on the river show us the wonderful possibilities of one-to-one interaction between teacher and student, the reappearance of Tom Sawyer (along with the introduction of Aunt Sally) suggests the fragility of those possibilities when same-age peers begin to exert pressures on the mix. Once Huck has his old playmate back again, Jim doesn't stand a chance.

Poor Jim, but he has made me richer. He reads the water for me, and he tells me where the dangers are. He still castigates himself for striking his little daughter, who he thought was obstinately ignoring him when it turned out she was deaf. Sometimes a kid really can't hear you, Jim reminds me. It isn't the kid's fault. As for the wisdom of Solomon, who'd cut a baby in half just to settle an argument, Jim has no use for it:

> "De 'spute warn't 'bout a half a chile, de 'spute was 'bout a whole chile; en de man dat think he kin settle a 'spute 'bout a whole child wid a half a 'chile, doan' know enough to come in out'n de rain. Doan' talk to me 'bout Sollermun, Huck, I knows him by de back."

Jim has never taught school, but he knows how school policies can take precedence over kids. He's never met my students either, but he knows what they're worth. He'd perform dismally on the Gates-MacGinitie reading test, but he knows the value of books.

Even if he can't read them himself, he knows it's still sweet to hear the stories, sweeter still if you have the company of lively young people, as I do, and the pleasure of a good cigar, as (alas) I don't.

Maybe thanks to Jim, maybe because my limited time in this job has finally been confirmed, and certainly because she has proven herself the most approachable of colleagues, I finally open my heart to the school librarian about the banished Library of America books.

Since their brief farewell appearance in a display window, they've sat like unclaimed luggage in the squat wheeled shelves on which they were ignominiously rolled from the library to the rear of Sara's classroom last September. In grim moments I've thought of soliciting permission to erect shelves in some corner of a stairwell, of adding a lamp and an easy chair to create a makeshift reading room, an alternative library as it were, where passing students could camp out and at least pretend to read the books. I've thought of organizing an extra-credit project in which students would each adopt a volume of the Library of America, familiarize themselves with it, and then in a culminating procession conduct the exiled collection to its new home under the stairwell like the banished Furies being installed under the hill of the Acropolis, only with more of a Mardi Gras flavor. But in addition to being too much work, such measures are likely to be interpreted as an affront to the librarian. Or as evidence that I've gone completely over the edge.

So I tell the librarian what's been weighing on my mind for months, prefacing my remarks with deferential disclaimers about not wishing to presume on her authority or disrespect her good work—needless precautions given that she has done everything

short of walking about the school with a suggestion box and a
retriever monkey to garner input. But I know I can come on
strong, and this is a subject about which I feel passionate. It
turns out I do not have the passion all to myself.

"I felt terrible about moving those books from the library,"
she tells me. "They'd been collected over all those years." But she
needed the shelf space for new books, and no one had checked
them out or asked their students to consult them. In the end
she'd done her triage in the most sensible way, by feeling for a
pulse. There wasn't one.

I spare her any condescending spiels about the prerogatives
of great literature though I do tell her about the student I had
who read Montaigne and Saul Bellow in her free time and went
on to write her doctoral dissertation on Keats. I can't resist adding one appeal to the heart by saying that every time I think of
those books "not belonging in the library" I feel as though I
don't belong there either. I'm not speaking as an author but as an
English teacher. In fact, I go on to tell her, every time I remember that several of *my* books remain in the library while these
others remain in exile, I feel embarrassed. If it made a difference, I'd be happy to see mine removed in order to make room
for a few of the others. A bit melodramatic, that, but I'm about to
make my pitch.

"If you were to find a space in the library for a narrow, upright
bookcase—and I confess to having a location in mind—I would
like to leave as my legacy to the school a bookcase that could be
devoted to those Library of America volumes. If you were willing to readmit them. I'd pay for the shelves myself, no purchase
order necessary, and you would choose the catalog and the
shelf."

She doesn't say she needs time to think about the idea. She
wants to do it. I'm relieved she doesn't suggest a brass plaque with

my name. I'm even more relieved when she says I won't have to pay for the shelves.

Spring break marks the first school vacation when I have not been ill, and I celebrate with a free-for-all of physical work. I stack firewood. I burn brush. I prune trees, including the crab apple tree my expository writing students gave to me in 1985 as a housewarming gift. It was about twenty inches high then and now stands a good twelve feet, with a span of branches almost as wide. It will be awash with white blossoms by the time of final exams. "Time to plant trees is when you're young," wrote the Vermont poet James Hayford, "So, aging, you can walk in shade / That you and time together made." Several years ago I realized I had heard from no fewer than seven of my former students in a single month: a gay anarchist agitator, a hairdresser, a college professor, a guidance counselor, a dairy farmer, a Web designer, and a felon, three females and four males, all very different but all contributors to the shade that I and time together made. I continue to wonder how much richer my life might have been had I never left teaching. I've met people willing to wonder the same thing on my behalf.

One of the more remarkable and, I think, telling things about the teaching trade is the number of people who need to believe that you love it. Ever since I left the classroom in the midnineties and throughout the past year people have asked if I missed teaching or had plans to take it up again. They didn't want to know; they wanted to hear me say yes. Some didn't bother to ask. "I know the pay is not the greatest, but of course you love it," says a former student, now a thriving local entrepreneur whose income is probably triple mine. The sentiment always puts me in mind of the trope of the happy slave. In fact, our word *peda-*

gogue derives from a Greek word for a type of slave who led children to school. Jim is Huck Finn's teacher not only in spirit but
in accordance with an ancient tradition. I am not suggesting
that contemporary teachers are slaves or that I was ever treated
like one, only that I am inclined to distrust people who expect
me to work for love or who need a sentimental mythology to
gloss over the impossibilities of teaching and the daily injustices
it lays bare.

Mr. Messier never asks me if I love my job. He does often say
that he hopes I am enjoying my year at Lake Region. He tells me
that I was important to him when he was a high school student
and that I am having a similar impact on students this year. He
says that he thinks of me as the school's "artist in residence";
apparently he does not think the artisan teacher needs to die. Or
that the pastoral principal is a relic of the past. At the close of
every day, he walks the students to the buses, his figure unmistakable even with the hood of his windbreaker up. He walks
back into the building when the last bus is gone, and I feel that I
know exactly what he is thinking, that he has seen his kids off
for another day, only wishing he could see every one of them
safely home, especially the ones who dread going.

Though my role in his formation is minimal at best, I am
unabashedly proud of him, and I would be even if he never got
to be Principal of the Year. I can't say with wholehearted conviction that I love teaching. I do love him, and others I have taught
who are very different from him. Yet, even with that love and its
incomparable satisfactions, I am counting off the days until I
can go home for good.

Scores of days and hundreds of "teachable moments" remain
before that can happen, however; every week something new. I

almost can't believe what I'm seeing when the door to my class-room opens during my fourth-period Popular Fiction class and a teaching colleague of mine delivers a small boxed pizza and several other takeout orders to some girls in my class, including at least one of the sparkly girls who were identified for me as "the posse." He does not knock before entering nor does he say a word to me coming or going. The girls coo their thanks—speaking his surname as though it were his first, no Mister, no big deal—and that is that. None of them open up their parcels. No one can accuse them of eating in class. I let go of my breath and continue teaching.

After doing a reality check with Sara, who seems more infu-riated by the incident than I am, I approach the teacher after school. I see no point in taking up the issue with the girls, who would only use it as a pretext to foment the collegial tiff I am hoping to avoid. The teacher has been kind to me in the past; on several matters of technological difficulty, he's been an invalu-able help. I do my best to give the word *disrespectful* a friendly context. I am careful not to ask if the delivery was his idea or the girls'. It's a minor point anyway: he is the adult and my colleague, the one who should have known better.

He apologizes immediately. He says he never meant to show me any disrespect. He seems surprised that anyone could think so. No, no, he never intended that. From someone else I might regard the apology as disingenuous, but from him I can only regard it as sincere. In other words, I find him almost too naive to be disingenuous. If he doesn't know how capable his pizza-eating protégées are of turning on him in an instant, he's a babe in the woods.

Before that happens, they will turn on me. Or one of them will. I'm not sure if the pizza incident lit the fuse on a bundle of tensions or if they'd have exploded anyway, but I think of it as the ominous sizzle that precedes my worst day of the year. It begins the day after the delivery and in the same class.

We start the period with a Mickey Mouse quiz on the previous night's reading assignment. I have repeatedly asserted in all my classes, both orally and in writing, that I will never, except in cases of sudden illness, negotiate an individual postponement of a quiz or test once a class is in session. Negotiations of that kind should take place in the morning, before school begins, not only out of respect for the student's privacy but also in recognition of the rights of those students who come to class prepared and are entitled to expect something better than auditing someone else's (usually lame) excuses. Nevertheless, I have six students, exactly one third of the class, attempt to talk me out of taking their quiz. It is the last week of April. They have had three and a half months to learn the rule about in-class negotiations, three and a half months to adjust to my bizarre expectation that students taking a "reading elective" are actually going to read. Those with better than spotty attendance have also heard me say that I consider preparedness a matter of social responsibility. Students who don't read the assignments don't just lower their grades; they deprive their classmates of their insights. I know I wasn't dreaming when I said this, but I wonder for a moment if I'm dreaming now.

Only a sadist would subject the reader to an account of all half dozen excuses; I will confine myself to the prize. One of my students has spent her April break and another week besides vacationing with her family in Jamaica. Prior to beginning her extended absence she had all her teachers sign the official sheet indicating that she had received the assignments she would miss, a school requirement for any student with a planned absence. I signed her sheet, gave her the homework, and told her to have a good time. I never raise an eyebrow at absences like these, though some teachers do and perhaps I should. But I can't help seeing them against the background of mortality. Years ago a boy approached me and asked what I thought about his taking some days off from school to go duck hunting with his father. I told him that I hoped his father would live to a ripe old age, but given the tendency of fathers to check out of this world unexpectedly, he probably ought to go hunting with his father while he could. "Get yourself some ducks, and when it's too dark to shoot, read your book." He did both.

In this case, though, the girl appears dumbfounded that I would have expected her to read. "I was in Jamaica!" she whispers wide-eyed. (Later in the day she will vent to another teacher: "How can you expect somebody to read in Jamaica!") For a moment we must resemble one of those cartoon encounters between an alien and an earthling. We don't scream and our hair doesn't stand on end, but it's a similar instance of mutual incredulity. A reader possessed of no more than the very crudest class consciousness probably pictures some spoiled rich girl scowling as she twists the ends of her hundred-dollar haircut with her manicured fingers. In fact, this girl is neither spoiled nor rich nor given to scowling, though I suppose that if her family can spend two weeks in Jamaica she hardly qualifies for the lumpen proletariat. Still and all, I wonder if any spoiled rich girl would stoop to such an excuse. A trip to Jamaica would be no big deal to such a kid. She'd have no sense of a once-in-a-lifetime opportunity profaned by a teacher's reading assignment. It flashes through my mind that, once again, I'm dealing with poverty even when I'm not, strictly speaking, dealing with poverty.

For the most part, though, what flashes through my mind with the numbing repetitiveness of a strobe light is that I'm dealing with farce. I have a class full of high school juniors and seniors for whom *required* reading remains a novel idea. I have at least some students for whom placing a fast food order with a teacher is a perfectly tenable idea. I have a colleague ready, willing, and able to deliver the order piping hot to their desks. Worst of all, I have a class full of students who, in spite of all kinds of cooperative learning exercises, not to mention the most ostentatious displays of "school spirit," seem not to have much care for one another's welfare. Time and again I break them into heterogeneous groups to tackle some task, urging them to leave no one out, *rewarding* them for leaving no one out, only to watch as the strongest show the least regard for the weak, isolating them not only from the work at hand but from any part in the shenanigans that enliven the work. And now two of my brightest are talking with the quiz still in progress. And now you are going to see me not at my best.

I start out well enough, though I'd have done better merely to make note of the infraction, collect the quizzes, and give each student the zero she knows is the consequence for talking during a test. Instead—call this mistake number one—I ask the two to speak to me outside the room. I'm concerned by what I perceive as the brazenness of the infraction; it wasn't something I "caught" so much as something I felt I was meant to see. Need I say that none of this has to do with cheating? Both students had turned their quizzes face down on their desks when they began to talk. Neither was among the six who tried to excuse themselves from the evaluation. What this has to do with is the common courtesy that I expect even the smartest kid to show and even the slowest kid to enjoy. In a feeble attempt to make the concept of mutuality better understood, I try putting it on a different footing.

"Have I ever disrespected either of you?" I ask. "Because if I have, I want you to tell me when and how so I can apologize." Both say no. Why then have they broken a rule that they know is important to me? One girl, who broke the silence merely to answer the question put to her by the other, is obviously regret-ful, maybe for my sake, probably for the sake of her grade. (And I wonder later if she was thinking to herself: He tolerated the effrontery of having hot food delivered to certain special charac-ters during a class discussion without a single word of protest, and now he's lecturing me about disrespect?) The other girl is of a more explosive temperament. "Go ahead and give me the frig-gin' zero," she says. As I ought to surmise, her ire probably has very little to do with me. More likely it has to do with whatever set of intolerable conditions prevented her from reading her assign-ment, perhaps with the fact she is *never* one to make excuses or ask for a break. Possibly she is also losing patience with a man she perceives as a tiresome pedant, utterly oblivious to the world out-side his precious books.

In any case she goes on to say, "I'm the type of person who when she wants to say something she just says it." In other words, I counter, the type of person who makes her own rules. "Yes," she says. Before I can check the impulse to sarcasm, I say, "Then I wish you luck in the world as it is." "Oh," she says, "I imagine I'm going to be pretty lucky." Does she really? I'm not sarcastic when I say, "I hope you truly are."

That's the end of the discussion, during which I'm sure there have been further, much more egregious interruptions of the testing session—to say nothing of the tension I've added by step-ping out of the room. (As an aside, I'll note that Mr. Messier is out of the building today, and though the school always runs smoothly on the rare occasions when he's absent, I sense a psy-chic ripple in the building when he's gone.) Even here, I have the opportunity to cut my losses if I'll take it, but I don't. Part of my problem is that I'm not sure there's all that much to lose. Respect? Good will? I'm granting requests from the sublime to the ridicu-lous from the minute I step into this building until the minute I go home; is it too much to ask that a couple of mine could also be granted?

I've not been keeping count, but by this point we must be up to my fourth or fifth mistake, which consists of turning from my hallway conference to vent my frustrations (not a mistake unless you do it *while you're frustrated*) by telling the entire class I've just about had it with the lack of preparation, the constant excuses, the flouting of a few simple rules, and not least of all the smug attitudes of people who either can work faster than their peers or else are beyond caring one way or another about their own academic performance. Is this what our much-touted school spirit comes down to, yelling at pep rallies and then treating our classmates as though they're beneath contempt?

"You're judging us!" a student calls out, though I suspect she has already judged herself in the light of what I've said and is not happy with what she sees. "You don't know what we're thinking!" She's right, I say. I am judging, and I don't know what other people are thinking. But I'm not judging *people* or attempting to read their minds. I'm judging the only thing I can judge. I write two words on the blackboard, rapidly and in large letters: THOUGHTS and ACTIONS. In the process my chalk breaks in my hand. I pick up another piece and finish. I point to the second word and say, "This is all anybody can judge. Listen: all your life you're going to meet people who *think* they're not racists—'Don't get me wrong, I've got nothing against black people'—but if their actions say otherwise, what are you left to conclude?"

Mistake number whatever-we're-up-to-now: using analogies with people who almost always see them as literal comparisons. Add to that the mistake—perhaps the worst of the bunch—of addressing an entire class on matters that do not, in all particulars, refer to every member of the class. The problem with the mind-set that would seek the one lost sheep at the expense of the ninety-nine is the real risk of haranguing the ninety-nine for always getting lost. And if that happens to be accurate, as is close to being the case here, it's a piss-poor way to say thanks to the one or two sheep who've never once given you a lick of trouble.

I might be able to acknowledge these exceptions, but nothing I have to say is permitted development, qualification, half a chance. For one thing, I'm still susceptible to bouts of coughing. For another, I'm being challenged before I can complete my thoughts. Finally, one of the students—the one who's the type of person to say what's on her mind no matter what—becomes so abrasive that I ask her to go to the principal's office, something I've not done with any student since the beginning of the year. On her way out she refers to my breaking of a piece of chalk as evidence that I am "out of control." When a friend gets up to go with her, I remind her that I've not given her permission to leave. She doesn't care. Sensing the potential for momentum, a third girl stands up from her desk—one of the pizza recipients from yesterday—walks to the door, and exhorts the entire class to follow her to the office. "Come on, guys," she says. She has no takers. When the other girl who'd been talking during the quiz meekly asks if she can go to the guidance office, a request I never refuse, the number of exiles grows to four.

Suddenly the room feels eerily quiet. The silence is broken by a young man who sits near the back of the room, not my best student but possibly my most mature and without a doubt my volunteer fireman of choice (he has a beeper on his belt and the insignia of his town squad tattooed on his shoulder) should I ever be so out of control as to yell "Fire!" when I'm burning alive. "Well, now that they've left," he says dryly, "we can get something done."

Everything in our brief history leads me to believe he is saying this in support, though it might also be his politic way of saying that I have allowed a few students and a few of my frustrations to waste a lot of our time. I will pay for that mistake in kind. So will other students, who will lack my full attention in the classes that follow. First, I need to find time to speak to my department head. I can always count on her to be in my corner, but I never want her blindsided by any action of mine. She sizes up the incident even before I can finish my account. It's part of a larger pattern, she says, and I'm relieved to discover she doesn't mean any pattern of mine. By her count this is the third time one of these girls has attempted to stage a mass walkout and the first time it didn't succeed. In one instance the walkout accompanied— Sara does not say it caused—a teacher's termination partway through the year.

I'm glad she tells me this. Without that information I might be even more stunned than I am when a girl from the class asks me later in the day if I'm "going to be fired." "Why on earth would you think I was going to be fired?" I ask. "I don't know. I just don't want you to be." I'm also glad when a teacher from another department sticks his head in my door and says, "You're not the first to have a run-in with this crew. Hold the line."

But there is no line to hold, not really. I give my account to the vice principal, who has already heard my defectors' version, in which the broken piece of chalk figures prominently. I'm momentarily stunned when he says he's randomly asked other students in the class for an account of what happened. Sara later tells me that given the individuals involved this was a prudent move on his part. For now, I can't help but feel hurt that my word is not enough. "And what did the other students tell you?" I ask. "Exactly what you told me," he says, adding that he is not surprised. He's already decided on his course of action. The students who left class without permission will be given a "cut" and disciplined accordingly. The student sent to the office for rudeness will serve a detention or face further consequences. Parents will be notified of the actions taken, as will Mr. Messier when he returns to school.

In my account of what happened I felt I should mention the pizza incident of the day before. The vice principal is keen to know the name of the teacher who delivered the goods—adding that "Mr. Messier would very much want to know this"—but I say I can't tell him. The teacher apologized to me when I approached him, and it would be disgraceful to name him now. I only brought up the incident, I say, to describe the climate in which these events occurred.

No doubt I also brought it up to look as sympathetic as possible. The matter has been settled so definitively, and so clearly in my favor—but with a cool objectivity, too—that I'm feeling uneasy. Any teacher might, and any person who thinks that schools will always take a teacher's side (or should) has never worked in a school. Some years ago in a school very close to mine, a teacher's aide went to her principal to report that she'd seen one of the eighth-grade boys exposing himself and urinating outside the school. She hoped to report her observation anonymously but the principal would have none of that. An accomplished practitioner of "conflict resolution," he told the aide to remain right where she was while he called the boy down to the office to confront his accuser.

"Mrs. Miller says she saw you expose yourself and urinate in front of the school. Did you do that?"

"Nope."

"Then why did Mrs. Miller say that's what you were doing?"

"Dunno."

"Do you think it's possible," the principal offered in complete seriousness, appealing to Mrs. Miller as well as the boy, "that you were holding a bottle of soda and spilled some of it accidentally in a way that made it look like you were doing what Mrs. Miller thinks you were doing?"

"That's it!" said the boy. "That's what happened." Problem solved, though that is not the punch line. Mrs. Miller happens to have a husband and four sons, which, though it hardly qualifies her to sit on the Supreme Court, does give her impeccable credentials as an expert witness in any case involving the difference between a urinating penis and a spilling bottle of soda. I don't take it for granted that I've fared much better than Mrs. Miller.

And still I'm uneasy. In the course of our conversation, as he's giving me all the support any teacher could want, the vice principal makes an observation that takes me aback no less than "I was in Jamaica!" and "Are you going to be fired?" Conceding that the students who came to the office were exaggerating for effect, he notes: "Now if you'd broken a piece of chalk deliberately because you were upset, I could understand how they might be afraid."

Really? Not if I'd thrown the chalk across the room or aimed it at one of them, or forced the chalk into one of their hands, or chalked an insult on their desks or persons, but if I broke a piece of chalk deliberately, in my own hand, in my own frustration at being ignored, provoked, and then defied, that might give a person pause? *A piece of chalk?*

Well, I know I did not break the piece of chalk deliberately, and none of my students would be frightened if I did. I'm actually more prone to break chalk in a good mood than in a bad one. I teach with fervor, I write with vigor, and I write my words large. I'm as likely to drop my chalk into the tray as to place it there when I'm done. I'm breaking chalk all the time. My classroom floor is littered with it. Most days my clothes are covered with dust. The ghost of my scrawl remains on the blackboard even after I've erased the words.

And yet, like Twain's Jim, who's ready to believe that he dreamed his separation from Huck until he sees the condition of the raft, I actually go to the chalk tray in my classroom to see if it looks as I remember it. I examine its contents like a cancer candidate checking his stools for blood. It is full of white and yellow nubs of chalk, many of them worn to uselessness. But is there broken chalk? Yes, there is a quantity of broken chalk—not a single accusatory piece, implicating me in a trauma, but the humdrum litter of fragments I expect to find. I am not an evil teacher. I do not deliberately break chalk.

At the close of what feels like the longest day of the school year, I stand outside my classroom as the students make their way down the hall to the buses. It's my customary place at this time of day, as is true for a number of my colleagues, who use the opportunity for an extra word of cheer, a final reminder, the swooping up of an assignment that was due "no later than three this afternoon." It feels like a good day to remain at my desk, I've had enough interactions to last me a month, but I'm determined to show I'm still here, still spiffy and shameless in my chalk-dusted jacket and tie.

As the last stragglers begin to pick up their pace to a slow run, a girl halts in front of me and blurts out, "You're the greatest, Mr. Keizer!" That's all. The final stun-gun moment in a day full of them. I don't ask why she would say this, though I might well wonder. She's not in any of my classes. I'm not even sure I know her name. We've had a few friendly exchanges, many of them outside the door of the special education classroom where she spends a good part of each day, nothing beyond a few words.

But I bet I know what she's trying to tell me. In fact, I'm in the mood this afternoon to place all kinds of bets. I bet, for example, that she heard about my little set-to less than an hour after it happened. I bet she knows all the key players by name. I bet she knows them better than I do, and I bet she knows at least one of them better than she wishes she did. Oh, but these are all bets I could lose. Best put my money on surer things. I bet nobody ever fetched this kid a pizza in the middle of her fourth-period class.

11

MAY

"Think about something cheerful, old man," he said. "Every minute now you are closer to home."

—Ernest Hemingway, *The Old Man and the Sea*

Osama bin Laden is killed on the second day of the month. I'm expecting a barrage of comments, in anticipation of which I decide to let Homer speak my piece. From top to bottom on my blackboard I write a dozen lines from *The Odyssey*, what Odysseus says after he has slain the suitors and his faithful servant Eurykleia is about to rejoice. "No crowing aloud," he tells her, though he's willing to add that the suitors got what they deserved. "To glory over slain men is no piety."

The last time I did something like this was back in September, when two soldiers from a Northeast Kingdom town were killed in Afghanistan. I chose the Who for my spokespersons, writing the names of the soldiers on the blackboard "in memoriam" before playing the song "Young Man Blues" (the live version from Leeds). That was a matter of five minutes between classes, just enough time to permit Roger Daltry a few feral repetitions of the "nuthin" that is a young man's allotted portion "these days." I leave the lines from Homer up for the better part of a week.

Still, no one asks me what they mean or what they are doing on my blackboard. As nearly as I can tell, no one reads them. For that matter, no one mentions Osama bin Laden. At the close of the third day there is nothing left for me to do but erase the lines and go for a haircut, which in my case involves reducing a half inch of salt-and-pepper thatch to a maintenance-free quarter and which I know will infallibly arouse keen interest and lively comment (all of it sweet) the next day.

On other fronts, the written word is holding its own. We're doing drama now and soon to start poetry. I wish I hadn't put them off until late spring. I discover how much the students enjoy reading aloud—especially what was always meant to be read that way. Girls vie for the part of Emily in *Our Town*; the unlikeliest boys take a shot at Whitman's *Song of Myself*. I come to suspect that it is not reading my students hate so much as reading in isolation. The same radical privacy that I seek in books, my mind's way of eating its lunch alone, is what turns their stomachs. I learn of two girls in my tenth-grade classes who got through *Ethan Frome* by reading aloud to each other over Skype, not unlike George Gibbs and Emily Webb chatting between their upstairs bedroom windows, just with different kinds of windows. They are acutely *social* creatures, these kids, and it is a slow learner indeed who fails to grasp that fact even as he prattles on about building a more social democracy.

The relative brevity of the genres, as well as the empty spaces on the page between poetic stanzas and lines of dramatic dialogue, works in our favor too. For several years now (perhaps as my closeted answer to the question "Do you miss teaching?") I've kept a notebook for a reading curriculum I hope to develop someday. It would be aimed at the most marginal teenage readers and incorporate some of the world's most venerated texts. The linchpin of the program would be the use of radically short genres: the aphorism, the slogan, the haiku, the epigram, the epitaph, the joke, etc. The twin objectives would be to put the noses of nonreaders in books for part of each day and to lift their chins the rest of the time. When college-bound peers turned aside from their SparkNotes summaries of *Beowulf* long enough to ask, "So what're you reading, Rodney," Rodney could answer, "Nothing much. Just Pindar and Lao-tzu and them guys." A mere three lines of text could easily inspire as many pages of prose and as many periods of class discussion. Instead of giving remedial readers baby bottles of formula fiction you'd be giving them shot glasses of 100-proof insight. This week "Awake and sing, all ye who dwell in dust," next week "Workers of the world unite!" As I said, someday. Right now I have gems aplenty with Emily Dickinson's packed quatrains and the more imagistic pieces of William Carlos Williams, who also gives us plums "so sweet / and so cold."

Reading poetry with my sophomores reminds me of reading it when I was a sophomore myself, when a twenty-two-year-old raven-haired beauty named Miss Pombo inspired me to raze "electrical engineer" from my future horizon and write "poet" in its place. I can hardly hope to have the same impact. Her enthusiasm for her students and for what she taught was irrepressible; even my skeptical father was prompted to say to her after a parent-teacher conference, "You were born to teach." And he hadn't even had the experience of listening to her read from Lawrence Ferlinghetti's *A Coney Island of the Mind* as she dangled her dusky legs from the edge of her desk. I wasn't the only boy who took a keen interest in all things literary that year. Ferlinghetti marked the beginning of my lifelong love affair with New Directions paperbacks, and I suppose that for a time I also

had a crush on my teacher. Perhaps it showed; a female classmate rubbed my back consolingly after we saw Miss Pombo take
the arm of the business education teacher one night after the
showing of a film in the school auditorium. "Poor Garret," she
sighed, seeming to hint that I might consider paying more attention to women my age. Eventually I would come under the wing
of the business teacher too, who lent me Sartre's *Nausea* to read,
another New Directions paperback, and who made the administration itchy by growing a beard. When the couple married a
few years later, they invited me to write a poem for their wedding. I was out of high school by then and publishing poetry in
little magazines, but I owed my initiation to Miss Pombo, who'd
also set me up for Sartre by writing the word *existentialism* on
her blackboard.

In past years this would be around the time I'd be introducing the same word to my Advanced Placement English class, a
bonus lecture as we worked our way through Beckett, Kafka,
and Camus. I have no hankering to do such a thing this year, no
more than I have to be teaching AP, but the lecture comes to
mind with the scent of cut grass wafting through my classroom
window. Most of my seniors were less than enamored with the
Continental authors, less impressed than I thought they'd be by
Gregor Samsa's metamorphosis, but they loved the existential
stuff. It wasn't unusual to have a few of them claim to have
found, at long last, an identifier they could live with. Their
fathers were hippies or Republicans; they were existentialists. At
the time I construed their enthusiasm as of a piece with their
enjoyment of Anne Rice and Stephen King, their counterpart to
my classmates' fascination with the Hell's Angels and the Doors.
It was scary and dark, this stuff about a godless universe
(Kierkegaard never impresses an adolescent imagination so well
as Nietzsche) and radical free will, the imperative to make one's

own meaning in the face of death, the decision to stay in bed on a school day clarified as the destiny of creatures *condemned to choose*. This year, though, I find myself wondering if the existential leanings of those AP kids had more to do with the similarities between their daily routine as students and the notion that existence is absurd. What better title for an anthology that included *The Myth of Sisyphus*, *The Penal Colony*, and *Waiting for Godot* than *Three Ways to Look at High School*?

Such thoughts as these come with the season. May can be an absurd month, fraught with seemingly meaningless interruptions, a feckless teacher's windfall but a conscientious teacher's nightmare come true. No upended cockroach ever felt so immobilized; all my little legs are going at once, but I'm going nowhere. A guidance counselor informs me that over half my third-period sophomores will be fifteen minutes late for class in order to complete their course sign-ups for next year. The day before that, a science class canoe trip—the rivers are finally iced out—took a quarter of my first-period Composition class. Other field trips dependent on spring weather and clear roads are sure to follow. Next week classes have been shortened to accommodate AP exams. The NECAP practice essays remain an ongoing part of the English regimen, and I'm still arranging makeups for the kids who missed all or part of the Gates-MacGinitie reading test we gave in April. Graduation practice, the prom, and "senior skip day" (as hallowed as it is unauthorized) are still a ways off, but preparations are already in the air.

For all that, I take a particular pleasure in this May, and I think it owes to more than balmy weather and the realization that—to paraphrase Shelley—if May is here, June can't be far behind. I've accomplished most of what I hoped to, and I have enough experience under my belt to know that "most" is the best a teacher (or any other mortal) dares hope for. I also know from past experience to approach the end of the year with diminished expectations—to plan for it as though it contained fewer days than the calendar indicates, which in point of fact it does.

The Popular Fiction class I feared I might have lost has pretty much come around. I've approached the "mopping up" of last month's debacle with the best strategic combination I know: scrupulous preparedness, a touch more formality, zero tolerance for the slightest testing of the rules, unflappable calmness when meting out the consequences, and unconditional acceptance of every step taken toward reconciliation. I've not adjusted a single one of my classroom requirements, nor would I consider doing so—first, because I continue to believe they're right, and second, because any retreat now would be disastrous. That said, I try to remember what I have too often forgotten to my peril: as far as teaching goes, when all you are is right, what you really are is in trouble. As the Israeli poet Yehuda Amichai wrote: "From the place where we are right / flowers will never grow." Had I managed to be just a little more than right when things started blowing up in my face, perhaps nothing more than a bit humorous, I might have had a few flowers to pick for consolation.

As it turns out, I get the flowers anyway. They arrive in May, when the other north country flowers begin to bloom. One of them comes from a private conversation with one of my former mutineers, whom I discover walking the halls one day with tearstained cheeks and bloody knuckles. I have nothing to do with the reason she punched the girls' room wall, but perhaps she's able to see me as someone who might understand how a person could. I am, after all, a man who writes with enough passion to break chalk. I try to help her put her troubles in perspective. I recall (but do not quote) a school bus driver who told me once that the reason young people commit suicide is that they haven't lived long enough to realize that most situations improve if we wait another day. That sounded wise, though not all of us will manage to live as long as the driver did. I hope this young woman will. I praise what I've observed of her integrity, her intelligence and fierce heart—what I wish I'd expressed more emphatically before now. I also coax her to let me escort her to the nurse's office. I wish her luck as I take my leave, but not aloud. I wouldn't want to sound sarcastic or give the impression that the best thing she has going for her is luck. It isn't.

Other flowers come from the same rocky May schedule in which it seems nothing will grow. A combination of absences, some of them prom-related, reduces the Popular Fiction class to a motley handful, including some of my poorest-performing students and some of my brightest. Not all of them will skip the prom but apparently none of them feel any need to skip school the day before. We're in the midst of discussing Jon Krakauer's *Into the Wild*. (As it's been taught in recent years, Popular Fiction includes popular nonfiction whose authors have taken discernible imaginative liberties.) Suddenly what I've thought of as my weakest class yields one of the best discussions of the year. Almost everyone participates. No one seems cowed by anyone else, and some of the questions raised are as good as anything I used to get in AP. It's like watching a pickup game of basketball where the only object is to keep the ball in motion and to see it swish through the net as often as the laws of physics allow. The students pass ideas from one to another; they're quick to lift any player who falls. "This is what I think Justin might be trying to say." Dribbling faster than anyone on the court, taking the longest shots, snatching one another's rebounds almost as soon as they're off the rim are the two girls who zeroed out for talking during last month's quiz. They're not vying for points, merely showing what they can do, perhaps seeing if they can make me smile. They can. And laugh for joy.

My cough is back, not that it ever went away. It's become more noticeable, though. An X-ray is ordered but my lungs are clear. I'm told to "keep an eye on it," words that some malign power seems to take as an invitation for a practical joke. I come down with conjunctivitis, pink eye, first in one eye and then in both. After everything else I've caught, it's almost amusing. I look like a rabbit on a bender.

Always finicky where my eyes are concerned, I'm hopeless at using my prescribed eye drops. Kathy does her best to put them in at night and recommends I get help with the daylight dose from the school nurses. There are two of them, Joannie, who does the review of blood-borne pathogens at the start of the year, and Jeannette. They draw a curtain around me, instructing me to lie down on the couch. They give me a spot on the ceiling to watch as they sneak in the drops. They dab at the missed shots, a hint of how they must dab tears and disinfect bruised knuckles. I don't wonder that some of my students are constantly asking to see the nurse. I never refuse them permission, though I always call down to the nurse's office in advance of their arrival, just in case they pass out on the way or, as is far more likely, are tempted to go on walkabout for the next half hour. But the nurse's office is the main draw, and I get requests backed by explanations that I'd have thought would embarrass most high school kids: a Band-Aid for an invisible paper cut, a checkup for a stubbed toe, each but a notch or two below a kiss on a boo-boo. I'm grateful they have the option.

In later life my students will seek the same consolations from

masseuses and hairdressers, bartenders and truck-stop wait-
resses, always at their own cost and on their own time and often
without that gentle affirmative nudge to "go back to work because
you're just fine, really." Something we can all stand to hear now
and then. In my version of the perfect world, every workplace
would have, in addition to basketball hoops and a marching
band, the equivalent of a school nurse. And every school would
have a cosmetologist and an athletic trainer; I couldn't begin to
guess how many "discipline problems" originate in a student's
hatred of his or her appearance. But at the moment not all schools
even have nurses. Their elimination for the sake of fiscal auster-
ity, along with that of art and music teachers and guidance counselors, evokes a world very different from the one I conjure, a
world in which any attempt at loveliness is suspect and every
form of meanness is the rule.

For now, at least, Lake Region and its "extras" seem relatively
safe, its sports programs safer still. I'm glad. On my way to the
faculty parking lot I pass the boys' baseball team doing a fielding
drill on the grass. It's a balmy day; the side doors have been
propped open to take advantage of the breeze. I don't know for
sure, but it's possible the diamond on the upper campus is still
soggy from snowmelt or a recent shower. Or maybe the JV squad
has it today—I'm the last person who would know. These are the
varsity players in any case, some of them students of mine. One
by one their coach smacks each of them a ground ball, the player
on deck catches or retrieves it, throwing it to the captain, who
stands, glove at the ready, beside the coach. The rhythm is brisk
but unhurried, punctuated by the crack of ball on bat, the slap of
ball on glove, and short exclamations, mostly of praise and mostly
from the coach.

In these after-school hours, "Coach" is what he's called, but
he also happens to be the school's vice principal. Not that many

years ago he was an outstanding player for Sacred Heart High School, one of our two rivals to the north. He was captain of his team and also its catcher, details I've gathered as the year's progressed. So I understand now, as I didn't understand last August, that when he appeared before the faculty in his catcher's outfit on that second dreadful staff development day, he was not in costume so much as in his most familiar second skin. It's possible he was needing as much armor that day as I was. "This is who I really am," he might have been telling us, not the school's hatchet man down in the office but a player on your team whose job it is to catch anything thrown at him, sometimes one of your pissed-off students and sometimes the assignment of coming up with a staff development exercise that's bound to piss at least one of you off.

I shouldn't be putting words in his mouth. But I know from our conversations that he lives for these afternoons. They're part of what keeps him sane, perhaps the better part of what entitles him to still think of himself as a teacher. I'm glad he has this reward at the end of the day. It lifts my spirits to see him enjoying it.

I envy him too, as I do coaches in general. They work long hours for little pay, and they get more scrutiny and flak in several months than many teachers get in as many years—especially in seasons when losses outnumber wins—but they can count on their players' motivation. They don't have to hawk their wares. They set up their booths and the customers come, all of them willing and most of them able. Coaches save some of the most endangered kids and make heroes out of the most gifted. Yes, and some coaches are perfect jerks. But the ones who know what they're doing, who keep their eye on what's most important as zealously as they want their players to keep their eyes on the ball, can be magnificent. If gifted teachers are the great prose authors of a school, its novelists, orators, and essayists, gifted coaches are its poets.

Once I'm to my car it occurs to me that I haven't taken a single photograph all year that wasn't connected to a project or a field trip. Most of the time, I've been too focused on doing a good job and keeping things straight to take in the sights, much less to catch any with a camera. Still, I'm glad I have no camera with me this afternoon. That would make it too easy to lose a picture I intend to keep. I fix my pink eyes on the image and snap a mental photograph of "Coach" and his "men" before backing out of my space, a memento of May days at Lake Region, and as good as any yearbook to me.

By popular demand and for several of my own reasons, not the least of which is to give as many students as possible the chance of a strong finish, I do a reprise of the museum project I did the previous fall. I gave the assignment in March, with a preapproval date of April 1 and a completion date of May 11—plenty of time for the more conscientious students to peck away at the task, but also, as I know only too well, plenty of time for the others to procrastinate. Whether we ought to spend time doing something like this again is another question altogether.

The impetus to repeat an assignment that went reasonably well the first time around is at once risky and irresistible. Risky, because it's likely to go less well the second time, after the novelty is gone. Irresistible, because one wants the chance to make a good thing better. In a different situation, I could say, "Next year, I'm going to do the 'museum' this way," but there is no next year for me. I want my students to have a second try as well, the importance of which I'm not sure I grasped fully as a younger teacher. If students who fell down on their first attempt because of poor time management, shoddy workmanship, or an ill-conceived partnership take a better tack this time, then their sense of success will be doubled. They'll have the good grade and the satisfaction of having risen above their deficiencies.

With all of this in mind, I try to devise the widest possible array of project suggestions. I retain the options for students to engage with the literature in a hands-on way by doing paintings, sculptures, dioramas, board games, needlepoint or, in a more literary way, by composing fiction, poetry, a dramatic monologue, or a screenplay based on the novels we've read. As in the fall, I appeal to special interests with options to create a computer game, a scrapbook (a popular hobby of late, at least in the hinterlands), or a song. New to the list are a 4-H-style project connected to Lennie's rabbits in *Of Mice and Men*, a lecture (for example, "The Influence of *Huckleberry Finn* on American Literature"), a debate ("Is *Huckleberry Finn* a racist novel?") based on research, and a full-scale model of a Mississippi river raft, also based on some research. Obviously, I'm hoping for a few second tries in that area as well.

The results, when they come in, are on the whole a level above the ones I received in October. The enthusiasm is at least as strong, no small achievement given the lateness in the year. It doesn't surprise me that I get no lectures or debates; nor does it surprise me that I do get rabbits, or one rabbit anyway, so for several days my classroom has some of the earthy sensations of a kindergarten or a biology lab. (Has there been any research, I wonder, comparable to what's been done in nursing homes and prisons, on the stress-reducing effects of having animals in a school environment?) Two boys undertake to build a life-sized raft and truck it to school, upping the ante by using hand axes to fell and shape the trees for the sake of authenticity. "Huck wouldn't have had a chainsaw," they tell me. The raft includes a wigwam made of evergreen branches and a sand-bottomed fire pit. The boys park their replica outside the side door of the building with a sign on the wall of the stairwell inviting passersby to step out for a look. It feels like the perfect symbol of our mission: to get away from the prim Widow Douglas and float free for a while.

Even so, we are no farther from the riverbank and its cruelties than Huck and Jim are. Not all the students have adults to help them with their projects. One of the boys who builds the raft tells me he still plans to join the marines after he graduates. Another student turns to one of the school custodians for help in restoring an old sleigh that he identifies as Ethan Frome's for our museum and will give to his little sister when he takes it home. Perhaps there's a marine sergeant who'll take a custodial interest in his classmate, moved by the *Semper Fi* already tattooed on his arm.

We get a steady stream of visitors. Some come merely for the refreshments, but most seem impressed by the handiwork and leave their compliments in our guest book. We have sprawling dioramas of the dream farm that George conjures for Lennie, a homemade DVD abridgment of *Ethan Frome*, and a cut-paper mosaic of the sun rising over the old man and the sea that arrests the attention of nearly every visitor who enters the room and proves for anybody who ever doubted it that inexpensive materials combined with care and talent can produce marvelous results.

The museum takes up several days. It fortifies grades, as do the dreary NECAP practice essays, five in all. I'm surprised that most of the students do not seem to mind the latter. They brainstorm the one about how to instruct a new student to use the cafeteria as enthusiastically as if we were engaged in writing a recipe for success in love. I suppose I shouldn't be so amazed. If they are anything, my sophomores are good sports. And sports may provide the best metaphors for explaining their enthusiasm. The trouble with school is that we divide too much of a student's work between tests that "count" and practices that don't—not unlike the way we regulate athletics. Granted, it would be absurd to do the reverse, to grade students when they're still at the practice stage or to give exams that are "just for fun." But occasionally to combine the carefree intensity of practice with a guaranteed high score for good-faith effort has definite benefits. The kids are secure in their spontaneity and secure that it will bring them some reward.

I confess I'm not completely comfortable with the custom of giving an automatic 100 to every student who addresses the prompt and fills the space in a more or less satisfactory fashion. I don't begrudge the students their 100s, but I resent the overall implications. You can blow off Mark Twain so long as you play ball for us on the standardized tests, the reason being that while the first has to do only with your progress toward becoming an educated human being, the latter has to do with your teachers' ability to remain gainfully employed at an accredited school. Surely the matter is not so cynical as that, but it comes close. I take care not to let my cynicism show. I return each set of practices with a few comments on each paper—the volume permits little more—and a more substantial set of general comments (printed on a handout for everyone), all derived from repeated strengths or mistakes I've observed on the papers. I tell students that they should study these sheets for their final exam. No automatic 100s for that.

For the most part, their efforts on the NECAP practices are not depressing. Since the writings are done by hand, the word processor is not able to give the false impression of a finished product or enable speed of composition to outstrip careful thought. Predictably, some students do not complete all five practices. Not even the promise of an automatic 100 is enough to entice them. If you can get such a high grade for one paper, maybe you only need to write three. That Exeter teacher who said that laziness was the curable learning disability and stupidity the incurable may have erred not so much in his taxonomy as in his prognosis. If stupidity and laziness are truly all we have to contend with, then I'll take the task of curing stupidity. Only a less lazy man than I would try to find a cure for the other.

As if in homage to the season, babies in carry-on car seats begin to appear in the hallways, life-sized baby dolls, as it turns out, a project for a class in parenting. I recall a similar assignment from my previous teaching stint, though then it was done with a swaddled egg in a cigar box. The symbolism was obvious, emphasizing the fragility of a newborn. In the updated, higher-tech version, the students, all girls as far as I can tell, are expected to attend to the artificial infant's simulated needs, responding promptly whenever it cries and keeping close watch over it, though the dolls don't break as easily as the eggs did.

The parenting class is offered only to juniors and seniors but lo and behold a sophomore girl shows up in my last-period class with baby in hand. It seems the "mother" has absented herself from school for a day or two in order to handle her prodigious prom arrangements and has left the baby with a round-the-clock sitter, teasing out the simulation, to say nothing of the irony, more than she probably knows. But I have to say, her choice of a sitter is impeccable, a girl I'd surely have chosen were I needing one for any child of mine. Meredith already has the experience, for one thing, routinely caring for her little niece, who lives with her on the family farm. She also works part-time at McDonald's,

competes as an amateur wrestler (a pursuit I find hard to recon-
cile with her diminutive height and demure behavior, though
I've been told she can "beat the shit out of any boy in this school"),
reads her drowsy big brother's English assignments aloud to him
as he drives her to school in his truck (he's up at 2:00 a.m. doing
barn chores and occasionally nods off in my first-period class),
and can always be counted on to bring a pan of home-baked
cookies for an after-school study session (even when she herself
can't stay) and to deliver A+ speaking assignments, like the one
on historical infatuation entitled "How I Stalked J.F.K." A pearl
of a girl, in other words, so I'm glad she has charge of the "baby,"
not only because she'll see it gets the right care but also because I
hope she'll see, if she hasn't already, that this is a responsibility
she doesn't need for a while.

Midway through the period the doll erupts in a fit of wailing.
My first thought is to ask who has their blasted cell phone on
and whatever possessed them to choose such a perverse ring-
tone. Then I notice Meredith, clearly mortified by the outburst—
this is a kid who waits patiently until everyone has finished
speaking before putting her pencil into the noisy electric sharp-
ener. Smiling, I offer to rock the doll for her while I teach. "No,"
she says, "I'll take care of it," and hurries from the room.

Five minutes later I am still doing my teach-at-Armageddon
routine and the baby is still screaming out in the hall. Finally,
one of the students says, "Mr. Keizer, I think maybe you better
go out there."

When I do, I find Meredith frantically trying to turn a black
plastic key into the control box at the back of the doll. She is visibly distressed. I feel a bit rattled myself at this point—the cry is
"fake" but up close it arouses a very real and even primal
response. I also try the key to no avail, noticing that there are
written directions (and we know how much good they do) to

turn the key clockwise. What I also discover is that the lady wrestler or some caretaker before her has succeeded in twisting the key into a worthless corkscrew of plastic. It turns only on itself. Can you get in touch with the student who gave this to you? I ask, raising my voice to be heard. She can't. She adds that if the crying is deactivated by any other method than turning the key it could compromise the other student's grade. I couldn't give a fig, I want to say, but instead ask if she knows the teacher in charge of the parenting class. No, she's somebody up at the career center ten miles to the north.

The doll keeps wailing, louder, it seems. I am indignant on behalf of Meredith and on my own behalf as well. We have been handed "a situation" for which we have not been prepared. Somewhat beyond what the assignment intends, we are feeling what every parent feels at one time or another: overwhelmed, clueless, and (needlessly) alone.

I tell Meredith what I think we should do and reluctantly she nods her head. I pop the voice box from the doll's plastic back. Like something out of Poe, the box continues wailing in my hand as I stare at it dumbfounded. Wanting to stomp the thing under my boot, I pull the ribbon that expels the batteries and the noise finally stops.

But the simulation continues, at least for one deathly moment. In real life, in a predicament not too far removed from the experience of many of my students, I would not have been this girl's teacher. I would have been her boyfriend, perhaps the baby's father, perhaps not. I couldn't have pulled out the batteries, because there wouldn't have been any batteries to pull out. Instead, I would have taken up the infant in a fit of frustration and shaken it until it either died or became permanently eligible for special services. I, in turn, would have become eligible to have my deer-in-the-headlights mug shot appear in the police blotter of the local paper. Another stupid redneck loser gets his. Or, if you prefer, another shaken, stunned, and stunted baby boy comes of age in the richest nation in the world.

I do not have to wonder if any of my students are thinking these same thoughts. I do not have to wonder because, when I step back into the classroom, I tell them exactly what I think.

12

JUNE

> Our school was not the worst. It certainly did teach me a few things: elementary knowledge, the habit of methodical work, and outward discipline. . . . The same school, however, sowed in me, contrary to its direct purpose, the seeds of enmity for the existing order. These seeds . . . did not fall on barren ground.
>
> —Leon Trotsky, *My Life*

June is the accordion month of the school calendar: its final day remains tentative almost till the end, when the total number of unanticipated school closing days is finally known along with the number that will have to be made up to finish out the contracted year. Beyond that, teachers will each have their own informal ending dates, depending on their ability to put their affairs in order prior to the summer recess. Especially for heads of departments, the last day of the term can fall late in the month or even early in July. I remember those extra days from my own tenure as a department head, when it seemed I'd never get out.

I have determined that whatever it requires, the official last day will be *my* last day. In this I have both Sara's and Mr. Messier's support. I'm also determined that nothing will cause me to leave under a cloud. I feel like a soldier counting down the days remaining in his tour of duty: lucky up till now, he waits for the bullet to come out of the blue, the street to explode under his feet. I try not to be superstitious. More than that, I try not to be careless. This is especially important at this time of year, not only because it finds me tired but because there's a type of student whose last-ditch attempt to earn credit for a course he's failing is to discredit its teacher. I don't have many of that ilk, but I know from the bad experiences of other teachers that I have at least one or two.

I did my best to see that, at least in terms of new material and major grades, the marking period effectively ended at Memorial Day. I use the rest of the time for review, for enrichment, and for catching up those students with a few missing assignments— though I deliver repeated, strenuous warnings that I'm taking no deathbed confessions, answering no question like "What assignments am I missing?" two minutes before I'm out the door. I tell myself and I tell the kids that this is my due for a year of diligence. I go directly to "my old job," not the beach, the day after school lets out, and I intend to go unencumbered.

Say what I will, I know the boundaries are going to be pressed. More than a week after I've closed the gate on journal assignments, on an afternoon when a rare tornado is predicted for northeastern Vermont and an announcement has come over the intercom giving teachers permission to leave at three, two girls come up from one of the academic support areas to see "if you can tell us what journal assignments we're missing" (something I've been doing for weeks, both by way of general announcements to my classes and by written invitation to individuals who've fallen behind) and "if it might be possible for us to make them up" and "if you can tell us if we'd pass if we did" and "if we could do a few others for extra credit if we won't."

Without the predicted tornado, I might simply be irritated, but in this case I'm flabbergasted almost to the point of laughing aloud, which I'd surely do but for fear of seeming to mock the girls. Instead I say yes to their first two requests and no to the others. Admittedly, I'm eating some of my words and lowering some of my standards; admittedly, these girls are almost sublime in their fecklessness, but I remember what Huck's friend Jim had to say about the wisdom of cutting a child in half just to prove a point.

These aren't my last or best surprises. They'll continue, good and bad, until the year ends. The drudgery of completing the agreed-upon five NECAP practice essays is lightened by a few surprises beyond the jolt that comes when I learn at a department meeting that the very teachers who set the bar at five during a previous meeting have decided to interpret the number figuratively. I've held to the five in what I thought was a spirit of colleagueship. I swallow hard but say nothing; I sometimes wonder if, after nine months of bridling my tongue, I will spend the last weeks of June standing in my backyard screaming. But, as I said, the practice essays are not all a waste, especially the installment for the "reflective essay." Recalling the prompt on last October's NECAP, I ask students to write an essay based on a quotation. I ask them to do it at home and invite them to take their time with it. Hoping to make the assignment do double duty, I choose a quotation from *Our Town*: "Wherever you come near the human race, there's layers and layers of nonsense." I'm not casting aspersions on my students when I choose it—though I do expect that it will set some of them thinking about school.

It does, but not exclusively. One girl does some research (after having done virtually none for her research paper) and comes upon the example of a perfectly grammatical but utterly nonsensical sentence constructed by a man she identifies as Noam Chromsky. "I bet I'm the only teacher in the state who got a reference to the famous linguist Noam Chomsky on a <u>NECAP practice essay</u>," I write on her paper. It so happens I've recently purchased a black-and-white postcard of the very same Noam, looking skeptical and a tad cadaverous, and I attach it to her paper in lieu of a gold star. Another girl writes about the way she's been mocked for preferring to hang out with boys, many of whom are Future Farmers of America like her. She has little patience, she writes, for the "layers and layers of nonsense" that attend social interactions among more "typical" girls, and she could do without their snide remarks. Still another student writes of the loss of her cell phone, followed by the awesome discovery in the weeks thereafter that she enjoys her life more without it. She says she probably won't bother to get another. I wonder if Thornton Wilder could have anticipated the layers and layers of sense in these papers.

I have my sophomores do the last practice essay as part of their final exam, noting that I'll evaluate it by how well they've incorporated my feedback on the previous four. I give them the question ahead of time, as I do with essay questions for all my exams, and allow them to bring notes and an outline. Some of the best performances on the final exam are from students under the special ed umbrella, a credit to their aides and teachers but no less a credit to their own grim diligence. (Anybody who believes that special education is about coddling underachievers needs to get his ass into a school.) The highest exam grade in my sophomore classes goes to a boy who's repeating the course. I'm not surprised. He's a bright kid. I suspect many of his difficulties have to do with factors outside school. He shines when we do our review for the exam, often supplying the correct answer no one else seems to have. There and on the exam itself I suspect he wants to give me one last proof that I've been right in my overall assessment of his abilities. I'll miss him, a soft-spoken boy who never passes me in the hall without a kind word.

It's a truism that exams evaluate the teacher as much as the students, and on that score I pass as almost all of them do, though I hardly pass with distinction. "Patriotism is abstract, but a flag is _____," reads one of my sentence-completion items, drawing on the illustration I've used repeatedly throughout the year to clarify the distinction between abstract and concrete. One girl writes *cement*. As was sometimes true for her teacher, she got heartbreakingly close to the right answer but not quite close enough for it to count.

Except for an imaginative question or two, my exams are pretty much the traditional written deal. My colleague who teaches Advanced Placement Language and Literature has his students write essays and give a reading in the library after school, either as part of their final exam or as a major project for the last quarter, I'm not sure. But I attend, always interested in what a student can do, especially under the guidance of a master teacher like my colleague. Notwithstanding one father who attends the occasion in a muscle shirt, I'm struck by the visible difference between these college-bound seniors and many of the upper-classmen I teach. Part of it is clothing, part of it is poise; much of it is a greater tendency toward slenderness. Not all of what I see can be attributed to class—the ability levels don't sort themselves out that neatly—though I suspect some of it can.

What also impresses me, in the awkward schmoozing that takes place before and after the reading, is the reticence of some of the students as I attempt to make conversation. They hardly know me, of course; they're young, they're shy, and some of them have to be a little nervous—but there is something else I recognize, remember actually, from the days when I taught the upper track and could count on greater attentiveness to my overtures. Many students, especially grade-conscious students and "top-level students" most of all, are quick to discriminate between adults who matter and those who don't. On the one hand are teachers who might conceivably have something to say to them, by way of instruction, or for them, by way of a letter of reference; on the other hand, those less deserving of notice. I may be overstating the case, but I'm not the first teacher to do so. Even at this age one detects in certain ambitious students the first traces of a subtle snobbery. One need go no further than to remember that the courses they take are referred to as "honors level" to figure out where they're getting it.

This is not an observation I feel free to share. I confine my remarks to praising the essays, which are praiseworthy to say the least, and praising the teacher. He is highly dedicated and opinionated in what he does, but I've never found him pompous or vain. I suspect his students trust him, and they should. My private observations go to Kathy, as hers come to me. Her transitional year has gone reasonably well. She likes her colleagues at the elementary school and at Dartmouth, though she misses working in a preschool setting, and the systemic intransigence of elementary school is thrown into increasingly sharper relief by the colleagueship she experiences at the hospital. If she needs something at the latter, be it materials or a day off to attend a professional conference, it's assumed she's working to improve the program. If she expresses the same needs at the elementary school, it's assumed—or at least responded to as if—she may be trying to pull a fast one.

"I'm not sure I can let you go for this," says a since-departed principal when Kathy asks permission to attend a two-day workshop in order to maintain her professional license. "If I allow you to take the time, our students will be without speech services for two days." And if she doesn't take the time, the students will be without a licensed speech pathologist—but this requires further explanation from Kathy and a day or two of additional contemplation on the part of the principal before the imprimatur is granted. One of the administrators at the hospital is a former school speech pathologist and explains her change of careers by dryly noting that she got tired of working in an environment "where nothing gets done." Kathy tires of that too, though she's quick to add that many of her colleagues have it worse. At present they're straining to develop alternative NECAP examinations, as required by law, for special education students, some of whom are nonverbal and lack the most basic social skills—yet another example of taking time away from teaching in order to test what you lack the time to teach.

Probably the year's big story for her was the adoption of the iPad. By the end of the year, her colleagues remain more sold on it than she. As she predicted, the needs of the children are as likely to be reinterpreted in relation to the machinery as the format of the machinery adapted to them, assuming their needs are even noticeable beside the glare of the digital bling. On the positive side, the devices are powerful motivators for some kids and status symbols too, something cool in the hands of an "uncool" kid. Not that this is allowed to stand without comment. In one class a substitute teacher sees a special ed student working on an iPad and quips to the student's aide—in the presence of the student—"So that's why our taxes went up, so these kids can have their daily schedules written on an iPad."

There are probably more implications about the nature of public schools packed into Kathy's experience with the iPad than there are apps. But, unlike technology, human ingenuity has no limits. A technical consultant tells one of Kathy's colleagues that dish drainers make ideal storage racks for classroom sets of iPads. So, one afternoon, while the tech crews are once again reconfiguring the school's computers—and probably nullifying most of Kathy's downloads and creations in the process—she and her sidekick head down to the Dollar General to look for dish drainers. Soon I'll be saying good-bye to the world of schools, not only to the frustrations contained in the story of the iPad but also to enchanted mornings where teachers get out of their cars like a theophany of peddler goddesses, dressed up and cheerful in spite of bulging sacks on both shoulders, sections of varicolored foam rubber tubing (for what, God knows) waving from their sacks, snowmen on their sweaters for winter and pumpkins on their stockings for Halloween, and—as if this weren't vision enough—a dish drainer tucked under each arm.

Graduation occurs before the last official day of school, a bow to the special needs of seniors, who've already made plans around the unrevised calendar. I'll attend in spite of my temporary status and the load of work I still have to complete if I want to graduate too. I consider staying away but then learn that Mr. Messier plans to quote from my first book in his remarks. (He asks me ahead of time if I'd mind.) I probably ought to be there in case he has anything else up his sleeve. I also feel an obligation to the handful of seniors I taught. On the most basic level, I feel that I don't deserve to stay away.

As in the past, I view commencement exercises as an act of penance for the sins of the teaching year. Not a full expiation, for sure, but at least an act of contrition. The lengthy monotony of the proceedings, the stifling heat of a gymnasium in mid-June, the oxygen deprivation that comes of sitting with hundreds of spectators in a scarcely ventilated space—what else besides a guilty conscience could keep a person coming year after year? Add to these the inevitable if unintended insult that

comes of being publicly "thanked" for an education whose quality is thrown into doubt by every other sentence accompanying
the thanks, the self-congratulatory tone and smug insider jokes
of the valedictory speakers, the steady deflation of making the
rounds afterward to congratulate students in whose eyes it's
clear that anything you might have meant to them or they to
you is dissolving like a mirage. Most of all, the oppressive loneli-
ness that is relieved only by remembering that any number of
the students up on the dais are feeling lonelier still. At the conclusion of what many of them have repeatedly been assured are
the best years of their lives—which in some cases will prove sadly
true, the relative crappiness of those years notwithstanding—
small wonder that more than a few of them will be stone drunk
by nightfall.

Of course, there's plenty to move even a jaded heart: the sight
of kids who are the first in their families to graduate high school
or the first to be going on for further study, the pride in their
eyes and in the eyes fixed on them. The kids overcome with
more emotion than the occasion would seem to warrant, as if
this were their first encounter with transience. The kids who
unashamedly give flowers to their mothers, embracing the only
individuals in the world besides themselves who truly know
how hard it was to get to this day and how close they came to not
making it. The uncanny self-possession of those students who
put their high school years in perspective a long time ago, who
will go on to do the quiet useful work they've set their sights on
all along, who will keep their yearbooks but not open them
often, who have instinctively understood that life gives a person
several true friends at most and who will remain true to their
friends all their lives. One imagines them looking beyond the
few graduation parties they'll attend this weekend to a road trip
planned for November or a year's stint on an uncle's fishing boat

somewhere in Washington State. They will give only a little time to finding themselves because they've never felt any great need to go looking for someone they already know.

I don't take a seat but stand near the door, at the edge of the bleachers, where few people will notice if I duck out to the men's room or drop to my haunches at the mention of my name. The sight of Mr. Messier at the podium moves me, as does his decision to quote from my book, though the passage he chooses and the question with which he introduces it amount to a conundrum. He reads my opening description of the region, as seen through the eyes of a new teacher, its natural beauty and stultifying poverty, its isolation and heartache, and asks the graduates to think how much has changed at the school and in their community since the book appeared in 1988. I'm almost certain the answer he's implying is "a lot." I'm less sure that everyone in the audience would give the same answer. To the degree that he himself represents a positive change at the school, he is fully entitled to his optimism. The author of the passage, though, has his doubts.

My mind begins to wander during the other speeches. It slips outside the gymnasium and drifts downhill to the underpass where senior art students have recently painted the mural that each successive graduating class leaves for a legacy until a new one requires the space. During the week I watched it take shape in the form of a rural landscape, with an image of Lake Region High School atop a green hill and the words RANGER PRIDE written in the blue sky above it. Then, when I drove up to school over the weekend to retrieve my misplaced grade book, I noticed in alarm that someone had painted an enormous fist breaking through the center of the cement "canvas," its knuckles aimed at the viewer and the background torn into stylized shreds around it.

My first thought was that a group of talented graffiti guerrillas, perhaps kids from the rival high school to the north of us, had stolen down one night and defaced our mural, symbolically punching us out on our own turf. There will be consequences for this! The fists won't be symbolic either. I considered calling the principal in the hopes of averting an incident. Was it possible no one else had noticed what the vandals did? Well, it was a Sunday and they could have made their raid in the wee hours of that same morning. Several minutes passed before I understood that the fist was part of the design, a realization that felt like a fist punching through me. Why put a fist through the landscape that supposedly inspires your pride? I suppose that, taken as a paradox, it made a kind of sense: a senior wants to punch his way free of the place he also loves.

Come Monday, praise for the completed mural was widespread and fulsome, especially among the faculty. There was no attempt and apparently no felt need to give it any interpretation. My uneasiness was my problem. This is how students must have felt in my classes some days: What on earth is he talking about? Am I the only person who doesn't get it? Why do Ethan and Mattie run their sleigh into a tree? Why do people call things tragic that are just plain stupid? Or is the stupid one me?

I return my attention to the order of ceremonies on my program; I do a visual count of the rows remaining to receive their diplomas. My faults are more than I can number, but my penance is about two-thirds done.

Had I been invited to speak at graduation, as teachers sometimes are, and had I accepted, what might I have said? Probably nothing too heavy. High school graduations are not the place for diatribes or manifestos. Neither are high school classrooms. I have always believed it is a teacher's duty to teach the curriculum

and not to pontificate, to inspire debates and not to settle doc-
trines. I did on one or two occasions tell my students that the society they were living in valued people of their age, region, and class
primarily as cannon fodder, cheap labor, and gullible consumers
and that education could give them some of the weapons necessary to fight back. Those things I did say, and I might have ventured at least that far in a graduation speech. I find myself wishing,
though, that I had had a simple refrain, some terse slogan I could
have repeated to my classes day after day, like the Roman senator
Cato, who is supposed to have ended every speech by saying "Carthage must be destroyed."

In fact, Cato's refrain might have done nicely. As it happens,
the people of Carthage worshipped the same god their Phoeni-
cian ancestors had, a Canaanite deity they called Moloch, whose
signature burnt offering was the dearest thing his worshippers
had. When the Romans eventually took Cato's advice, they found
within the walls of the doomed city a multitude of clay urns con-
taining the tiny charred bones of children. The Romans worshipped their own version of Moloch, needless to say, as do we if
our poets are to be believed. "Moloch whose love is endless oil
and stone! Moloch whose soul is electricity and banks!" So wrote
Allen Ginsberg when I was a mere three years old, half a century
before the financial meltdown of 2007–08, an unknown number
of years before the last American soldier leaves Afghanistan.

Carthago delenda est. I couldn't say that to kids without more
explanation than I had time for and more trouble than my long-
suffering hosts deserved, but at least I can say it to you. The sentimental hypocrisy that holds children to be our most precious
resource even as every indicator from the conduct of foreign
policy to the debate over guns puts them several notches down
in value from the availability of cheap oil and the goodwill of
the NRA—*delenda est.* The fatuous assurance that children are

happiest when their parents behave as if no happiness matters so much as their own and that of their live-in lovers—*delenda est*. The two-headed effrontery of believing that equal opportunity in the society at large can be promoted merely by reforming schools and that schools can be reformed without radically transforming the structures of society—*delenda est*, both heads at a single stroke.

And who better suited to wield the sword than we who are charged with giving our students a "head start" only so that—as one civil rights worker put it years ago—the most disadvantaged of them can run sooner into a brick wall? Who better than us to demand the wall's destruction? May I live to see the day when a teachers' strike is at the vanguard of a general strike.

Till then, I have a room to straighten and grades to turn in. I have an inventory to complete. I have one last installment of my productivity rubric to enter on PowerSchool. I have a few scattered opportunities to tell a few drop-by visitors that I hope they'll have a safe and happy summer.

On my last day, Mr. Messier takes me to breakfast and the English department takes me to lunch. The breakfast is at the same café in Barton where I've been meeting my lone student for months. He and I have already had our year-end breakfast and agreed to have at least one encore after he starts at a local college this fall. I trust Mr. Messier knows what I've asked Sara to pass on to anyone who suggests marking my departure in some special way—"no party, no presents, no fuss"—and he has chosen this quiet way to say good-bye and thanks. I can hardly imagine one better. Though we've had many occasions to chat throughout the year, most have had some agenda, and all were subject to the interruptions that come at a principal like a barrage of driving snow. Now we're able to relax, take stock of the year, and look to our respective futures. I know how much of his heart and sense of vocation are involved in Lake Region and so it comes as more than a pat on the shoulder when he tells me that I have been good for the school. He hopes my time there has also been good for me. I'm not lying when I tell him that it has.

In addition to picking up the tab for my coffee and double portion of bacon, the principal hands me two gifts. One is the library's hardbound copy of my first book—"We'll replace it," he says—with yearbook-style farewells and accolades from a hand-ful of my students written inside the covers. It would seem he has tried to seek out the kids who've meant most to me during the year or to whom I've meant the most, though both of us know those categories can never be better than an educated guess. He includes himself among them, repeating something he'd said to me early in the term when I gave him my diagnosis of a troubled young man in one of my classes: "You may have been away for fifteen years, but you still have it!" There on the dust jacket is my author photo from over twenty years ago, unsmiling, earnest, with darker, longer hair and beard, someone I would not recog-nize if I passed him on the street.

The other present is a letter to the principal from a colleague with whom I've had the most perplexing relationship, a person who will greet me affably on some days and hardly acknowledge me on others. Though of late there have been unexpected com-pliments about the good preparation I've given to the students we share, I have always assumed that my mercurial colleague regarded me with suspicion at first, perhaps even with distaste. I note from the date on the letter that it was written early in the term. It nominates me for the school's Teacher of the Year. The honor rightfully went to someone else and probably ought never to go to someone passing through a school system on a temporary gig. But the letter gets my nomination for Surprise of the Year, yet another example of how easily we misjudge others—and, let's face it, how easily they misjudge us.

My lunch with the English department is at the restaurant at the Orleans Country Club, already in operation when Kathy and I first came to the Kingdom, though I often forget it's there. Perched invisibly above the town and the furniture factory, the greens lie close to the houses built at the crest of what some people call Snob Hill. It is hardly Beverly Hills, nor is life in the valley altogether desolate, though several months from now the local paper will report the arrest of one of our citizens for the theft of "some sausages and a ham."

Once everyone is seated—the guidance counselors have come too—I receive my cordially inscribed card and perfect gift: a small shrub with varicolored leaves that I'd like to set in my garden straightaway. I'm impressed for one last time by the dedication of my peers, still inclined to talk shop on this rare chance to be away from it, and by the sobering recognition that all of us have already moved beyond our temporary partnership. I have been among these people for no more than a year, never a permanent fixture, and the year is effectively over. Any messes I've made will be theirs to clean up. Any improvements I made were built on their prior successes and will need their further efforts to maintain. I wonder how many of them are as anxious as I am for the food to get eaten and the check to come, how many feel forgivably resentful at this added obligation, one more thing to stall their passage to the well-earned summer break. School is like this: awards and citations, trophies and send-offs, wave upon wave, lest anyone feel unacknowledged—but how restless one can feel at the banquet.

I'm glad that most of my good-byes to my students are behind me. I said a formal good-bye to all of my classes before handing out their final exams. I told them that I had hoped to leave with some words of wisdom but that I could come up with none that suited me beyond a simple statement of their own preciousness as human beings. I thanked them for their overall kindness and told them that any stray thing they might regret having done or said to me was already forgiven. I hoped they'd find the where-withal to extend the same forgiveness to me.

Then I reminded them not to talk until all the exams were concluded and wished them luck. I could not tell if they were saddened by what I said or mildly offended by its terseness—already it felt as if there was distance opening between us. Less formally, I shook hands with the bearish freshman in my teaching roommate's class, who'd made a point of saying good morning to me nearly every second period as he was coming into the room and I was gathering up my stuff to leave. I wished him luck too, not knowing he'd be killed in a car accident before the end of the year. To one of his reticent classmates, a long-haired boy I'd made stay after school for covering his desk with graffiti, I gave an inexpensive sketchpad. No hard feelings, I meant to say, and your graffiti shows promise.

With those of my own students who came back to see their corrected exams or dropped in to say their good-byes on the day of their last exam there was more to say, some of it poignant. I'll draw a curtain on those, but I can't resist sharing one brief exchange that happened near the end, a little thing, though it left me with a sense of benediction.

On the final day of exams—a half day for students with the afternoon reserved for makeups—an announcement came over the intercom a few minutes after the buses left that there was Chinese food in the upstairs faculty workroom for any teachers who wanted some. I happened not to and continued my correcting. Within the minute two boys poked their heads into my room, one of them the boy I chewed out for tailgating me that November afternoon when I was going to see my daughter in Burlington.

"Hey, Mr. Keizer," he said, "did you hear that announcement about the Chinese food?" I did, I said, touched by their concern that no teacher miss out on a free lunch. I added that I wasn't hungry.

"Do you think you could snag some for us?"

I was touched even more that they judged me fit for such buccaneering—though apparently they'd spoken in jest. "You're going to do it?" the other asked incredulously as I sprang up from my desk. "Are you kidding? This is the best idea I've heard in a month."

I filled a plate with some of every entrée, nuked it in the faculty microwave, and made off with the booty and two clean forks. My guys were waiting at my classroom door like spectators at a finish line. They could bring the dirty plate to me, I told them, not so much out of kindness as out of fear that a colleague of mine might wind up poisoned if they gave it too Platonic a wash. They were back in what seemed like a minute. "That was so good!" they said, handing me the dirty plate and thanking me, though I might as well have thanked them. Funny thing about Chinese food: ever notice that an hour after you steal some for a couple of hungry rascals your heart still feels full?

My last chore after grades are done is to put my room in order. I place my exams and practice NECAP essays in neat, sorted piles. I empty the desk of everything but the office supplies and stationery that were left for me when I arrived, with a few additions: a new stapler, fresher felt-tip markers, butterfly paperclips in assorted boxes, the remote control and instruction booklet for the computer projector. I take my tin of mints, my jar of ocean pebbles, my framed photographs of patrons scanning the stacks of a blitzed London bookstore and the Rose Room at the New York Public Library. Between the pages of an art book, I tuck a mixed CD of Japanese "noise music," a parting gift from a once-sour young poet, lately turned sweet. I bequeath my daughter's lime tree, which she bequeathed to me after college and which has thrived remarkably in the close air of my classroom, to Sara along with my poster of Eleanor Roosevelt. They would have been fast friends, Eleanor and Sara; they've been something like my patron saints this year, two smiles I could always count on during the toughest days. Malcolm X doesn't smile, so he's going home with me. Sara comes by to ask if there is anything she can do—besides the hundred and one things she's already done—to help me leave on time. If there is anyone at the school I will miss, anyone who I think will genuinely miss me, it is Sara. I believe we both know that when we assure each other that we're not really saying good-bye.

It takes me several trips to get my crates of books and decorations to my car, along with my new plant and several of my old ones. I fold forward my backseats and fill my hatchback to the ceiling. When everything is loaded, I close the car and head back toward the school. I have one last thing to do before I can leave. I took away the doorstop on my last trip to the car, and I turned my keys in to the main office half an hour ago, but there's no need for me to get inside. I need only stand within arm's length of the building. Even under hands as callused as mine, the bricks are warm.

So I'm free. I head home past the Crystal Saloon and along Crystal Lake, not for the last time but very probably for my last time as a teacher going home from school. My windows are open, my music is loud. Though I'm driving the same car I've driven all term and for six years prior to that, I feel as though it's been returned to me after a year's impoundment. I can drive it wherever I want to now and at any hour. Better still, I can keep it parked in the dooryard below my office windows, its inertness the visible sign of every blessed moment I can stay put. I hope I'll never have to take another job besides writing, but I know I'll never regret the teaching I did this year.

The Sunday after our last day of school Kathy and I head down the interstate for a celebratory outing, an early Eucharist (from the Greek for "thanksgiving") in Littleton, New Hampshire, followed by breakfast at the diner there, a stroll around town to walk off the pancakes and take in the farmers' market, and anywhere our hearts fancy after that. There are no papers to grade, no lessons to plan. The day's a beauty—"so cool, so calm, so bright," to quote George Herbert, "the bridall of the earth and skie." But apparently not perfect. For a quarter mile or so I worry I'm going to have car trouble or some kind of roadside altercation—why else is the driver behind me gesticulating so wildly at seven o'clock on a Sunday morning? As he pulls hard to my right to take the third St. Johnsbury exit, I slow down to get a look at his face and a sense of his meaning if I can. If my tailpipe's sagging, if he flips me the bird, I'm not going to let it wreck my day.

He turns out to be one of my former sophomores, a newly minted junior, his learner's permit exchanged for a license. He's at the wheel of the used car that I know from an early composition to be his pride and joy. For reasons I could never learn, the final draft never got handed in. He did manage to finish his research paper, though, in spite of his bid to stack my firewood instead. It was a fine piece of work for which he earned an A. He's beaming at us now, still waving as his car turns down the ramp and away from our direction. He must have noticed me a ways back and only wanted to be sure I noticed him.

ACKNOWLEDGMENTS

I owe a great debt to those students and staff members at Lake Region Union High School whose kindness sustained me during the year recounted in this book. I wish especially to thank Erikka Adams, Timothy Chamberlin, Danielle Conley, Eric Degre, Michelle Hubert, Sara McKenny, Andre Messier, Cathy Sargent, and Chastity Urie, lacking whose frequent ministrations I might not have survived to "tell the tale." That said, the tale is mine, written entirely without the aid, knowledge, or permission of anyone in the Lake Region community. It amounts to one small slice of one man's experience at an extraordinary school. Any faults in the telling belong to me alone.

I also wish to thank Ellen Rosenbush, my longtime editor at *Harper's Magazine*, who shepherded the essay on which this book is based, and my agent Jim Rutman, for his representation of that project. To his colleague Peter Matson I owe much of my good fortune in having Sara Bershtel as my relentless, astute, and ever-gracious editor at Metropolitan Books. Her assistant, Connor Guy, and my copy editor, Roslyn Schloss, also made invaluable contributions to the text, as did Christopher O'Connell to the book's production. Not least of all, I'm grateful to Kathy Keizer and Howard Frank Mosher, my first readers for this and every other book I've written.

I dedicate *Getting Schooled* to teachers, thinking particularly of my own, a list that includes the individuals mentioned above, as well as many former mentors, teaching colleagues, and students. Foremost in their company are my wife, Kathy, and my daughter, Sarah, both dedicated teachers in our public schools and constant teachers to me.

ABOUT THE AUTHOR

GARRET KEIZER is the author, most recently, of *Privacy* and *The Unwanted Sound of Everything We Want*. A contributing editor at *Harper's Magazine* and a former Guggenheim Fellow, he has written for *The New York Times*, the *Los Angeles Times*, *Lapham's Quarterly*, *The Village Voice*, *Mother Jones*, and *Virginia Quarterly Review*, among other publications. He lives with his wife in Vermont.